RHODE ISLAND

RHODE ISLAND

ISLAND

≈§ The Independent State ₹≈

George H. Kellner and J. Stanley Lemons

"PARTNERS IN PROGRESS" BY

Linda Loteridge Levin

PUBLISHED IN COOPERATION WITH THE RHODE ISLAND HISTORICAL SOCIETY

WINDSOR PUBLICATIONS, INC., WOODLAND HILLS, CALIFORNIA

PAGE TWO: Upon dispatching the General Washington *in 1787, John Brown became the first Rhode Islander to enter the China trade. Pictured here is the second of his ships named after the first President of the United States, the* George Washington. *Brown's commitment to the national government was symbolized by his naming some of his ships after its leaders, such as the* President Washington *and the* John Jay. *Courtesy, Rhode Island Historical Society (RHi x3 3085)*

PREVIOUS PAGE: The "Independent Man" stands on top of Rhode Island's capitol. Sculpted by George T. Brewster and cast by Gorham, the statue was raised to its place on December 18, 1899. Courtesy, Rhode Island Department of Transportation/Earl H. Goodison photo

to
Ellen and Nancy

Windsor Publications
History Books Division
Publisher: John M. Phillips
Editorial Director: Lissa Sanders
Administrative Coordinator: Katherine Cooper
Senior Picture Editor: Teri Davis Greenberg
Senior Corporate History Editor: Karen Story
Production Manager: James Burke
Art Director: Alexander D'Anca
Art Production Manager: Dee Cooper
Composition Manager: E. Beryl Myers

Staff for *Rhode Island: The Independent State*
Editor: Phyllis Rifkin
Copy Editor: Bernice Lifton
Editorial Assistants: Phyllis Gray, Susan Block, Susan Wells, Karen Holroyd
Compositors: Shannon Mellies, Barbara Neiman
Proofreaders: Clareen Arnold, Doris Malkin
Designer: Laurie Handler
Production Artists: Shannon Strull, Beth Bowman, Ellen Hazeltine

Published 1982
Printed in the United States of America
First Edition

Library of Congress Cataloging in Publication Data

Kellner, George H., 1940-
Rhode Island, the independent state.

Includes index.
1. Rhode Island—History. I. Lemons, J. Stanley. II. Rhode Island Historical Society. III. Title.
F79.K44 1982 974.5 82-50181
ISBN 0-89781-040-6

CONTENTS

FOREWORD

BY ALMOST ANYONE'S standards 350 years is a considerable length of time. When something attains that age in the western world, it is a cause for remarks and reflection. Rhode Island will be 350 years old in 1986. Of course, native American civilization predates this anniversary by perhaps a thousand years, but few could argue that the date of 1636, marking the arrival of Roger Williams and his associates, is not a reasonable beginning for all the events which have flowed since to shape life in our state as we know it today.

This history of human life in the lands surrounding Narragansett Bay is not significant as an endless, unbroken march of progress and uplifting human experience. If we are candid and honest, even those of us most disposed to put a bright face on everything would have to admit we have had our ups and downs. What really is remarkable is that Rhode Island survived at all. Smallest of all the states, limited in natural resources on its mainland—though blessed with a 400-mile shoreline and a magnificent bay and harbor—Rhode Island was settled by fiercely independent thinkers who were driven from other communities. They didn't seem to be the sort to agree on anything, let alone the kind who could build a community which would withstand internal squabbles, the land-grabbing appetites of stronger neighbors, the extreme dangers of annihilation by enraged natives, or the powerful discipline of their "dread Sovereign" in their homeland across the sea.

The community did survive, however. Its colonial commerce flourished, first as exporters of agricultural surplus, then as carriers of rum and slaves. As quarrelsome as they were with their own people, Rhode Islanders were even more prickly with outsiders who wanted to do them in. Rhode Island could be pragmatic and even hypocritical in altering its policies to accommodate the changes in British imperial politics. This erratic course was designed to preserve its independence. When it came time to cut away from royal allegiances, the Rhode Island colony was one of the first. When it came time to give up some independence to be a part of the new American nation, it was one of the last.

As highly as Rhode Islanders prized political independence, they held economic liberty in even higher esteem. With a limited and uncertain future associated with maritime enterprises facing them at the beginning of the 19th century, Rhode Islanders threw themselves energetically into the promise of prosperity offered by industrialization and manufacturing. Cloth and metal products consumed the state's imagination and energies for over a century. Waves of non-Yankee populations periodically brought transfusions to the body politic. Irish, French-Canadians, Italians, Jews, and Portuguese were among the largest of the new immigrant groups. Manufacturing cities grew up along the state's fast-moving streams. Farm townships eventually became suburbs. Cycles of prosperity and recession marked the state's history.

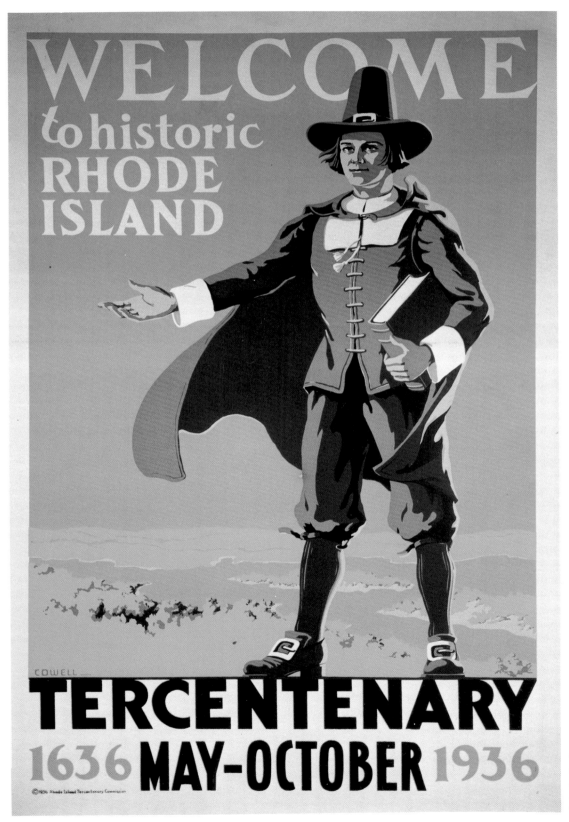

The 1936 Tercentenary celebration was one of many such events held annually in historically conscious Rhode Island. Courtesy, Rhode Island Historical Society (RHi x5 44)

In the 20th century enormous forces threatened Rhode Island's independence: two world wars and a national depression. An accelerated life-style, defined by autos, airplanes, computers, and televisions, has tended to make everything and every place in our country think, act, and look pretty much like everyplace else. Rhode Island has had to surrender a lot of its uniqueness, but it has also managed to keep a good deal of it.

As Rhode Islanders approach the 350th anniversary of their community's existence, there is much to consider. In order to provide the community with ample time to ponder its long and varied past, The Rhode Island Historical Society decided not to wait to celebrate it. Rhode Islanders will have two or three years to enjoy and comprehend this summary of their past before the anniversary. It is hoped that this advanced look will result in a more meaningful commemoration. We are delighted to be joined in this enterprise by the major businesses and corporations of our state. Their own histories have been ably presented by Linda Lotridge Levin of our Society.

Local historians George Kellner and J. Stanley Lemons have performed well this task of providing us with a thoughtful and interpretive look at our past. Their observations and judgments no doubt will be challenged by some. Others will question the book's emphasis or note that some topics were omitted while others received only passing attention. Professors Kellner and Lemons have broken new ground by providing a more thorough look at our late 19th century and 20th century history than we have had before. Their thematic approach to Rhode Island's recreation and its spirit of patriotism is different from the approach of other books.

All of this, of course, demonstrates why there can be no "official" history of anything. History is constantly being rewritten by those who are not satisfied with the points of view of their predecessors or by those who discover new information. In any event, it would be too much to expect Rhode Islanders to have a complete consensus on anything, especially their own history. It would be out of character—against the tradition of individualism and independence.

It is in the spirit of a birthday gift that the Historical Society offers this book. It is our commemorative gift to our fellow citizens, conveyed in a spirit of "hope."

Albert T. Klyberg, Director
The Rhode Island Historical Society

ACKNOWLEDGMENTS

MANY PEOPLE have aided us in a variety of ways to make this work possible. Several read portions of the manuscript and have saved us from errors of fact and expression; these include Joseph Conforti and Norman Smith of Rhode Island College, William McLoughlin of Brown University, Patrick Malone and Tom Leary of Old Slater Mill Historic Site, and Albert Klyberg, Glen LaFantasie, and Paul Campbell of The Rhode Island Historical Society. Jay Coughtry made valuable comments and suggestions about the slave trade and race relations. The staff of the Library and Museum of The Rhode Island Historical Society came to know us well, but we owe particular appreciation to Maureen Taylor and Joyce Botelho for their aid and patience in selecting the many pictures from the Historical Society's collection. Joseph Mehr, Librarian of the Providence Journal Company's picture collection, helped us to locate many of the photographs of the recent era. The hardest picture to secure of them all was the picture of "The Independent Man." At last we had Governor Joseph Garrahy to thank for intervening to get it taken and Earl Goodison, photographer of the Rhode Island Department of Transportation, for doing the actual photography. Chet Browning of the Rhode Island Department of Economic Development was extremely helpful in securing pictures for the contemporary color section. Jeanne Richardson, Rhode Island Collection Librarian, gave us freedom and support in the use of the Providence Public Library. Mrs. Edmund Wordell of the Newport Historical Society and Rowena Stewart of the Rhode Island Black Heritage Society were generous in their time and consideration. Sally Wilson, Special Collections Librarian of Rhode Island College, bore our impositions with wonderful cheer and supported our efforts in more ways than nearly anyone. Gloria Ricci and Irma Morettini helped greatly by transforming scribbles and scratches into clean drafts. The copy editor for Windsor Publications, Bernice Lifton, deserves much credit for ironing out wrinkles in the organization and prose of the academic historians. Our strongest word of appreciation is reserved for Albert Klyberg, Director of The Rhode Island Historical Society, who stayed with this project all the way to see that it was truly a work of history and scholarship. Finally, we appreciate Ellen and Nancy who wondered if we would ever get finished.

Chapter One

THE HERETIC COLONY

Anne Hutchinson (1591-1643) was tried by the magistrates for "traducing the ministers" of Massachusetts. Convicted of this and heresy, she was banished to Rhode Island. From Scribner's Popular History of the United States, 1897. Courtesy, Pawtucket Public Library

THROUGH MOST OF THE colonial era Rhode Island* was condemned by many. A Dutch Reformed minister declared that it was "the receptacle of all sorts of riff-raff people, and is nothing else than the sewer of New England." A Congregational minister wrote that the colony was "a hive of hornets, and the sink into which all the rest of the colonies empty their heretics." Plymouth colony complained that Rhode Island was an "asylum to evil-doers" and existed as an affront to all who tried to live an orderly life. In 1668 the Town of Stonington declared in a petition to the Connecticut General Assembly, "Our condition is truly deplorable to have persons of such corrupt principles and practices to live near us." Some denounced Rhode Island as "Rogues' Island."

Beginning as an unpromising collection of outcasts, malcontents, squatters, and dissenters, followed by a century and a half of internal dissension and external hostility, Rhode Island emerged as a special place. In a world of religious orthodoxy, conformity, and intolerance, it began and developed as an oasis of religious liberty. As a tiny and almost forgotten parcel of the British Empire, it governed itself with greater independence than any other North American colony. Its diminutive size, unfriendly neighbors, unique religious climate, and tradition of self-governance produced a people that were unusually sensitive to power and adept at securing an advantage. But in the beginning its founders were stiff-necked individualists, runaways, and exiled heretics from religious and political authority, who agreed on little more than religious liberty for everyone.

By the late 1620s, the religious establishment in England had squelched most dissenters, and the Puritans resolved to create a society in the New World where they could set up a purified church and godly government. A thousand Puritans sailed to Massachusetts Bay in 1630 to found a colony. Roger Williams and his wife, Mary Barnard, arrived on the *Lyon* in February 1631. Boston welcomed the young man, as he was well known to the leading Puritans as a good preacher and devout Puritan. Invited to become the second minister in the Boston church, Williams confounded the Puritans by rejecting the offer because the church had not separated itself from the Church of England. As the purpose of the Massachusetts experiment was to create a purified Church of England, the Boston leaders found Williams to be unreasonable.

One problem that any highly charged movement faces when it comes to power is how to balance the drive of its zealous members with the need to govern ordinary people. Williams was one of several settlers who sought to maintain a higher, purer standard. He was the Puritan of Puritans and became the ultimate sectarian in his effort to cleanse the worship of God of all

*To avoid confusion, the name Rhode Island is used for the whole colony or state, while the original "Rhode Island" will be called by its prior and present designation "Aquidneck."

worldly corruptions. He believed that the compromises that the leaders of the Bay Colony had made in establishing a government actually polluted the worship of God. For him, logic led to separation of church and state in order to safeguard the purity of worship. Such a principle, however, would destroy the Holy Commonwealth that the Puritans were trying to build in Massachusetts.

Williams went first to Salem and then to Plymouth Colony, where he became assistant minister and supported himself through farming and trading with Indians. A born linguist, fluent in many languages, he quickly learned several Indian tongues and developed permanent friendships with Massasoit, sachem of the Wampanoags, and Canonicus, grand sachem of the Narragansetts, who came to view Williams almost as a son. These relationships were remarkable because the Wampanoags and Narragansetts were enemies, but Williams traveled freely around Narragansett Bay. Eventually finding the Plymouth church to be insufficiently separated from the Church of England, Williams returned to Salem and became the minister there in August 1634. His sweet, winning disposition swayed the congregation to his unorthodox ideas. He preached "Soul Liberty" which denied the right of town authorities to punish breaches of religious discipline, force religious beliefs, or compel church attendance. He condemned civil

interference in the church, saying it would render "the garden and spouse of Christ a filthy dunghill and whorehouse of rotten and stinking whores and hypocrites." Even worse in the magistrates' view was Williams' impugning the Christian character of the King and his charge that the King's charter was invalid in granting their land. As the charter was then under attack in England by the colony's enemies, they feared that news of Williams' unorthodoxy would be used to void it.

The magistrates remonstrated with Williams, browbeat his congregation into withdrawing support, and finally ordered him banished on October 9, 1635. Williams could remain until the following spring provided that he cease preaching seditious doctrines. But he would not be silenced; and learning that the order was to be carried out, he fled Salem in January 1636 to the camp of Massasoit at Sowams (present-day Warren, Rhode Island). There he spent the winter in the company of a few followers who had joined him. In April Williams led his little band to the bank of the Great Salt Cove and began the first of Rhode Island's four original towns. He wrote, "I, having made covenants of peaceable neighborhood with all the sachems and natives round about us, and having a sense of God's merciful providence unto me in my distress, called the place Providence; I desired it be for a shelter for persons distressed of conscience." Unfortunately, such was not the purpose of most of Williams' companions. Above all, they wanted land.

The settling of Providence is a fascinating study in the clash between the hopes of a God-intoxicated young man with no political or administrative experience and the individualism and land hunger of his "loving neighbors." Williams was only about 33 and had no plans to establish a colony. He was full of an uncompromising idealism that was untested by the reality of governance. He wanted to dwell in peace and harmony with the Indians, but lived to see Providence burned to the ground by them. He sought to create a place "for such as were destitute, especially for Conscience sake," but some took this to mean the end of all government or the right to grab as

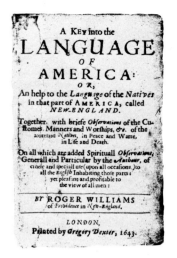

ABOVE: A Key into the Language of America *by Roger Williams was published in London in 1643 while Williams sought a charter for his colony. The printer, Gregory Dexter, returned with Williams and later became the pastor of the Baptist church. From the Imprint Collection, Rhode Island Historical Society (RHi x3 774)*

LEFT: Though no actual likeness of Roger Williams (1600?-1683) exists, F. Halpin engraved this portrait of him in 1847 for Benedict's History of the Baptists. *RIHS (RHi x3 19)*

much land as possible. He believed that "selfless benevolence" should prevail between neighbors, but he found bickering, litigation, and even brawling in the streets. He welcomed refugees from Massachusetts and made them coproprietors of the land that his Narragansett friends, Canonicus and Miantonomi, had given him, but some of these men betrayed him by summoning the authority of the Bay Colony. The resulting tangled land claims, lawsuits, and dissension jeopardized the independence of Providence Plantations.

Living as squatters beyond the jurisdiction of any colony, the settlers drew up a formal covenant in August 1637. The 13 who signed agreed to obey majority decisions of the heads of households "and all others whom they shall admit unto them only in civil things." This meant that religion was to be free of governmental interference. By 1638 enough of Williams' followers from Salem had joined him that they organized a church. Anne Hutchinson's sister, Catherine Scott, convinced Williams that only converted adults should be baptized; so when the church was gathered in late 1638, it rejected infant baptism and adopted baptism by total immersion. Having founded the first Baptist Church in America, Williams soon doubted this organization and resigned to become an unaffiliated preacher for the rest of his life. Only about a dozen of the 60 householders joined the only church in town, highlighting the individualism and religious anarchy that characterized the settlement.

"Rhode Island was purchased by love." This expressed Williams' relationship with the Indians, and no dispute ever arose between him and the Narragansetts who freely gave him land. But he had many problems with his fellow settlers. Chief among the land hungry was William Harris, whom one historian has described as "without doubt one of the most litigious of the early New England colonists." Harris had come destitute and Williams admitted him "out of Pity." Yet Harris eventually attempted to steal 300,000 acres from the Narragansetts by arguing that the original land grants, which were intended to be a few square miles, extended far inland.

When challenged by Williams, Harris began lawsuits which dragged on beyond his death in 1681. In the struggle with Connecticut over possession of the southern half of Rhode Island, Harris acted as Connecticut's agent. Likewise, William Arnold and other coproprietors demanded more land and received a special concession below the Pawtuxet River. When this group fell into dispute with their neighbors, they submitted themselves to the jurisdiction of Massachusetts, giving the Bay Colony grounds for asserting control over part of Providence Plantation. From 1642 to 1658 the Arnold group regarded itself as part of Massachusetts, and Arnold registered his land deeds there.

Arnold was wise because Williams' Indian purchases were invalid in English courts. The Crown and the other colonies

John Hutchins Cady drew this map in 1936 showing the 1636-1659 boundaries of Rhode Island. RIHS (RHi x3 855)

recognized land as being conveyed by royal charter, and buying land from the Indians without a charter's sanction was not valid. As Plymouth, Massachusetts, and Connecticut extended their claims over the Narragansett Bay, the Rhode Island towns were hard pressed to prevent them. In August 1642 the Massachusetts court summoned Miantonomi, sachem of the Narragansetts, to Boston to deny his sale of land to Roger Williams, to submit himself and his land to Massachusetts Bay jurisdiction, or to show what right he had to his lands! Miantonomi was deeply offended, as he considered his authority to be equal to any colonial government; and he rejected all demands. The court responded by forbidding him to sell land without its permission and ordered the Narragansetts to be disarmed. In the summer of 1643 war erupted between the Narragansetts and the Mohegans of Connecticut. When Miantonomi was treacherously murdered by the Mohegans with Puritan complicity, Rhode Island lost an important ally.

Williams had not meant to begin a colony, but his activities opened a door to a stream of refugees. He welcomed Anne Hutchinson and the Antinomians, who established Rhode Island's second town, Portsmouth. This group represented a far more serious threat to Massachusetts than Williams, and they became the strongest part of the heretic colony on Narragansett Bay. Williams had only a handful of followers in the outlying town of Salem;

the Antinomians constituted a large group in Boston. Antinomians were opposed to being ruled by other men, believing that God was the one true Ruler. The name, Antinomian, means "against the law." They were not truly anarchists, but they represented another of those purist challenges to Massachusetts Bay. The Puritans tried to balance the demands of external behavior and internal piety. The ministers and magistrates emphasized obedience to the laws of the church and state as a way of creating a well-ordered, well-regulated society ruled by visible saints. The tendency always existed for this to lead to empty form and ritual. Anne Hutchinson thought she detected such a tendency in Massachusetts; and she charged the ministers with preaching a "covenant of works," which emphasized right behavior. She preached a "covenant of grace" which

FACING PAGE: Roger Williams had exceptionally good relations with the Indians, and his Narragansett friends, Canonicus and Miantonomi, granted him the land for Providence Plantations. From Providence: The Southern Gateway to New England, Commemorating the 150th Anniversary of the Independence of the State of R.I., 1926. Courtesy, Providence Public Library

LEFT: The Narragansett sachem Miantonomi was captured by the Mohegans in 1643. He was later murdered by them with the approval of Puritan authorities. Engraved by F.O.C. Darley from History of the Indians of Connecticut by John W. DeForest. RIHS (RHi x3 634)

stressed the individual's direct apprehension of God's love and forgiveness. In fact, she was a mystic who believed that she received revelations directly from God. She preached a higher purity and declared that only two of the colony's ministers were truly saved. Her individualistic theology had particular appeal to certain leading Boston merchants, who felt confined by the corporate, communal nature of the colony. It also gave a sense of assurance to people who found no comfort in the stress upon pious behavior and practices.

William and Anne Hutchinson arrived in Boston in September 1634; and as Hutchinson was a successful merchant, the couple entered the highest levels of society. They built their house near the homes of Governor John Winthrop and William Coddington, the richest man in New England. An experienced nurse and midwife,

Anne's charisma won many friends among the women of Boston. She began holding meetings in her home with several women to discuss the ministers' sermons, but soon attracted so many men and women that she held two lecture days. As her ideas became known, her opponents called her an Antinomian.

In 1636 the Antinomians elected one of their group, Harry Vane, governor, defeating Winthrop. The church and town divided into factions. When the Antinomians refused to join the military expedition against the Pequot Indians in 1637 because the chaplain was not one of their men, the religious division took a dangerous turn. In May 1637 the towns outside Boston rallied to reelect Winthrop, and by November his forces had complete control and disarmed and disenfranchised the Antinomians. Defeated and facing exile,

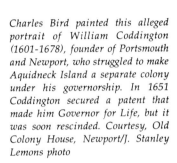

Charles Bird painted this alleged portrait of William Coddington (1601-1678), founder of Portsmouth and Newport, who struggled to make Aquidneck Island a separate colony under his governorship. In 1651 Coddington secured a patent that made him Governor for Life, but it was soon rescinded. Courtesy, Old Colony House, Newport/J. Stanley Lemons photo

William Coddington and other Antinomian leaders searched for another settlement. One of them, John Clarke, learned from Roger Williams that Aquidneck Island was available; and Williams arranged to buy the island from Canonicus and Miantonomi. The following spring the exiles began a town called Pocasset (later renamed Portsmouth). Anne Hutchinson joined them in 1638 after trials which banished and excommunicated her from Massachusetts. She was part of the turbulent history of Pocasset until her husband died, and she removed to Long Island in 1643. The next year she was massacred by Indians, an event which Puritan Massachusetts regarded as God's just punishment.

The leading figure at Pocasset was Coddington. He was by far the most important and powerful of the exiles from Massachusetts. He had been one of the original Assistants to Governor Winthrop in 1630 and later became treasurer. Winthrop sought to dissuade him from leaving when the Antinomian party collapsed. Nevertheless, Coddington took the lead in locating a new settlement and in organizing the exodus to Aquidneck. Since the wealthy exile supplied most of the purchase price, Roger Williams put the deed in his name.

Ironically, Coddington had been one of the judges who banished Williams from Massachusetts and would subsequently be a major obstacle to Williams' efforts to unify the Narragansett Bay towns. Coddington eventually connived with Plymouth, Massachusetts Bay, Connecticut, and the Dutch on Long Island to gain recognition of his separate and supreme authority on Aquidneck Island.

Exasperated by the machinations of Coddington, Williams wrote that he was "a worldly man, a selfish man, nothing for public, but all for himself and private." Coddington was actually a public-spirited man who devoted nearly 50 years to governance. However, he was deeply conservative and believed that deference was due him as a consequence of his wealth and social station. When the Antinomians signed a compact creating a government for their settlement, Coddington was elected "Judge." He expected to rule in Old Testament style over a Bible Commonwealth, but was thwarted and frustrated by the individualism and democratic tendencies prevailing in Rhode Island. He neither attained the order he wanted nor was he accorded the deference he expected. While he had the support of most of the "better sort," he was rebuffed by the ordinary people led by the Hutchinsons. When the chronic troublemaker, Samuel Gorton, appeared on the scene, Coddington lost control entirely and withdrew with some supporters to the southern end of Aquidneck. There in April 1639, he founded Rhode Island's third town, Newport. Those remaining at Pocasset adopted a new compact which restricted the magistrates to "civil things," required jury trials, and forbade a religious test for office. Finally they changed the town name to Portsmouth. However, by November, Coddington forced Portsmouth into a common government for Aquidneck by controlling the land titles.

The fourth of the original towns resulted from the gyrations of that cantankerous character, Samuel Gorton. He was so unorthodox and aggressive that he was driven successively from Boston, Plymouth, Portsmouth, and Providence before founding his own town at

Shawomet (soon to be renamed Warwick). Arriving in Boston in March 1637, he departed for Plymouth within two months, but the authorities there expelled him in December 1638. His bickering with Coddington's Aquidneck government led to his banishment after a public whipping in March 1641. Next he vexed Providence and Roger Williams, who wrote, "Master Gorton, having foully abused high and low at

The presence of the Gortonites and the argument with Roger Williams over the interpretation of the Indian deeds led the Arnolds, Harris, and others to appeal in September 1642 to Massachusetts for redress. Gorton thought it best to remove himself, so in October 1642 he purchased land (Shawomet) to the south from Miantonomi. But this came after Massachusetts had arbitrarily forbidden Miantonomi to

In the fall of 1643 Massachusetts dispatched soldiers to Shawomet (Warwick) to arrest Samuel Gorton. The Gortonites held off the soldiers for two days before surrendering and being marched away in chains to Massachusetts for trial. Engraving from Scribner's Popular History of the United States, *1897. Courtesy, Pawtucket Public Library*

Aquidneck, is now bewitching and bemaddening poor Providence both with his unclean and foul censures of all the ministers of this country ... and also denying all visible and external ordinances." Denied admission as freemen (voters) in Providence, Gorton and his followers purchased land but soon became embroiled with the Arnolds and William Harris over its possession.

sell his land. The Arnolds also wanted Shawomet, so they appealed to Massachusetts, which issued a summons to Gorton for trespassing on Massachusetts territory. Gorton ignored the summons. In October 1643 soldiers arrested him and took the Gortonites to Boston for trial. Gorton was sentenced to six months at hard labor in chains. When released and forbidden to return to Shawomet, he sailed to London and there, with the aid of the Earl of Warwick, secured a charter in 1646. The Gortonites returned, renamed the town in honor of their patron, created a government, and in May 1647 joined the other three towns as part of the "Province of Providence Plantations."

Roger Williams had labored seven years

to establish a community where no one could be persecuted for his religious beliefs, and he had built solid ties of trust with his Indian neighbors. But all was threatened by his greedy fellow settlers and by the formation of the United Colonies, a military alliance of the Puritan colonies of New Haven, Hartford, Plymouth, and Massachusetts (noticeably excluding the heretic towns on Narragansett Bay). Since the Puritans frequently asserted that the Rhode Islanders had no authority for civil government, Williams took a ship to England in June 1643 to secure a patent. He returned triumphantly to Providence in September 1644 with a patent establishing the "Province of Providence Plantations in Narragansett in New England." Undeterred, neighboring colonies continued their efforts to take the territory, basing their actions on treaties with Indians, submissions from both settlers and Indians in the area, fraudulent land claims and mortgages, arbitrary expansion of existing charter grants, and eventually by right of conquest in King Philip's War in 1675-1676.

William Coddington did not welcome the Charter of 1644 on Aquidneck Island. Portsmouth and Newport debated for two years as to whether to join Providence in a government under the Charter. When Plymouth suddenly asserted that Aquidneck Island belonged to it and threatened the inhabitants if they recognized Williams' Charter, Portsmouth broke with Coddington's Aquidneck government and cast its lot with Providence. Coddington was deeply opposed to federation and sought recognition from Plymouth or Massachusetts for a separate government on the island. Having been thwarted in America, Coddington sailed to England, secured his own patent, and returned in the summer of 1651 as Governor for Life over Aquidneck and Conanicut islands with virtual dictatorial authority.

The mainland towns rejected Coddington's patent and dispatched Roger Williams to England to confirm the Charter of 1644, and the freemen of Aquidneck sent John Clarke to seek revocation of Coddington's grant. Coddington, unable to govern, had to flee to Boston for safety. The

British Council of State rescinded Coddington's commission in 1652; however, the four towns did not reunite in a single government until 1654. Williams returned to be President for 1654-1657, while John Clarke remained in England as the colony's agent. At last Coddington ended his efforts to rule a separate colony and returned to Newport in 1656, apologized, was for-

Charles II, King of England from 1660-1685, granted the Charter of 1663, which created the English Colony of Rhode Island and Providence Plantations. His motives for permitting such independence and freedom of worship are not clear. RIHS (RHi x3 4247)

restoration of the monarchy in England in 1660, ending the Cromwellian Commonwealth, caused Rhode Islanders to question the Charter's legality. Charles II nullified all actions of Cromwell's government, making the validity of the Charter of 1644 doubtful. Just as Roger Williams had turned his personal acquaintance with Oliver Cromwell and Robert Rich, Earl of Warwick, into the Charter of 1644, so John Clarke found an advantage for Rhode Island in the new political situation in England in the 1660s. He secured a new charter in 1663 for "The English Colony of Rhode Island and Providence Plantations in New England in America."

The Charter of 1663 was amazing. It gave Rhode Island the freedom "to hold forth a lively experiment, that a flourishing and civil state may stand, yea and best be maintained ... with a full liberty in religious commitments." No person was to be "molested, punished, disquieted, or called into question, for any differences in opinion in matters of religion ... ." Rhode Island could elect its own governor and assembly and control its own military affairs. Essential power remained in the town meetings, which elected the General Assembly members and reviewed Assembly actions. This was a grant of freedom beyond that of any other colony and permitted it to become virtually self-governing.

No one knows why Charles II granted such a liberal charter as he was no advocate of dissenters and heretics. Perhaps he took some delight in twitting the noses of the neighboring Puritan colonies which grudgingly recognized his accession and which continued to harbor some of the regicide judges who had condemned his father in 1649. On the other hand, Rhode Island had been the first New England colony to proclaim its allegiance to the new monarch.

Unfortunately, the Charter did not end the United Colonies' efforts to seize most of Rhode Island. Their intrusions accelerated a land rush that had gathered momentum in the 1650s and pushed toward the catastrophe of the last great Indian war in southern New England, King Philip's War. Some Rhode Islanders joined the rush and

Depicted in this 1834 wood engraving is Metacomet, called King Philip, sachem of the Wampanaog Indians. He led the rising of his people against Plymouth Colony. The war spread to become the worst Indian war in New England history, 1675-1676. RIHS (RHi x3 771)

given, and served in various offices, including governor under the Charter of 1663, until he died in 1678.

The confirmation of the Charter of 1644 and the submission of Coddington to the unified government of Providence Plantations did not end the travail of the heretic colony. Its neighbors still behaved as though the Charter were invalid; and the

Benjamin Church (1639-1718) adopted Indian-style tactics to defeat Metacomet's warriors in King Philip's War. This questionable likeness was engraved by Paul Revere to accompany the publication of Church's account of King Philip's War. RIHS (RHi x3 559)

in 1657 bought claims to the Pettaquamscutt Purchase south of Wickford and by 1660 to the Misquamicut tract in the Westerly area. These acquisitions established a Rhode Island presence in territory that Connecticut and Massachusetts maintained was theirs by right of treaty, charter, and conquest.

The most notorious and fraudulent land grab was perpetrated by the Narragansett Proprietors, a group of businessmen and officials from Boston, Plymouth, and Connecticut. Ignoring Rhode Island laws against unauthorized purchases of Indian lands, they began buying land from the Indians in 1658. In 1660 the Narragansett Indians declared war against the Mohegans, but the United Colonies intervened and imposed a humiliating treaty and levied an impossible fine on the Narragansetts. The Indians were allowed four months to raise 2,000 fathoms of wampum on condition that they mortgage their lands to the New England Confederation as surety. The Confederation exchanged the mortgage for the fine with the Narragansett Proprietors. When the Indians failed to meet the payments, the Proprietors foreclosed in 1662 and claimed ownership of all Narragansett lands. The Proprietors felt secure because Connecticut's new charter of 1662 placed the eastern boundary of Connecticut on Narragansett Bay. On the other hand, Rhode Island's Charter of 1663 defined its western border as the Pawcatuck River. The conflicting charter claims of both colonies to all of southern Rhode Island went unsettled for 60 years as both sides tried to assert control, even to the point of absurdity. In one instance a homicide occurred and Connecticut officers arrived first, examined the corpse, and buried it without letting the Rhode Island representatives see it. After the Connecticut officers left, the Rhode Islanders dug up the body and conducted their own investigation. Some of Connecticut's strongest claims, however, grew out of King Philip's War on the grounds that it had conquered the Narragansett Indians.

King Philip's War brought to a bloody climax more than 50 years of English-Indian relations in New England and eliminated the Indians as a major factor in southern New England. One cannot read of the encroachment of the settlers upon the native population, the whittling away of their lands, dignity, and independence without a sense of sorrow; but it is difficult to see how it could have turned out differently. The Indians did not understand until too late that the straggling white settlements were the vanguard of a dynamic, expanding civilization. The settlers saw the natives as heathens and the land vacant for the taking. For their part, the Native Americans were not pawns of the settlers; and they had their own reasons for cooperation or hostility.

The English-Indian confrontation was, in reality, an English-Indian-Indian struggle. Each tribe used the settlers to gain an advantage over old adversaries, and the colonists seized this division to advance their interests. Massasoit made a treaty of mutual assistance with the Pilgrims at Plymouth because the Wampanoags wanted help against their traditional and more powerful foes, the Narragansetts. Historians have suggested that the Narragansetts welcomed Roger Williams in Providence and the Antinomians on Aquidneck to create a buffer zone between them and their enemies, the Wampanoags and Plymouth to the east. Canonicus and Miantonomi could then give more attention to the threat posed by the Pequots to the west. The Pequots had invaded New England from the upper Hudson River area in the late 16th century and reduced most southern Connecticut tribes to tributaries. They had a fearsome reputation for cruelty and cannibalism, and they had defeated the Narragansetts in a fierce battle near Westerly in 1632. For their part, the English feared an Indian uprising. In 1622 supposedly friendly Indians suddenly massacred 347 colonists at Jamestown, Virginia; consequently the Virginia Company lost its charter and the Crown took over. Fear of such a massacre and the loss of their precious charters haunted the New England colonists throughout the 17th century. No weakness could be shown the natives; the colonists used force repeatedly to secure submission.

The Pequots sought to stop the advance of the English into Connecticut in 1637 and appealed to the Narragansetts to join them. They warned that if the English prevailed the Narragansetts would soon be subjugated. Massachusetts authorities now begged Roger Williams, banished under pain of death one year earlier, to prevent the alliance. He succeeded in this mission; and in the ensuing war the Narragansetts sided with the Bay Colony. The Pequots were defeated and most of the survivors sold either to the West Indies or given as slaves to the Narragansetts, Mohegans, and Niantics. Ironically, Massachusetts then used the victory to claim Rhode Island lands and moved to reduce Miantonomi to subordination.

When the Pilgrims arrived in 1620, the Wampanoag country extended from Narragansett Bay to Cape Cod, but by the time Massasoit died in 1661, the Indian lands had been reduced to Mount Hope Neck, Tiverton, and Sakonnet. The Puritans assumed after the Pequot War that Indians had to obey their laws. Violations were tried in Puritan courts, and the Indians often had to sell their lands to pay the fines. One of the principal grievances stated by Massasoit's son, Metacomet, was that the English "undertake to give law to the Indians and take from them their country." He declared at last, "I am determined not to live until I have no country." He would lose both his land and his life.

Massasoit, friend of Plymouth and Roger Williams, had kept the peace during the 40 years before his death; but his sons, Wamsutta and Metacomet (dubbed Alexander and Philip) burned with accumulated hatred and grievances that Wampanoags felt toward Plymouth. King Philip's War began in June 1675 in Swansea, spread to engulf most of New England, and 15 months later wound down to the Mount Hope Neck again. Plymouth failed to pin Philip at Mount Hope or in the Tiverton area, and he escaped to central Massachusetts where he gained the support of other tribes. The Narragansetts harbored Wampanoag refugees, giving the United Colonies an excuse to make a preemptive assault on the Narragansett stronghold. A 1,000-man army under Plymouth Governor Josiah Winslow invaded Rhode Island, and with the help of a traitor from within the tribe made a surprise attack upon the Narragansetts in the Great Swamp on December 19, 1675. Casualties were heavy on both sides, and many Indians died when fires destroyed their dwellings. After the battered colonial army withdrew, the Indians swept the mainland clean of settlers in the following months. All but 28 men fled from Providence; and on March 29, 1676, the Indians, despite entreaties from Roger Williams, burned the town, including Williams' house.

The Indian victories were temporary. Metacomet sought support as far west as New York, but the Mohawks drove him out and launched devastating attacks upon other Indians in western New England. One historian has said that the Mohawk attack "was the blow that lost the war for Philip." In the final phase, Philip and his remnant flitted through the woods and swamps near the place where it all began; and they were hunted by a force that included many Wampanoags commanded by Colonel Benjamin Church. At last in August 1676, one of Church's Wampanoags killed Philip.

The war broke Indian power in southern New England, and the tribes declined into dependency or disappeared entirely. The remnants of the once-powerful Narragansetts merged with the Niantics of southern Rhode Island, lost nearly all their land, and eventually settled on a small reservation in Charlestown. The destruction of the Narragansetts eliminated the only ally Rhode Island had had in its struggles with its neighbors, and Connecticut reasserted its claims to much of Rhode Island by right of conquest. During the war, Aquidneck became almost all that remained of the colony because by April 1676 not a single white family remained between Providence and Point Judith. Most of the population fled to the islands, as suggested by the Quaker-dominated General Assembly, which had refused to provide any military defense for the mainland towns. At war's end, people began drifting back, rebuilding, and staking out new claims in the interior. While Providence was rebuilding, Newport entered its period of dominance in the colony.

Chapter Two

THE ENGLISH COLONY OF RHODE ISLAND

Sir Edmund Andros (1637-1714) served as Governor of the Dominion of New England. Rhode Island was temporarily merged with the other New England colonies under the governorship of Andros. He was deposed in 1689 after the fall of King James II. From Scribner's Popular History of the United States, 1897. Courtesy, Pawtucket Public Library

WHAT WAS THE pivotal event in Rhode Island's struggle for survival in the 17th century? Some choose Roger Williams' patent of 1644, others pick John Clarke's Charter of 1663, and others single out King Philip's War of 1675-1676. One historian maintains that it was the first arrival of the Quakers in 1657. They assured the economic survival of Rhode Island by creating a commercial network within the British Empire which reduced Rhode Island's dependence upon its covetous neighbors. The Quaker majority on Aquidneck and their commerce helped Newport become the dominant town in the colony. However, these advances were made in the face of continuing threats to the independence of Rhode Island and even its temporary disappearance as a separate colony.

Other colonies thought that it was bad enough that Rhode Island had Baptists, Antinomians, Gortonites, Seekers, and other exotic religious groups, but admitting the Quakers was going too far. In 1656 Massachusetts treated roughly and then expelled the few Quakers who surfaced there. In 1658 the colony enacted a law that condemned to the gallows any Quaker who returned a third time after being banished twice. Under this harsh statute four Quakers were hanged in 1659 and 1660. Connecticut and Plymouth also enacted anti-Quaker laws; and the Commissioners of the United Colonies requested that Rhode Island banish its Quakers, threatening reprisals otherwise. The governor replied that there was no law

by which "men could be punished in Rhode Island for their opinions, and that the Quakers being unmolested, were becoming disgusted at their want of success." In fact, many leading Rhode Islanders, including William Coddington, John Coggeshall, Nicholas Easton, and William Harris, became Quakers in the 1660s. By 1690 Quakers were nearly half the people of the colony, and they dominated the government for years.

As neighboring colonies applied economic pressure, Rhode Island became more independent of them because the Quaker network provided connections in the British West Indies, Pennsylvania, Ireland, and England. Although the Quakers were a small minority in Britain's American possessions, they were dispersed more uniformly throughout the colonies than any other religious group. Fundamental to commercial success in the colonial era was a network of sound and trustworthy associates. What ties of family and friendship provided for some, religion supplied for others. Both the Quakers and later the Jews of Newport relied upon coreligionists to conduct their business in distant ports.

Aquidneck Island had developed a successful agricultural economy within a half-dozen years of its founding. Some pioneer families, such as the Coddingtons, Coggeshalls, Brentons, and Hutchinsons, were fairly wealthy; and moving from Massachusetts and Plymouth, they brought most of what they needed to get reestablished. Their agricultural land was among the best in southern New England, and the islands

"The Silver Fleece" was the first seal of the Town of Newport, 1696. The selection of a long-tailed sheep symbolized Aquidneck Island's commercial agriculture, the basis for Newport's prosperity. Courtesy, Newport Historical Society/John Hopf photo

were ideal for commercial livestock grazing. In addition, unlike Providence where Williams attempted to distribute land equally to inhabitants, Coddington and his friends created landed estates with tenant farmers, which soon produced agricultural surpluses for export. Newport had an excellent harbor, and a lively agricultural commerce was conducted with New Amsterdam, Salem, and Boston. The trade paid for a modest amount of imported British goods and provided capital to invest in mercantile activities. By the time the Quakers arrived, the colony was exporting hogs, cattle, sheep, and horses. The Quakers substantially improved the commercial opportunities. Rhode Island did so well that by the 1690s it probably had a favorable balance of trade, which was unique among the colonies because most imported more than they sold. The establishment of a thriving economic base for Newport in the 17th century allowed it to dominate the colony and to provide the leadership which preserved Rhode Island from threats to its charter privileges after 1663.

The greatest menace to the separate existence of Rhode Island came when it was reduced to a county within the Dominion of New England under Governor Edmund Andros. The Dominion was intended to embrace all the English possessions from New Jersey to Maine, and in 1686 King James II dispatched Andros to collect the charters of the New England colonies and begin the administration of the Dominion. The Crown hoped to rationalize the confused colonial administration and exert greater control. Rhode Island passively resisted the Dominion by ignoring directives and failing to carry out orders, and it and Connecticut hid their charters from Governor Andros. The Glorious Revolution of 1688 which drove James II from the throne also aborted the Dominion as armed citizens overthrew Andros in Boston in April 1689. The following month Rhode Island officials who had been in office in 1687 summoned a meeting of freemen in Newport, the charter was brought out of hiding, and the old government restored.

The reemergence of the colony brought a return to its independent ways and renewed attacks on the charter. Though this effort extended well into the 18th century, the period of greatest threat began in the 1690s and ended in 1707. Critics mounted an effort in England to revoke Rhode Island's charter privileges. The chief justice of New York wrote that Rhode Islanders "did in all things as if they were out of the dominion of the Crown." Newport in particular was accused of being "a place where Pirates are ordinarily too kindly entertained." In fact, pirates did vacation and refit their vessels there. Captain Thomas Paine, soldier, pirate, and privateer settled first in Newport in 1683 and then in Jamestown in 1688. His friend, the infamous Captain William Kidd, also received a friendly reception in Newport. In addition, Rhode Island was charged with issuing privateering commissions of dubious legality which cloaked some of the activities of piratical characters. Moreover, those endless boundary disputes with Connecticut and Massachusetts and the undying but fraudulent land claims of the Narragansett Proprietors surfaced repeatedly. Finally, some disgruntled Rhode Island royalists longed for the good old days of the Dominion of New England and its "proper" government; and they complained that the colony was governed by illiterates, incompetents, Quakers, and other sectaries. Nevertheless, all these charges came to naught in large part because of the shrewd and vigorous leadership of Governor Samuel Cranston.

Cranston began his long tenure as governor in 1698, just as the winds of criticism were rising to gale force. When he died in 1727, after serving 29 terms, Rhode Island had been transformed into a fairly secure colony. By cooperating where required while maintaining Rhode Island's independence, Cranston defused external critics; and the colony's internal affairs were reformed to promote commercial activities. In particular, the central government was strengthened at the expense of the towns, the General Assembly asserted its power to tax, the first paper money issues eased the credit and specie shortage, and Newport emerged as a booming commercial center.

Across Narragansett Bay from Newport there developed a society with large estates and slave labor that was more like the South than any other part of New England.

Because many of its principal landowners came from Aquidneck Island, this area was tied by family, economics, and politics to Newport. A number of families, the Hazards, Potters, Updikes, Robinsons, Gardiners, Champlins, and Marchants, acquired farms with thousands of acres. These "Narragansett Planters," as they were called, raised livestock and produced dairy products for export. One lucrative effort was the successful breeding of horses, especially the famous Narragansett Pacer. These activities supported Newport's dominant position in Rhode Island.

Newport would become the fifth largest town in the colonies before the American Revolution. At the end of the 17th century, however, it was little more than a single street (Thames Street) with various lanes running off to nearby farms. Pigs

Mary Dyer, one of Anne Hutchinson's closest friends, was among the first Americans to convert to Quakerism. On her fourth invasion of Massachusetts in 1660 to spread the Quaker gospel, she was hanged by the authorities. Engraving from Scribner's Popular History of the United States, 1897. Courtesy, Pawtucket Public Library

scavenged in the streets, and wolves were a problem in town. The merchant marine consisted of some small vessels and a few dozen sailors. In 1681 Governor Peleg Sanford reported that the town had "several men that deal in buying and selling," but none could "properly be called merchants." He said "that most of our Colony live comfortably by improving the wilderness." Although Rhode Island exported agricultural goods to other American colonies, it still had no direct trade with England. As late as 1708 it sent products to England by way of Boston. This would change by the 1720s as Newport surged forward when the imperial wars among the European powers provided oceans of opportunity.

King William's War (1689-1697) stimulated Newport by bringing in loot from privateering activities; for example, the Wanton brothers began their fortune by successful privateering in 1694. Queen Anne's War (1703-1713) produced even more vigorous privateering as well as the entry by the colony's traders into the French and Spanish West Indies. Rhode Island fitted out more privateers than any other northern colony during King George's War (1739-1748). Rhode Island vessels feasted on enemy shipping, taking 20 ships in 1745 alone. The privateering tradition carried through the French and Indian War (1754-1763), to the extent that in 1760 Governor Stephen Hopkins reported that Rhode Island had 50 privateers preying on French shipping. At the same time, it probably had more ships trading with the enemy: an interesting arrangement in which it destroyed enemy ships and replaced them with its own. British officials singled out Rhode Island as the most notorious violator of the prohibition against trading with the enemy. Some of this trade was done through neutral Dutch ports on Surinam and St. Eustatius or, during the French and Indian War, with the port of Monte Cristi on the Spanish half of Hispaniola. In another device, sailing under a "flag of truce," a ship carried enemy prisoners to an enemy port to be exchanged for British prisoners. Some ships carried only one or two prisoners with an entire cargo of goods to be traded. Some enterprising merchants took captives by privateering and then returned them to the enemy under a flag of truce.

These operations greatly accelerated commercial activities and shipbuilding. In 1708 Governor Cranston reported to the Board of Trade that the annual export to England was six times as high as 20 years earlier; and whereas Newport had had only four or five vessels in 1681, it now had nearly 30. By 1721 Newport's trade had doubled again, and by 1740 the colony had nearly 120 vessels trading with other American colonies, the West Indies, Africa, and England. By the end of the French and Indian War, Newport merchants alone owned 200 trading vessels, and Providence and Bristol were also putting increasing numbers of ships to sea. Still, it was Newport's Golden Age.

Politically, Newport dominated Rhode Island. Every governor from 1663 to 1743 was from Newport except Joseph Jencks of Providence (1727-1732), and the General Assembly insisted that he live in Newport during his terms. "The colonial leaders ... were Newport merchants who took it for granted that what was good for Newport was good for Rhode Island." The town's population rose from approximately 2,200 in 1708 to 9,200 in 1774, despite having Middletown separated from it in 1743. The entire colony increased from 7,000 to nearly 60,000 in the same time span. Some 5,000 people were added in 1747, when Britain ruled in favor of Rhode Island on a boundary dispute and Massachusetts had to cede the towns of Cumberland, Warren, Barrington, Bristol, Tiverton, and Little Compton. The number of towns jumped from nine to 30 between 1708 and the American Revolution. It did not escape the notice of some by mid-century that Providence County's population was actually increasing more rapidly than that of any other part of the colony, and this demographic fact was driven home by the economic and political challenge mounted by Providence to Newport's supremacy after 1750.

Part of Newport's Golden Age was its cultural flowering. Its culture was provincial in that it imitated the styles of London, but the town's population was the most

Sea Captains Carousing in Surinam *by John Greenwood, 1755, shows a number of prominent Rhode Island ship captains drinking in a tavern in the Dutch colony. The artist depicted himself vomiting in the doorway to the right, while at the table were Captain Nicholas Cooke of Newport (dressed in grey, wearing Quaker-type hat), Captain Esek Hopkins of Providence (glass in hand), his brother Stephen (asleep, head in hand), Joseph Wanton of Newport (sleeping bald man, about to be drenched with wine), and Captain Ambrose Page of Providence (vomiting into Wanton's pocket). Lord Loudon, British commander in America, wrote to Prime Minister William Pitt that Rhode Island traders were a "lawless set of smugglers." Courtesy, St. Louis Art Museum*

Aaron Lopez (1731-1782), a Portuguese Jew, arrived in Newport in 1752. Beginning with little, he busied himself in oceanic commerce, slave trading, and spermaceti candle manufacturing. By 1775 he had become the richest merchant in Newport. Courtesy, American Jewish Historical Society

diverse of New England. Religious freedom and the spirit of enterprise had attracted Quakers and Jews. Both groups had been made unwelcome in the English and Dutch colonies elsewhere, and the first of them arrived in Newport just a year apart. While the Quakers flourished and dominated Rhode Island, the original contingent of Jews dwindled until a new influx in the 1740s brought at least 15 families. Some would become leading merchants, and Aaron Lopez may have been the richest man in Newport on the eve of the Revolution. Newport was the home of America's first Jewish synagogue and of Rhode Island's first Anglican church, as well as a Congregational church established by missionaries from Massachusetts. The town's mild climate attracted people from many places, especially from the West Indies and the southern American colonies. So many planters from South Carolina came each summer to rest and repair their health that

by 1730 Newport was being called the "Carolina Hospital."

Growth and prosperity led the town's leaders to demand improved conditions and culture. A street committee worked to clear the streets and highways of garbage and filth, sought to control scavenging hogs and stray dogs, and had most streets paved by 1715. Newport opened the first poorhouse in Rhode Island in July 1723, thereby clearing the streets of cripples, beggars, and drunks.

Newport, both then and now, congratulated itself upon the visit in 1729 of the British philosopher and Anglican divine, George Berkeley. Discouraged by the skepticism, indifference, and immorality of Europe, he arrived in Newport on his way to Bermuda to found a college that he envisioned would promote education, religion, and morality in the New World. His entourage contained a number of literary men and artists, including the promi-

27

nent portrait painter, John Smibert, who inspired Newport-born portraitist, Robert Feke.

Berkeley's dream never came true. He waited in vain for three years in Newport for Parliament to appropriate funds for the proposed college before returning to England in 1732. He never traveled to Bermuda; in fact, his experience in Newport so disillusioned him that he never traveled again. Charmed at first by the community's religious diversity and vigor, he came to feel that sectarianism was as damaging to faith and morality as the skepticism and atheism of Europe. In addition to Anglicans and Quakers, he was confronted by four Baptist churches, the result of splits of other Baptist congregations, and two Congregational churches, also the result of a split. Still, he found the ministers to be among the most learned and interesting persons in the town. The leading intellectuals in post-Berkeley Newport would be the two Congregationalist ministers, Ezra Stiles, pastor of the Second Congregational Church (1755-1778) and later president of Yale, and the pastor of the First Church, Samuel Hopkins, who was Jonathan Edwards' most brilliant disciple.

Berkeley's influence is difficult to measure because he did not take part in town affairs and lived in Middletown in Whitehall, the home he built. While he frequently preached at Trinity Church and entertained the local ministers and others, he took no direct part in the founding of the Society for the Promotion of Knowledge, which was Newport's equivalent to Benjamin Franklin's Philosophical Society in Philadelphia; and no evidence exists to indicate that he attended any meetings. His greatest impact was to bolster the small but growing and influential Anglican community in Newport. He donated an organ to Trinity Church after leaving Newport. He brought some 2,000 books with him and shared these with local merchants, some of whom also had impressive libraries. This eventually spawned the Redwood Library in 1747, endowed by Abraham Redwood with £500 sterling.

Rhode Island's first newspaper appeared in Newport in September 1732 when James Franklin, the brother of Benjamin Franklin, published a fortnightly called the *Rhode Island Gazette*. It disappeared shortly and Newport did not support a successful newspaper until the *Newport Mercury* appeared in 1758. (Providence acquired its first newspaper in October 1762 when William Goddard began the *Providence Gazette and Country Journal*.) Newport enjoyed other delights of civilization: a voice teacher could make a living there by 1732, French lessons were available, one could attend a class in psalmody, and Mary Cowley advertised a dancing school for "Gentlemen and Ladies of Family Character" in 1764. The first theatrical troupe ever to perform in New England came to Newport in June 1761. Having been well received, they made the mistake of trying Providence the next summer. The more puritanical Providence was so upset that it convinced the General Assembly to ban stage plays and theatricals in the whole colony.

Handsome homes and public buildings were built, and the first steepled church in Rhode Island, Trinity Church, was erected by the Anglicans. Such buildings provided opportunities for architects such as Richard Munday, who designed Trinity (1726) and the Colony House (1739); and Peter Harrison, who was responsible for the Redwood Library (1748), Touro Synagogue (1759), and the Brick Market (1760). For furnishings the merchants called upon talented silversmiths, interior decorators, and furniture makers, such as the Townsend and Goddard families, who crafted a distinctive Newport style. Except for the Brick Market, all of the major structures were completed by 1763. It was mostly a wooden town, but nearly all of the 1,000 buildings were painted, which was unusual for colonial America. All Newport lacked was a college. When the charter for a Baptist college was approved in 1764, it was assumed that the institution would be located there. But, when the contest had ended and Rhode Island College (as Brown University was then called) permanently located, the College Edifice rose on a hill in Providence.

In the first half of the 18th century,

Rhode Island's economy shifted from agriculture to commerce, but it had little of its own that anyone wanted. The raising of livestock, especially horses for export, remained a profitable enterprise through three quarters of the century; other products, such as pork, beef, wool and mutton, lumber, barrels and shingles, cheese, and dried fish came from local sources, but the colony would not get rich on its natural products. These were simply too limited. Because it had a tiny hinterland from which to draw raw materials or in which to sell products, its commercial prosperity was painfully and tenuously built on the reexport trade. Most of the industries which developed in the towns, such as making spermaceti candles, twine and cordage, and distilling rum, were linked to the reexport business. The remarkable thing about Rhode Island's prosperity in the 18th century was how well it did given the deficiency of local products. Rhode Island had to work harder than most for its prosperity, and this prosperity was precarious at best.

Of vital significance was the import of molasses (mostly from illegal sources) and the export of rum. The Rhode Island Remonstrance of 1764 indicated the significance when it stated that molasses "serves as an engine in the hands of the Merchant to effect the great purpose of paying for British manufactures." Nearly 500 vessels called Rhode Island home, and they transported nearly a million gallons of molasses annually. By 1769 Newport had 22 distilleries and Providence had 31, causing Stephen Hopkins to write that "distillery is the main hinge upon which the trade of the colony turns and many hundreds of persons depend immediately upon it for a subsistence." A lot of this rum went to the Africa coast for slaves; and it is estimated that half of Newport's merchant marine was engaged in the rum-slave traffic by the 1760s. In the 30 years prior to 1764, Rhode Island annually sent out nine vessels to Africa carrying rum. However, "molasses to rum to slaves" was only part of the picture. Most of Rhode Island's shipping was not involved in the slave trade. Rum, however, was a staple item which merchants used in their indirect trade with

England. The refrain might as readily run "molasses to rum to bills of credit" because rum was exported to other colonies, the Caribbean, and South America for trade and sale.

The uncertain and difficult basis of the merchants' wealth drove Rhode Islanders in unsavory and illegal directions. After 1720 the slave trade became a significant enterprise of Newport merchants, some of whom piled up fortunes in this "iniquitous traffic." Also, they took advantage of the Anglo-French wars to enter a forbidden trade with the enemies of their Sovereign. One of the bitterest complaints against Rhode Island was this traitorous dealing with the enemy. Rhode Islanders argued that this commerce was positively good for the Empire because it secured products that allowed them to trade with England. Always short of specie, Rhode Islanders

The nine carved shells and rich mahogany of this desk and bookcase make it the grandest expression of the Newport block and shell style. The piece is believed to have been crafted sometime between 1760 and 1785 by John Goddard (1723-1785). Originally owned by Joseph Brown, it is now in the John Brown House Museum in Providence. RIHS (RHi x3 4328)

No. 65	District and Port of Newport, August 28th 1805								

List of the names, places of birth and refidence, and a defcription of the perfons compofing the company of the *Brig* called the *Hope* of *Newport* burthen *ninety seven* tons 3/4 feet, whereof *Thomas White* is Mafter, bound for *Africa*

NAMES OF SEAMEN.	STATION.	Ages.	Height. Feet. Inches.		Complexion.	Residence.	PLACES OF BIRTH. States and Countries.	Towns.	Country of which they are refpectively Citizens or Subjects.
William Spooner	1 mate	31	5	6 7/8	light	Newport	R: Island	Newport	
William Johnson	2. mate	28	5	5 7/8	light	ditto	Massachusetts	Salem	
George Washington Sanford	seaman	20	5	3 7/8	light	ditto	Rhode Island	Newport	
Isaac Shaw J.	seaman	14	5	6	light	ditto	Massachusetts	Taunton	United States of America
Titus Sheffield	seaman	21	5	3 5/8	black	ditto	Rhode Island	North Kingstown	apprentice to the Captain
Stephen Gardner	seaman	22	5	9	black	S. Kingston	ditto	S. Kingston	ditto
John Oxford	seaman	33	5	10	black	Boston	Massachusetts	Boston	
Ebenezer Underwood	Cook	20	5	6 1/2	black	Newport	Massachusetts	Boston	Apprentice to the Captain

Thomas White

The complex nature of the slave trade was demonstrated by the voyage of the brig Hope on August 28, 1805: half of the crew was black. Newport's Free African Union Society (the first black organization in the United States) sought to discourage black participation by prohibiting membership or association with those "of the African Race that do or hereafter be the Means of bringing, from their Native Country, the Males, Females, Boys & Girls from Africa into Bondage." (Free African Union Society, Proceedings, September 8, 1791. From the U.S. Customs House Records, Newport Historical Society/J. Stanley Lemons photo

got most of their gold and silver and good bills of credit in the Caribbean and South America, and these in turn paid the colony's bills owed to England for manufactured products and the comforts of civilization.

Slavery was slow to develop in Rhode Island; but once it became a commodity of commerce, the colony's involvement became sustained and deep. In 1652 the General Assembly sought to forbid black slavery, but Aquidneck, under Coddington's brief tenure as Governor for Life, refused to recognize the law. Rhode Island opposed Indian slavery, but King Philip's War ended with the captives being parceled out to the towns as indentured servants or being handed over to Plymouth for export to the West Indies. The first recorded instance of a slave-trading vessel visiting Rhode Island was in 1696, when the *Seaflower*, out of Boston, brought a cargo of 47 slaves and sold 14 in Newport. In 1700 three vessels, fitted out in Newport but owned and commanded by Barbados merchants, sailed for Africa; and until the end of Queen Anne's War, Newport purchased its annual supply of 20 or 30 slaves from Barbados. After the war some of the town's merchants began investing in the growing and generally lucrative slave trade.

Newport and later Bristol and Providence became major sources of the slavers, and by mid-century slaves sold in the Caribbean and in the southern colonies produced about £40,000 annually to merchants for remittance to England. Rhode Islanders participated in the African slave trade in a major way from 1725 to 1807. The peak year was 1805 despite the fact that Rhode Island law had forbidden its citizens to engage in the trade since 1787. Jay Coughtry's *Notorious Triangle* reports: "During that span of seventy-five years at least 934 vessels left Rhode Island ports for the west coast of Africa and carried away an estimated one hundred six thousand slaves." While it was a minor carrier compared with the British who transported 20 times as many slaves, "Rhode Island was the principal American carrier." Nearly every leading merchant of Newport, whether Anglican, Quaker, Jew, Baptist, or Congregationalist, profited from the trade. The number of slaves in Rhode Island rose from 426 in 1708 to a peak of over 4,700 in 1758. By then it had the highest percentage of slaves of any New England colony, and Newport's population was 15 percent black. Nearly half of the colony's slaves worked on the great farms of the Narragansett Planters in South County.

The first slave ship from Providence was dispatched in 1736 by James Brown, the father of the four Brown brothers, Nicholas, John, Moses, and Joseph. The result was only marginally profitable and 23 years elapsed before another Brown ship sailed to the Guinea coast, but it never returned. The four brothers attempted a third voyage in 1764 and lost nearly $12,000; and all except John abandoned the trade. Moses became a Quaker, freed his 10 slaves, led the abolitionist movement in Rhode Island, and pushed the state to gradual emancipation in 1784 and a law passed in 1787 forbidding Rhode Islanders to engage in the slave trade. His Abolition Society brought the prosecution against brother John in 1797 in which the latter's ship was condemned, but John remained an advocate of the African slave trade until his death in 1803.

Merchants determined to engage in the slave trade did not permit Rhode Island laws to stop them any more than British navigation acts deterred them from trading with forbidden markets. When the post-Revolutionary depression pushed merchants back into old commercial patterns, all major ports reentered the slave trade. More than one third of all slaving voyages from Rhode Island occurred after the trade had been outlawed. Particularly notorious were James and George DeWolf of Bristol, who remained in the business until at least the 1820s. When South Carolina reopened her ports to the Guinea traffic from 1803 to 1807, slavers brought 38,775 slaves to Charleston. Despite Rhode Island's law, 7,958 of these were carried in 59 vessels from Rhode Island, half in DeWolf ships. The United State Congress outlawed the trade in 1808; and this, plus Moses Brown's antislavery crusade and the dogged enforcement of state and federal laws by William Ellery, United States Collector of Customs, ended the slave traffic by most Rhode Islanders.

However, the DeWolfs got around the law. James declared himself a Republican, and after Thomas Jefferson took office, was rewarded by the appointment of his brother-in-law, Charles Collins, as United States Collector for a newly created customs district—Bristol and Warren. This ended the scrutiny of Ellery at Newport, who protested while Collins closed his eyes as the DeWolfs outfitted one slaver after another. James left direct participation after 1808, turned to other business interests, and became a United States Sena-

George DeWolf (1779-1844), the most notorious practitioner of the illegal slave trade, profitted until his illicit empire crumbled with the failure of his Cuban sugar plantation in 1825. Bristol investors lost so much that the town did not recover for two decades. Oil painting by unknown artist. Courtesy, Linden Place/J. Stanley Lemons photo

tor in the 1820s. Cousin George continued smuggling slaves into the United States or dumped them on his sugar plantation in Cuba until the price was right. He also engaged in privateering along the South American coast when that region was torn with revolutions. His illicit but profitable empire collapsed with his sugar crop failure in 1825, and his London broker lost about $700,000. Uncle James lost the $250,000 he had invested, and Bristol took nearly two decades to recover. The United States Congress passed increasingly stringent laws to combat the African slave traffic, making slaving a capital crime in 1820. The only person condemned under the statute was a Rhode Island captain in 1859.

Once Rhode Islanders found a profitable enterprise, regardless of its legality, they found it difficult to alter course. Their options were limited, and their reserves insecure; therefore, a change in conditions could mean success or failure. Just as earlier wars enticed Rhode Islanders to escape the confines of Narragansett Bay, the events of the French and Indian War and the new Imperial climate after 1763 offered new perils and opportunities. It brought hardship and disaster to Newport, but Providence gained a great advantage.

THE INDEPENDENT STATE

THE FRENCH AND Indian War ushered in a period of difficulty for Rhode Island which emphasized its independent, otherwise-minded character. Problems of financing and taxation related to the war aggravated a growing political split in the colony, and the postwar revision of the British Imperial system moved the colony into early rebellion. Rhode Island resisted the regulations and reorganization which led to the American Revolution. In the event itself, it contributed heavily to the effort and suffered considerably. However, while the colony was first in war, it was last in peace. The fears that drove it into rebellion kept it out of the Union created by the Constitution.

As usual, Rhode Islanders rushed to take advantage of an Anglo-French war. More privateers sailed to prey on enemy shipping; more flag-of-truce voyages cloaked trading ventures with enemy ports; more blockade-runners attempted to evade British efforts to close French ports. Rhode Island was so notorious that Sir Francis Bernard, Royal Governor of Massachusetts, complained to the Board of Trade, "These practices will never be put an end to, till Rhode Island is reduced to the subjection of the British Empire." However, the price was high: Providence lost 65 vessels and Newport 150 to French privateers and British patrols, and Rhode Island's share of the war effort created heavy debts for the government. The colony had met previous financial pinches by issuing paper money, but this had been done so frequently and the volume had risen so high that by 1750 the colony had £525,335 in depreciated paper floating around. Finally, in 1751 Parliament prohibited all issues of paper money; therefore, during the war Rhode Island footed its obligations by borrowing and issuing treasury bills redeemable in gold and silver. The royal treasury reimbursed part of the cost, but the rest had to be paid off by taxation. But who was to be taxed? Two strong political factions sought to place the burden upon each other.

Because of the Charter, Rhode Island had been virtually an independent, self-governing republic for a century. The Charter gave the General Assembly legislative, executive, and judicial powers, and authority to appoint all public officials not elected directly by the voters. As a consequence, political parties developed earlier in Rhode Island than in any other colony. These parties focused on their leaders, Samuel Ward of Westerly and Stephen Hopkins of Providence. In its simplest terms, however, the struggle was between Providence and Newport for ascendancy. Whoever controlled the General Assembly secured the spoils of office and determined how taxes would be apportioned. The election of Stephen Hopkins for the first of his nine terms in 1755 signaled that Providence was challenging Newport's political hegemony. While Hopkins got significant support from the Wanton faction of Newport, the base of his power was in the northern towns. Hopkins and Ward went head-to-head for the governorship for 10 straight years, and Hopkins won seven times. Because the elections were extremely close, vote buying became common.

The intense partisanship greatly distressed many in an age that considered factionalism to be contrary to good government. The vote buying, scramble for spoils, and blatant shifting of taxes to the towns of the losing party caused some to desire an end to Rhode Island's charter government. A group called the "Newport Junto," led by Martin Howard, Jr., favored greater British involvement in Rhode Island affairs and petitioned the King in 1764 to vacate the Charter.

The Ward-Hopkins feud ended in 1768 when the principals agreed not to run again, and the colony faced the newly aggressive enforcement of imperial regulations. Besides, the Hopkins faction clearly dominated now, electing Hopkins' former Deputy Governor, Joseph Wanton, annually from 1769 to 1775. One thing became apparent: in the end the issues which divided the colony were resolved in favor of Providence.

In 1763 Parliament transformed the wartime patrol along the Atlantic coast into an enforcement arm of the Navigation Acts. The Royal Navy was authorized to seize ships and goods under the British flag to check for compliance with the trade laws. Customs agents sent to America received one half of all ships and cargoes condemned as a result of seizures. Americans soon became thoroughly acquainted with "customs racketeering," the practice of selective enforcement of the laws to enrich the customs agents. Coercion arrived for Newport in the fall of 1763 in the form of H.M.S. *Squirrel*, followed by the schooner *St. John*. Within the year Britain announced the Sugar Act and the Stamp Act, and by that summer violence erupted between Newporters and the navy.

Enforcement of trade laws would mean ruin for Rhode Island merchants. The regulations had not been enforced for so long, and Rhode Islanders had created trade patterns that disregarded His Majesty's laws. With the announcement of the Sugar Act in 1763, the General Assembly responded with an official Remonstrance in 1764. They tried to demonstrate that the Empire was better off for

allowing them to trade where they could. Molasses was crucial; but of the annual import of 14,000 hogsheads, only 2,500 of it came from legal sources. If the Sugar Act were enforced and the new tax strictly collected, Rhode Island's trade would be devastated.

The *Squirrel* and the *St. John* not only began enforcement of the Sugar Act, they also recruited for the Royal Navy by impressing seamen coming to Newport. Local resentment of press-gang activities and the misdeeds of sailors led in July 1764 to an incident in which a crowd of townspeople stoned men of the *St. John* and the gunners of Fort George fired about 10 shots at the schooner. Despite promises

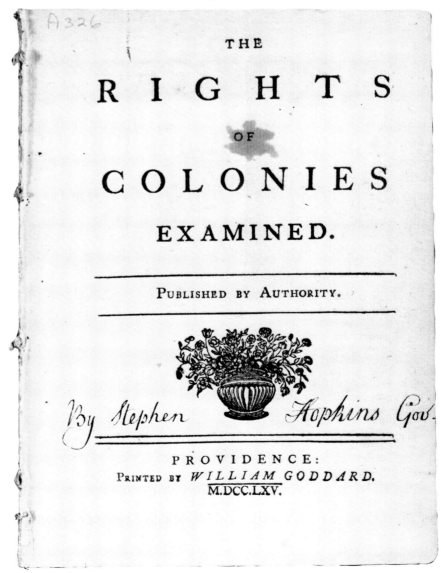

A326

THE

R I G H T S

OF

C O L O N I E S

EXAMINED.

PUBLISHED BY AUTHORITY.

By Stephen   Hopkins Gov.

PROVIDENCE:

PRINTED BY *WILLIAM GODDARD.*
M.DCC.LXV.

that no Newport resident or small boatman entering the harbor would be bothered, in the spring of 1765 the *Maidstone* actively pressed seamen from vessels outside the harbor and brought activity in the harbor to a standstill. Woodboats hauled no fuel, and fishermen refused to sail. When the *Maidstone* impressed the crew of a brig on June 4, a mob of 500 people seized one of *Maidstone's* boats, hauled it to the public commons, and burned it.

When Britain announced in 1764 that it would impose the Stamp Act in 1765, Stephen Hopkins wrote a pamphlet, *The Rights of Colonies Examined,* in which he asserted that Parliament had no authority to levy an internal tax. He argued that the

rights of Englishmen required that there be no taxation without representation and that the colonies had their own legislatures. Martin Howard, Jr., wrote a blistering reply to Hopkins; but as he was known to be behind the 1764 petition to the King, he became a target of a Newport mob in the Stamp Act riots that followed in August 1765. In Providence the reaction was confined to burning an effigy, but in Newport mobs burned effigies of Stamp Master Augustus Johnston, and of Newport Junto figures. The following night rioters destroyed Howard's home and threatened the house of Customs Collector John Robinson. All had fled to safety aboard *Cygnet,* a British man-of-war in the harbor.

Howard caught the next boat to England to urge the King to revoke the Charter. Johnston resigned the next day, Robinson eventually departed, and his replacement found being Collector a dangerous occupation. He was continually harassed in his duties and even severely beaten and dragged through the streets in April 1771. His subordinates fared no better: in Providence one was tarred and feathered and a second nearly beaten to death.

The General Assembly met in September after the riots and adopted resolutions declaring that its citizens were "not bound to yield obedience to any law or ordinance designed to impose any internal taxation whatsoever upon them." They authorized officials to conduct business as usual without the stamps and sent two delegates to the Stamp Act Congress which met in New York in October. All colonial governors were to swear an oath to support the Stamp Act, but Governor Ward of Rhode Island alone refused. No stamps were distributed and the law was repealed the next year. By then the Sons (and Daughters) of Liberty had organized in Newport and Providence.

The Empire's need for revenue led next to the imposition of the Townshend duties of 1767, and Rhode Island's reaction displayed its contrariness. On the one hand, at the dedication of the Providence Liberty Tree on July 25, 1768, Silas Downer, secretary of the Providence Sons of Liberty, gave his *Discourse Delivered in Providence.* Downer denied the authority of Parliament over the colonies, and declared that "we cheerfully recognize our allegiance to our sovereign Lord, *George,* the third, *King of Great-Britain* ... but utterly deny any other dependence on the inhabitants of that island." He said, "I cannot be persuaded that the parliament of *Great-Britain* have any lawful right to make any laws *whatsoever* to bind us." One historian has said that Downer was the first person in America to declare this position publicly six years before anyone else. On the other hand, Rhode Island's lack of cooperation with other colonies weakened the non-importation agreements against British goods. Four months after the rest had agreed, Rhode Island had not joined the effort and would not until merchants in

FACING PAGE, TOP: *Samuel Ward (1725-1776), member of the Stamp Act Congress, Continental Congress, and Governor in 1762, 1765, and 1767, was the leader of the Newport-South County faction that waged a bitter political war against Samuel Hopkins of Providence between 1755-1768. The controversy was characterized by intense partisanship and corruption. In 1762 the Ward-dominated Court denied naturalization to Aaron Lopez because Lopez favored Hopkins. From* Rhode Island Portraits. *RIHS (RHi x3 628)*

BOTTOM: *Britain's announcement of the Stamp Act prompted Stephen Hopkins to write* The Rights of the Colonies Examined *in which he argued that Parliament did not have the right to tax the colonies by levying "internal taxes" because the colonies were not represented in Parliament. It was "no taxation without representation." RIHS (RHi x3 4291)*

THIS PAGE: *Martin Howard, Jr., (d.1781) Rhode Island delegate to the 1754 Albany Convention, defended the Stamp Act. When a Newport mob destroyed his home in 1765, he fled to England. Appointed chief justice for North Carolina the following year, he was again driven into exile during the American Revolution. From a portrait by John Singleton Copley, 1767. Courtesy, Newport Historical Society*

New York, Philadelphia, and Boston boycotted Rhode Island trade. However, with the repeal of the duties, except the tea tax, the nonimportation movement broke down everywhere by October 1770; and Rhode Island merchants bore considerable responsibility for the collapse.

Meanwhile, Newporters continued their violent clashes with the Royal Navy. In 1769 the British sloop *Liberty* seized a brig

Narragansett Bay in March of 1772 and stopped everything, even woodboats carrying fuel to Aquidneck. The *Gaspee*'s crew abused the boatmen, stole livestock from farms, and cut fruit trees for firewood. While pursuing the *Hannah* from Newport on June 9, 1772, the *Gaspee* went aground. Late that night, eight boatloads of men led by John Brown and Abraham Whipple of Providence attacked the *Gaspee*, shot and

RIGHT: This somewhat romanticized, 19th-century depiction of the burning of the Gaspee, *Rhode Island's most famous incident of resistance to British efforts to enforce the trade regulations, shows several boatloads of Providence men capturing and burning the ship on the night of June 9, 1772. Steel engraving by J. Rogers after a painting by J. McNevin, published 1856. RIHS (RHi x3 119)*

FACING PAGE, TOP: The Stamp Act of 1765 occasioned outrage in every colony in America. Protesters burned effigies of Stamp Act officials in Providence and Newport, and mobs destroyed the homes and possessions of the Newport Junto. Drawing from Henry Davenport, Pictorial History of the United States, *1901. Courtesy, Providence Public Library.*

BOTTOM: Esek Hopkins (1718-1802) was commissioned by the Continental Congress to be the first commander-in-chief of the navy of the United Colonies from November 1775 to March 1777. Initially successful, Hopkins and the American navy became bottled up in Narragansett Bay when the British occupied Newport in December 1776, leading to Hopkins' dismissal from his command. Engraving by J.C. Buttre. RIHS (RHi x3 688)

off Block Island and brought it to Newport for condemnation. In port a scuffle broke out between crew members of the vessels, and the *Liberty* fired on the brig's men as they rowed to shore. An enraged mob scuttled the *Liberty* and the brig escaped.

The King's revenue cutters provoked the next outrage against the Crown's authority. The *Gaspee*, commanded by Lt. William Dudingston, took up station in

wounded Dudingston, and burned the schooner. The Crown appointed a commission with broad powers to investigate the incident and to transport to England for trial those responsible. Although a thousand people knew the culprits, only a deranged drunk and an unreliable indentured servant would testify; and nothing came of the investigation. Like every other incident, from the *St. John* in 1764 to the

Gaspee in 1772, no one was apprehended or punished for the offense. However, the intervention of the royal commission profoundly affected Rhode Islanders' perception of the threat to their independence, and they began to see the necessity of greater cooperation with the other colonies.

When the British enacted the Tea Act of 1773 to rescue the East India Company from bankruptcy, the colonies instituted another boycott and direct action against East India teas. The most famous incident was the Boston Tea Party of December 1773, which the British answered with the Coercive Acts in the spring of 1774. Rhode Island took the lead in giving aid to the distressed people in Massachusetts and in calling for a congress of the colonies. Before any other colony issued a call, the General Assembly urged that a congress be assembled and chose Stephen Hopkins and

Samuel Ward as delegates. The First Continental Congress met in Philadelphia that autumn and agreed to an embargo of all British products. This time Rhode Island heartily supported the embargo; and the Sons of Liberty, backed by mob violence and tar and feathers, enforced it. Towns sent donations and droves of sheep to Boston, and in October the General Assembly chartered the Newport Light Infantry,

Providence Grenadiers, Kentish Guards, Pawtuxet Rangers, and the Glocester Light Infantry. In December, four more militia companies received charters, and the cannons and ammunition at Fort George at Newport were removed to Providence.

The rebellion had begun. Extensive manufacture of firearms started, the Hope Furnace cast cannons, and enlistments in the militia proceeded rapidly. When Congress called for the suspension of the use of all tea, Providencians burned some 300 pounds in Market Square on March 2, 1775. Six weeks later came the battles of Lexington and Concord. When the General Assembly voted to send an "army of observation" of 1,500 men to Massachusetts, Governor Wanton refused to issue the commissions and was deposed. Within weeks the customs house in Newport was closed, and Rhode Island felt the oppressive weight of H.M.S. *Rose.* She harassed everything that sailed on the Bay, fired a few shots at Newport, cannonaded Bristol and Warren, and sent foraging parties ashore. The General Assembly authorized a small navy, commanded by Abraham Whipple; and it scored America's first sea victory when it captured a British vessel on June 15. The rebels built fortifications and observation points around the Bay and erected beacon towers. Defenders of British policy were arrested and roughly handled, and by the end of 1775 half of the population of Aquidneck had fled. John Brown's sloop *Katy* was sent to Philadelphia where she was rechristened *Providence,* becoming the first ship in the Continental navy. Stephen Hopkins had urged Congress to create a navy and secured the appointment of his brother Esek as first commander-in-chief. In 1776, the General Assembly commissioned 65 privateers, and before the British closed Narragansett Bay by occupying Newport in December 1776, privateers brought prizes worth £300,000 sterling into Providence.

It has become an article of state pride to maintain that Rhode Island was the first colony to declare its independence—on May 4, 1776—two months before the Declaration of Independence. But it is not true. The General Assembly repealed a test oath from 1765 which required government officers to swear allegiance to George III. Substituted for the King's name was "The Governor and Company of the English Colony of Rhode Island and Providence Plantations." Rhode Island still referred to itself as an *English* colony until July 18 when it ratified the Declaration of Independence. While Rhode Island had not declared its independence first, it was the first to renounce allegiance to the King. No public celebration accompanied the May 4th action; but when independence was proclaimed from the State House in Providence on July 25, jubilation reigned in the town. Most people readily supported the cause because they saw independence as a defense of their liberal charter privileges. They plunged into the fray, contributed proportionately more than nearly any other state, and suffered considerably.

The British occupied about a third of the state for more than three years and raided along the Bay. The great farms of the Narragansett Planters of South County were finished by the war. Already declining because of the British disruption of the West Indies trade, the Planters saw their markets disappear when the British occupied Newport and Conanicut Island and when British foragers killed their livestock, destroyed crops, and burned buildings. The British destroyed every house except one on Prudence Island, and at Jamestown they burned most of the houses in one raid in 1775. Then during the war, they cut down every tree for firewood, leaving Conanicut Island devastated and virtually depopulated.

Providence became the wartime capital

The effort to recapture Newport in August 1778 collapsed when the French fleet was crippled by a terrific storm, leaving the American troops stranded on Aquidneck. Though the British sought to capture the Americans as they withdrew, black soldiers in the First Rhode Island Battalion repulsed three assaults by Hessian mercenaries, allowing the Americans to make an orderly retreat. From Providence, The Southern Gateway to New England, *1926. Courtesy, Commonwealth Land Title Insurance Company*

and an armed camp. Fortifications were constructed at many points and a beacon tower perched on Prospect Hill. Although never attacked, Providence lived in continual fear during the British occupation of Newport. The town was disrupted by the presence of so many soldiers, whose principal leisure activity was drinking, but townsfolk made money off them. The number of taverns tripled between 1775 and 1778 so that Providence came to have one tavern or inn selling liquor for every 100 persons. Food shortages became critical in the winter of 1778-1779 with civilians and soldiers near starvation, causing two mutinies among the soldiers. University Hall was used as a hospital by the Americans and the French from 1776 to May 1782, and education was suspended at the college.

Rhode Island persistently urged the Continental Army to mount a major effort to expel the British, but always the attention was given elsewhere. The main attempt ended in the Battle of Rhode

Island, August 29, 1778. This battle was a rearguard action as the Americans extracted their troops from Aquidneck when French naval support failed to materialize because the fleet had been crippled by a hurricane. The most significant aspect of the engagement was the able fighting of the first black regiment ever employed in America.

While Providence escaped the ravages of war, Newport was severely damaged. Half of the population fled, many of its most enterprising merchants never returned, its wharfs and warehouses rotted and fell into ruin, and the British occupiers ripped down and burned 480 vacant homes and shops for firewood! When the war ended, Providence's population had declined slightly from 4,321 to 4,310, but Newport's had plummeted from 9,209 to 5,530. The contest between the towns was really settled, and by 1800 Providence counted 7,614 while Newport struggled behind at 6,739, considerably less than before the Revolution.

Because it rebelled to preserve its independence and because it felt slighted by the central government's lack of effort to dislodge the British from Newport, Rhode Island ended the war suspicious and hostile toward the new United States government. It blocked the attempt by Congress under the Articles of Confederation to strengthen the Union and then refused to ratify the Constitution. Rhode Islanders did not want to trade subjection to Parliament for subordination to Congress; consequently, it briefly became an independent republic.

When the Articles of Confederation were proposed, the General Assembly unanimously ratified it in 1778 because it created just the sort of central government they wanted, one with little or no power over the states. Rhode Island wanted to act without external restraint; but by behaving contrarily toward the Union, it helped to undermine the Confederation and produce the conditions that resulted in the Constitution, which reduced state independence. The Confederation government desperately needed revenue, but in 1781 and 1783 Rhode Island blocked the unanimous approval needed for an import tax. Instead it adopted a state import duty to pay the state debt. These actions caused other states to heap abuse on Rhode Island, and some sought to expel its representatives from Congress. One congressman declared that the "Cursed State ought to be erased out of the Confederation." Then when Rhode Island resorted to its favorite remedy for financial problems, another paper money issue, some states fairly roared with rage and denunciation. Rhode Island's self-absorption and the chorus of external abuse only served to weaken further its ties to the Union. By 1789 it would be outside the Union altogether.

The war debt had to be paid, but how? Because the commercial towns around the Bay had been occupied or had trade disrupted during the war, the burden of taxation had shifted to the rural towns. When the postwar commercial depression failed to generate much income from the state import duty, steep taxes were levied on real estate. These fell most heavily upon the farmers, who feared that they would be

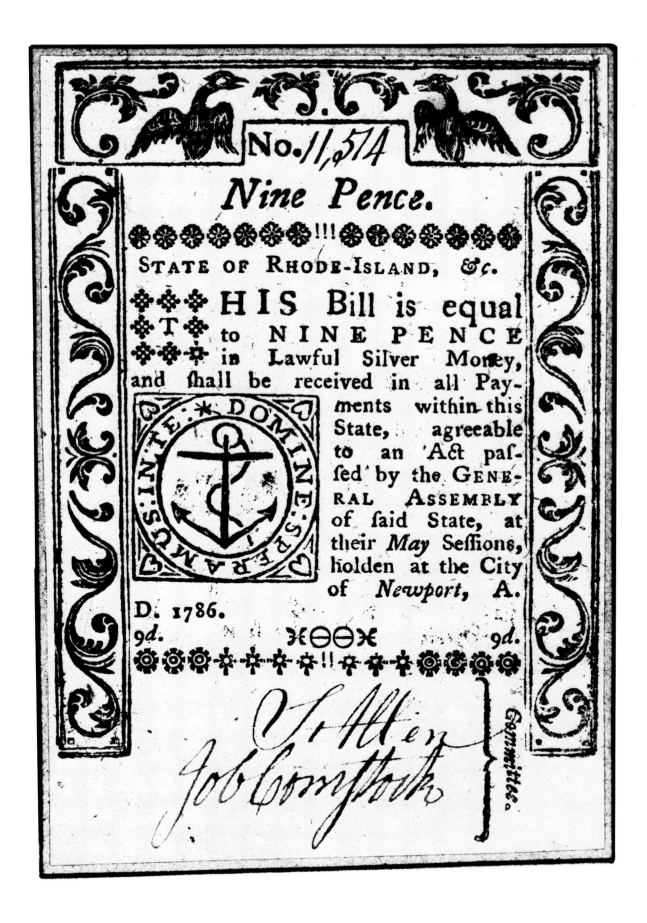

ruined unless relief were provided. They demanded the issuance of paper money based on land value. The Country party won on this issue in 1786 and held power until the state debt had been liquidated in 1790. Commercial interests bitterly opposed paper money, causing its value to depreciate rapidly. The Country party resorted to increasingly punitive measures to force creditors (some of whom fled the state to avoid accepting paper money for debts) to accept the money, including heavy fines for nonacceptance and trial without jury or appeal for violators. They even punished Newport. In 1784 Newport merchants had obtained a municipal charter, making it Rhode Island's first city. But the city council was anti paper money so, the General Assembly, under Country party control, revoked Newport's charter in March 1787.

The Country party opposed the Constitution and refused even to send a delegate to the Constitutional Convention in Philadelphia in 1787. Eleven times they rejected calls for a ratifying convention. Instead they presented the Constitution to a popular referendum, contrary to the recommendations of the convention delegates or Congress. James Madison said of Rhode Island: "Nothing can exceed the wickedness and folly which continue to rule there. All sense of character as well as of right have been obliterated." When the vote was cast in March 1788, Newport and Providence (pro-Constitution centers) boycotted the referendum, and the Constitution was smothered 2,708-237. The

rural towns were nearly unanimous in opposition: Foster voted 177-0, Coventry 180-0, Scituate 156-0, Glocester 228-9, and Smithfield 159-2 against ratification.

By late November 1789 only Rhode Island remained out of the Union, and the United States Congress began to move toward economic coercion. Meanwhile William Ellery of Newport, signer of the Declaration of Independence, was urging Congress to treat Rhode Island like a foreign country. In particular he urged them to levy duties on agricultural products so that the back-country farmers would "be compelled by a sense of interest to adopt the Constitution." Providence and Newport talked about seceding from the state! At last the General Assembly authorized a ratification convention, which in May 1790 approved the Constitution by two votes. The convention suggested 21 amendments to the Constitution; most would have weakened the central government. President George Washington made a special trip here in August 1790 to forgive and embrace the independent state.

Admission to the Union, however reluctantly accepted, closed one era. The state's economy had changed from agriculture to commerce in the 18th century and was on the verge of another transformation in the 19th. Rhode Island was on its way to becoming the nation's first urban, industrialized state.

FACING PAGE: Rhode Island turned to paper money to relieve the money crisis of 1784-1785, but this occasioned considerable resistance by local merchants and neighboring states. The Connecticut Wits denounced Rhode Island saying: "Hail! realm of rogues, renow'd for fraud and guile,/ All hail; ye knav'ries of yon little isle./There prowls the rascal, cloth'd with legal pow'r,/To snare the orphan, and the poor devour." RIHS (RHi x3 1056)

THIS PAGE, TOP: James Manning (1738-1791) was president of Rhode Island College (Brown University) from 1764 to 1791, pastor of the First Baptist Church of America from 1771 to 1791, and a leading opponent of slavery. An ardent patriot accused Manning of being a Baptist Tory, but after George Washington attended his church, Manning became a staunch nationalist and a member of the Confederation Congress. RIHS (RHi x3 4288)

BOTTOM: At the dedication of the Providence Liberty Tree in 1768, Silas Downer of the Providence Sons of Liberty declared that the British Parliament had no right to legislate for the colonies, RIHS (RHi x3 1251)

Chapter Four

REBELS, RIOTERS, AND PARTYMEN

ADMISSION TO THE Union in 1790 brought Rhode Island into the fold of the states, but it did not settle its relationship with the United States. Its peculiar history and economic needs pushed the state toward secession a second time during the War of 1812. Just as its merchants in the 18th century had disregarded and then resisted the laws of the British government, so did the early 19th-century commercial interests contravene federal law. Meanwhile, the Charter of 1663, which had made Rhode Island the freest of the colonies, had now outlived its usefulness. The guarantees of religious freedom and democracy passed to the federal Constitution, but the old Charter was unsuited for an urban, industrial society. Rhode Island ran counter to the rest of the country: as most states became increasingly democratic, by the 1830s Rhode Island had become one of the least democratic. The result was an attempt to overthrow the state government by force. As Rhode Island modernized its constitution and developed as an industrial state, it turned from the freedom of the oceans to the ties of interstate commerce and the federal Union. Last among the original 13 states to ratify the Constitution, Rhode Island was first to pledge troops to defend it in 1861.

At the beginning of the 19th century, Rhode Island's economy depended upon oceanic commerce, so anything that disrupted it threatened the state's economic well-being. Still, the traders seemed to tolerate continued impressment by the British, hostile actions by warring European powers, and the perils of seizure and impoundment more easily than trade regulations of their own government. When the British warship *Leopard* fired upon the American frigate *Chesapeake* in mid-1807, killing three sailors, all America was outraged and clamored for war. Rhode Islanders flocked to large meetings and pledged their lives and fortunes to avenge this "flagrant insult upon our national honor." But instead of their lives, Jefferson asked for their fortunes. At his urging, Congress adopted the Embargo Act in December, which immediately cut trade and commerce. Exports from Rhode Island fell from $1.6 million in 1807 to $240,000 the next year. Experienced in disregarding or evading trade regulations, New Englanders tried to circumvent the Embargo; and the federal government, like the British before the Revolution, enacted increasingly punitive enforcement measures. The Rhode Island General Assembly protested in 1809, calling the Embargo and enforcement laws "unjust, tyrannical, and unconstitutional," and warning that a "dissolution of the union may be more surely, and as speedily, effected by the systematic oppression of the government as by the inconsiderate disobedience of the people." When Congress finally declared war on Great Britain in 1812, Rhode Island joined the condemnation of "Mr. Madison's War," refused to release its militia to federal service, and sent four delegates to the Hartford Convention in December 1814, where the

Henry B. Anthony (1815-1884) was Governor of Rhode Island from 1849 to 1851, U.S. Senator from 1859 to 1884, and editor and joint proprietor of the Providence Journal. *As editor, Anthony elevated the paper to dominate the state and supported the Republican party and the economic transformation of Rhode Island. RIHS (RHi x3 1987)*

EMBARG

Office of the Newport

Embargo LAW.

the 2d day of March, 1799 ; and such penalties may be examined, mitigated or remitted, in like manner, and under like conditions, regulations and restrictions, as are prescribed, authorised and directed by the act, entitled " An Act to provide for mitigating or remitting the forfeitures, penalties and disabilities accruing in certain cases therein men-

des affaires at papers mentio Ships. *This* may appear, *War against E* that it is only we can propiti

unhappy New England states contemplated secession from the Union.

With nearly 400 miles of coast, Rhode Island felt exposed to the power of the British. It feared another occupation of Newport and the devastation of the Bay towns that had occurred in the Revolution. So, even while resisting the demands of the federal government, Rhode Island moved energetically to defend itself by constructing coastal fortifications and calling up the militia. The federal government expanded and strengthened Fort Adams at the same time. Rhode Islanders were probably relieved when the British chose instead to bombard Fort McHenry at Baltimore and to chase little "Jamie" Madison right out of Washington.

The state's honor was upheld by the 500 men who enlisted in the national army in 1812 and by Oliver Hazard Perry and the many Rhode Island seamen at the Battle of Lake Erie in September 1813. Oliver's younger brother Matthew, best remembered for opening Japan to western contact in 1853, also served in the navy and won a promotion to lieutenant at age 18 for his part in the first sea battle of the war. While some Rhode Islanders were sacrificing their lives on Lake Erie, others were earning their fortunes in a most traditional

manner—privateering. The state commissioned 31 vessels. Spearheaded by James DeWolf, Bristol became the principal privateering port. In July 1812 the *Yankee* began the first of six successful voyages which would seize 40 British vessels with property valued at $5 million, bringing DeWolf over one million dollars in profit.

The War of 1812 hastened the national trend toward greater democracy in state governments, but Rhode Island ran contrary to the tide. Of all the original states only Rhode Island and Connecticut had retained their colonial charters after the American Revolution. In 1818 Connecticut adopted a constitution, but it required nothing less than a civil insurrection to force Rhode Island to abandon its antiquated charter.

Complaints against the Charter of 1663 boiled down to two: malapportionment and disenfranchisement. The Charter fixed representation in the General Assembly, giving Newport six delegates, Providence, Portsmouth, and Warwick four each, and all subsequent towns two each. Although population growth shifted to the northern towns, representation remained fixed. By 1820 Providence had almost 12,000 people while Portsmouth had only 1,645, but both had four General Assembly representa-

& WAR!
ercury, April 13, 1812.

e English | perhaps to ultimate defeat, if *they* may | in order to ripen and bring it to perfec-
of Eleven | be saved from shame and disgrace. | tion, we are pledged to assist in crush-
range as it | FREEMEN OF RHODE-ISLAND, do you | ing the feeble exertions of Spain in de-
urried our | subscribe to *such* doctrines,—do you | fence of her liberties.
understood | approve of *such* measures, dictated by | In the name of Heaven, what has be-
bargo that | *such* motives.—Are you ready to see | come of our Constitution? The fram-
d Tyrant." | your country involved in all the horrors | ers of that once-valued Charter endea-
| and calamities of war, to save from | voured to guard most securely the dan-
| shame and disgrace the nice feelings | gerous POWER OF MAKING WAR.—

tives. The rural-dominated legislature determined who could vote and how taxes were apportioned. It refused to remove the property qualification that disenfranchised the growing urban population. Consequently the expanding northern towns found themselves outvoted and overtaxed by the static, rural towns. Thus, as the state became more urbanized, its government became less democratic and more anachronistic.

Rhode Island was probably the most democratic state in 1780, as three-quarters of all adult, white males met the property qualification and were eligible to vote. As the state's urban population grew in the 1820s and 1830s, the percentage of eligible voters shrank. The requirement that a voter own $134 worth of real estate, or be the eldest son of a man who did, excluded the growing numbers of propertyless industrial workers. By 1840 the excluded equaled 40 percent in the state and probably 94 percent in Providence. Elsewhere the franchise was extended to nearly all white men in the 1820s, but Rhode Island resisted all efforts at constitutional reform. Consequently, it had the most conservative suffrage law in the nation.

The demands for constitutional revision arose in the 1790s over the issue of appor-

tionment as the growing towns in the northern part of the state resented the power of the static country towns. The town of Smithfield called for a constitutional convention in 1792, and Providence echoed this in 1796 after the General Assembly had quadrupled its taxes. George Burrill, an attorney, state legislator, and notary public for Providence County, argued that proponents of constitutional reform could bypass the General Assembly and go directly to the people to secure a

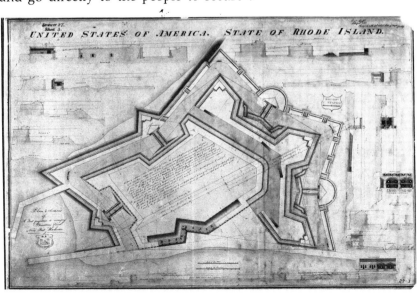

Supporters of Thomas W. Dorr probably carried this cotton banner of Providence's Sixth Ward during the People's Constitution elections and the inauguration of Dorr in 1842. Banners, stump speaking, and hard cider were symbols of the hoopla of the new political style of the 1840s. Courtesy, Rhode Island Historical Society Museum

enfranchised as propertyless Rhode Islanders paupered by "their own improvidence, extravagence, or vices," as "improvident adventurers" from other states, and as "degraded" foreign-born. Hazard expressed the prevailing sentiment of the state's southern and western landowners who resisted every effort of the industrializing towns to revise either apportionment or the franchise.

The geographical split on the constitutional questions was clear. In an 1821 referendum on whether to call a convention, Providence cast its votes 598-2 in favor, while the static and declining towns to the south and west voted just the opposite. The referendum lost by 300 votes. In 1824, when a convention was held and a constitution submitted to the voters, it was crushed by a two-to-one margin. Again the towns that were not growing overwhelmingly rejected the change: Foster (242-2), Richmond (90-0), North Kingstown (207-6), and Newport (531-5).

The suffrage movement intensified in Providence after 1833. Seth Luther, a housewright, led workers and artisans in demanding the right to vote. He and Thomas Dorr, son of wealthy China-merchant and industrialist Sullivan Dorr, organized a suffrage convention in 1834 and launched the Constitutional party. The new party contended for offices in April 1834, but fared poorly, though Dorr was elected as one of Providence's four representatives to the General Assembly. By 1837 the Constitutional party had folded, but the agitation continued.

In the 1830s the Democrats dominated the state government because of malapportionment and a coalition with the anti-Masonic party. Their base was in the rural, downstate areas while the urban northern towns shifted to the Whig party. The Whigs favored reapportionment, but not expansion of the franchise. Eliminating the property qualification might mean enfranchising the landless and the foreign-born, in particular, the growing numbers of Irish. Not only did the franchise issue strike fear in the hearts of those who believed that only the propertied should vote, but the influx of Irish Catholics stirred the antipopery feelings of native

constitution. While nothing came of his efforts in the 1790s, the Dorrites would follow this path in 1841 and 1842. Agitation subsided until 1811, when suffrage became a significant issue as a result of the political contests between the Federalists and Republicans for control of the state. A series of petitions followed from 1811 to 1823 which resulted in a proposed constitution in 1824.

The ferment was continued by a young journalist, James Davis Knowles of Providence, who declared that the people, sovereign and independent, could call their own constitutional convention if the General Assembly did not. About the time that Knowles surrendered political agitation for the Baptist ministry in 1820, the *Manufacturers and Farmers Journal* in Providence published articles attacking the state's constitutional system. The leading defender of the status quo was Benjamin Hazard, an attorney and General Assembly representative from Newport from 1809 to 1840. His 1829 attack, called *Hazard's Report*, dismissed the suffrage claims as demagoguery. He denounced the dis-

Americans. The number of unnaturalized, foreign-born residents in Providence increased from a mere 29 in 1820 to 1,005 in 1835. As the Irish tended to favor the Democratic party, the Whigs wanted to limit their influence. The Whiggish *Providence Daily Journal,* which had favored suffrage reform in the 1820s, opposed it in the 1830s, substantially on nativist grounds. With the rural-based Democratic party in Rhode Island wholly opposed to reform and the urban Whigs favoring only

HURRAH
FOR THE
OLD CHARTER.

THE OLD CHARTER IS SAFE!

All who voted for the new Constitution prefer law and order under the Charter to an unquiet government under the Constitution! *One thousand men* who voted against the Constitution did so because they preferred the Charter. It can now be maintained! Suffrage men have cheated themselves, and the Charter is triumphant!!

Friends of the Charter, to the polls! Vote against the Constitution and the extension of suffrage, and secure the old Government!!

reapportionment, the suffrage advocates turned to extralegal political action.

In 1840 a number of developments coincided to produce the final act in the suffrage agitation. In January the General Assembly passed a militia reorganization bill with a system of fines that fell heavily upon nonvoters who composed most of the militia. Second, Equal Rights Democrats from New York actively agitated in Rhode Island and published a brochure on how to call a constitutional convention by skirting the legislature and establishing another government. In March the Rhode Island Suffrage Association was formed and called for such a convention. That summer and fall Rhode Island witnessed the hoopla of the "Log Cabin and Hard Cider" campaign for President, which made those unable to vote more resentful. The Suffrage Association adopted some of the exciting presidential campaign devices, and the rallies for suffrage became bigger and noisier. Their great suffrage parade in Providence in April 1841 had two bands and more than 3,000 marchers. Thomas Dorr came under the influence of Equal Rights Democrats ideas and took the lead in 1841 in calling the People's Convention. The Convention wrote the People's Constitution, submitted it to a popular referendum of all voting-age men, and saw it approved 13,944-52 in December 1841.

Meanwhile the Whig-dominated state government summoned a Landowners

TOP: When the Charter government summoned a convention that drafted a constitution and submitted it to the legal voters, the latter rejected it by a 676-vote margin in March 1842. RIHS (RHi x3 4286)

BOTTOM: Exasperated with the old Charter government, Thomas Dorr attempted to overthrow it by force. On the night of May 18, 1842, the Dorrites tried to seize the state arsenal on Cranston Street in Providence; but the defenders, numbering some 200, protected the arsenal. The movement collapsed and Dorr fled the state. From "Scenes in Rhode Island during the Rebellion. Upper Room of the Arsenal," Bouve's Lithographers, Boston. RIHS (RHi x3 4301)

Convention to draft another constitution, which went to the voters in March 1842. Dorr urged the suffragists to reject it, and the Landowners Constitution lost 8,689-8,013. The suffragists, declaring that the old Charter had been superseded by the People's Constitution, held elections on April 18, 1842, and elected Dorr governor. Two days later the regular state elections were held and Samuel Ward King of Johnston was reelected governor.

Because the People's government was locked out of the State House, it assembled on May 3 in a Providence foundry and inaugurated Dorr. The next day the Charter government convened in Newport and inaugurated King. Now Rhode Island had a popularly-elected, illegal government and a legal, unpopular government, one trying to govern from Providence, the other from Newport. Even at this moment, support for the People's government was waning. The Charter government had met in special session in April and outlawed the People's government and levied heavy penalties on those who accepted its offices. Furthermore, the Charter government received assurances from President John Tyler of federal support in case of an insurrection. Much of Dorr's support collapsed in the comic-opera attack upon the state arsenal on Cranston Street on May 18. Dorr led 234 men and two old cannons against the arsenal held by 200 loyal volunteers. The cannons would not fire and most of the men slipped away in the foggy night. Dorr fled to New York.

Anticipation and fear swept the state when word spread that Dorr was returning to reconvene the People's legislature in Chepachet on July 4. In the northern mill towns People's militia units with names like Dorr's Invincibles, Johnston Savages, Pascoag Ripguts, and Harmonious Reptiles formed, drilled, and nightly patrolled the highways. Dorr arrived and greeted about 1,000 supporters on June 25, and the Charter government began mobilizing 3,500 troops. Believing that Dorr was going to attack Providence, the state army assembled there and marched out to do battle at Chepachet on June 27. By then only about 225 of Dorr's followers remained, and none of the People's legislators had

appeared. He disbanded his forces and fled to sanctuary in New Hampshire. Still, the Charter army stormed Acote's Hill, where the Dorrites had erected some fortifications, and found it occupied by a cow. Frustrated, they searched Chepachet and the roads to neighboring towns and arrested about 100 suspected Dorrites. Under martial law, which continued until August, others, including Seth Luther, were arrested and jailed.

Dorr surrendered himself in October 1843. The government, determined to make an example of him, sentenced him to life imprisonment at hard labor in June 1844. A Liberation party, born of political backlash to this harsh punishment, won the elections of 1845 and freed the rebel leader. His health broken, Dorr died at age 49 in December 1854.

Although he lost the "war," his cause was partially achieved. Bending to the pressures, the Charter government, calling itself the Law and Order party, summoned another convention in September 1842. It produced a constitution which the voters approved 7,024-51 in a November referendum. Reapportionment gave northern industrial towns greater representation, although it was less than would be required in a "one-man-one-vote" system. Rural towns still controlled the state senate since every one of the 30 towns, no matter how tiny, had at least one vote. The franchise was extended to native-born men, increasing the electorate by 60 percent. However, the property qualification was retained for the foreign-born, leaving

them still second-class citizens.

Rhode Island's blacks were among the native-born who won the right to vote. This development, too, ran counter to the national trend. Constitutional revisions in most states after the War of 1812 extended the franchise to all whites but took it away from blacks. Rhode Island's blacks had lost the vote in 1822 as part of this trend, but they hoped that the political agitation of the 1830s and 1840s might restore their suffrage. They felt a particular need for any political leverage that their small numbers might provide because discrimination and violence continually afflicted them. By the 1820s half of Rhode Island's blacks lived in Providence and 50 percent of them owned their homes. However, their houses were crowded next to the dwellings of immigrant laborers in disorderly, poor neighborhoods. In 1824 the "Hard Scrabble" riot saw a mob ransack the black neighborhood as constables watched because they did not "think it proper or prudent to interfere." In 1831 the Olney Lane Riot, a three-day rampage against blacks, ended only when the Rhode Island Light Infantry fired on the white rioters, killing four of them. This was the first instance in America in which militia had been summoned to quell an urban riot, and it convinced Providence to adopt a city charter in 1832.

Regaining the vote was a case of taking advantage of cracks in the white political structure because no party wanted blacks to have the vote. The People's Constitution was a whites-only document; and leading

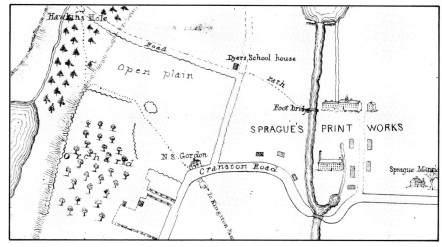

abolitionists, such as Frederick Douglass and Abby Kelley, campaigned against it for that reason. Rejected by the Dorrites, the black community supported the Law and Order party; and when the army marched to Chepachet, a volunteer force of 200 blacks patrolled Providence's streets to keep order. The Law and Order party rewarded them by including blacks in the expanded suffrage. As a result, Rhode Island's blacks generally voted for the conservative Whig party in the 1840s and 1850s.

While a Whig-Law and Order coalition dominated state politics in the 1840s, the period up to the Civil War was characterized by party instability, volatile alliances, shifting allegiances, and the rapid appearance and disappearance of parties. Some parties were temporary coalitions related to a state issue, such as the fleeting combination called the Liberation

ABOVE: A lithograph of A & W Sprague Print Works, 1844, shows the location of the Sprague Mansion and the home of John Gordon, who was convicted and hanged for the murder of Amasa Sprague. The affair triggered the crusade to abolish capital punishment in the state, but it was not until the Irish-supported Democratic party gained power in 1852 that it was abolished. When nativists and Whigs regained the governorship in 1858 they attempted unsuccessfully to repeal the statute. The area around the Print Works became the center of Irish settlers in Cranston. Lithograph by S.E. Cushing, from The Report on the Trial of John Gordon and William Gordon, 1844. RIHS (RHi x3 1039)

BELOW LEFT: The Law and Order army marched to the village of Chepachet and stormed Acote Hill searching for Dorrites on June 27, 1842. Lithograph by Thayer & Co., Boston, based on a drawing by H. Lord, probably an imprisoned Dorrite. RIHS (RHi x3 107)

The Providence City Guards

party in 1845 which gained Thomas Dorr's release from prison. Others reflected some single issue: the Temperance, Liberty, and Free Soil parties. The Know-Nothings erupted in 1854, swept the state in 1855, and then faded rapidly under the names of the American party and the American Republicans. Not until the rise to power of the Republicans in the 1850s did Rhode Island achieve a stable, two-party system.

As the national Whig party crumbled over the issue of slavery, the Rhode Island Whig party declined in the early 1850s. The Democrats won in 1851, 1852, and 1853 only to be driven out by the whirlwind of Know-Nothingism. While in power, Democrats supported election reforms, including the secret ballot and expanded suffrage, labor reforms, and abolition of the death penalty. The latter had been agitated for since 1833, when Rhode Island became the first state to abolish public executions but retained one of the lengthiest lists of capital crimes in the nation. The controversy over the execution of John Gordon for the murder of Amasa Sprague in 1844 only

added to the crusade. In 1852 Rhode Island became the second state in the nation, the first in New England, to abolish the death penalty and held fast despite several efforts to reinstate it in the late 1850s.

The Know-Nothing movement in the United States developed in response to the tide of Irish immigration and the rise of anti-Catholic bigotry in the 1840s. A major element in the anti-Dorr argument had been its nativistic appeal. One opponent declared that if the foreign-born were given the vote, Rhode Island would "become a province of Ireland: St. Patrick will take the place of Roger Williams, and the Shamrock will supersede the anchor and Hope." Such feelings developed as the Roman Catholic population, which was nearly all Irish, became more visible in the 1840s. Although nearly all foreign-born Catholics were excluded from voting, they favored the Democratic party. The triumph of political nativism meant the downfall of the Democrats in Rhode Island. Not until 1935 did Democrats regain control of both the governorship and the legislature.

The Know-Nothings worked in secret until they elected a candidate to the General Assembly in a special election in the fall of 1854. The following March they fielded a full slate for state offices. Governor William W. Hoppin, a Whig, was reelected with Know-Nothing backing, and they took all other state offices with nearly 70 percent of the votes. Yet, despite complete control, the Know-Nothings made no significant changes. In truth, most support for the Know-Nothing party came from voters dissatisfied with the failure of the Whigs or Democrats to take stands on the two major issues of antislavery and temperance, rather than from support for bigoted ideas. After winning nearly everything in 1855, the Know-Nothings faded rapidly in 1856 as the Republican party surged to power. Rhode Islanders gave the Republican candidate John C. Fremont 60 percent of their votes in the presidential election in 1856. A Republican legislature sent James F. Simmons to the United States Senate in 1857 and Henry B. Anthony there in 1858. The Senate voted to expel Simmons in 1862 for war-contract kickbacks, so he resigned; Anthony remained powerful in state politics until his death in 1884.

Despite the triumph of the antislavery Republican party, Rhode Island did not wish to aggravate the slaveholding South.

Too many ties of family, affection, and business existed between this state and the Cotton Kingdom. Newport had been a summer resort for southerners since the 1730s, and the state's number one industry, cotton textiles, depended upon the steady supply of cotton. While Rhode Island had been a leader in the antislavery movement in the days of Moses Brown, Samuel Hopkins, and James Manning, it had also been home port for some of the most notorious slavers. The abolitionist movement of the 1830s found greater sympathy in Providence than in Newport or South County. The Rhode Island Anti-Slavery Society was organized in 1836 in Providence, and abolitionist petitions to Congress emanated from there. By contrast, Newport's representatives in 1835 wanted the General Assembly to prohibit the publication of abolitionist newspapers in Rhode Island. The state denounced the Fugitive Slave Act of 1850, adopted a "personal liberty" law to thwart slave catchers, and voted for Fremont and Lincoln in 1856 and 1860. Still, when the Republicans nominated an abolitionist for governor in 1860, voters elected young William Sprague, a wealthy Democrat running under the Union party label. His coalition controlled the General Assembly and sought a compromise to the crisis of Southern secession. Rhode Island repealed the personal liberty law and sent five delegates to the Virginia Peace Conference that met in February 1861. At the same time it appropriated money for state military units in case of rebellion and Governor Sprague offered Rhode Island militia to President James Buchanan for the defense of Washington if it were threatened.

The compromise efforts failed. After the attack on Fort Sumter, Rhode Island immediately answered President Abraham Lincoln's call to arms, and the Rhode Island First Regiment was the first fully armed and equipped unit to arrive in Washington. Last to join the Union, Rhode Island was now first to defend it. Firmly in the Union, Rhode Island became increasingly aware that its economic life depended upon national markets for industrial products, a protective tariff, and a federal currency.

ABOVE: William W. Hoppin (1807-1880) won the governorship three times—1854, 1855, and 1856—by catching the winds of dissatisfaction and reform. Nominally a Whig, he came to power first with strong support from the temperance movement. He was reelected in 1855 when the Know-Nothings endorsed him; and he gained a third term with Know-Nothing and Republican support. After the Civil War he served as a Republican state senator. RIHS (RHi x3 4289)

BELOW LEFT: Anti-Irish, anti-Catholic nativism increased through the 1840s as the number of Irish in the state rose because of construction, industrialization, and the Irish potato famine. Nativism had a strong appeal to voters, and Governor Charles Jackson tried to refute the assertion that he favored expanding the franchise, which would allow naturalized citizens to vote. He lost the next election to the Whig candidate. (Broadside, 1846). RIHS (RHi x3 1266)

FRIENDS OF GOV. JACKSON, READ THIS!

IRISH VOTERS!!!

We have just been informed that the Country towns are flooded with *Infamous Handbills*, misrepresenting the views of GOV. JACKSON as to the *Qualification of Foreign Voters!*-- It is well known that Gov. Jackson PROPOSED the *FREEHOLD QUALIFICATION* in the CONVENTION. The whole story that *Gov Jackson* is in favor of ABOLISHING that qualification is *utterly* and *totally without foundation!* It is manufactured by SAMUEL CURREY, a *Naturalized Foreigner* from NOVA SCOTIA, who has been HIRED to *MISREPRESENT* the views of GOV. JACKSON *and his friends.*

People of *Rhode-Island* believe not these INFAMOUS LIES manufactured by this *HIRED TOOL* of the Providence ARISTOCRACY!-- They are *INTENDED to DECEIVE you*, and thus prevent the election of GOV. JACKSON AND HIS PROX. They dared not *circulate* one of them in Providence, for they *knew* it *would be refuted forthwith!*

Friends of CHARLES JACKSON, are you willing to see *him* crushed by the FALSEHOODS and *MALIGNITY* of his bitterest enemies?---- *We know you are NOT!*

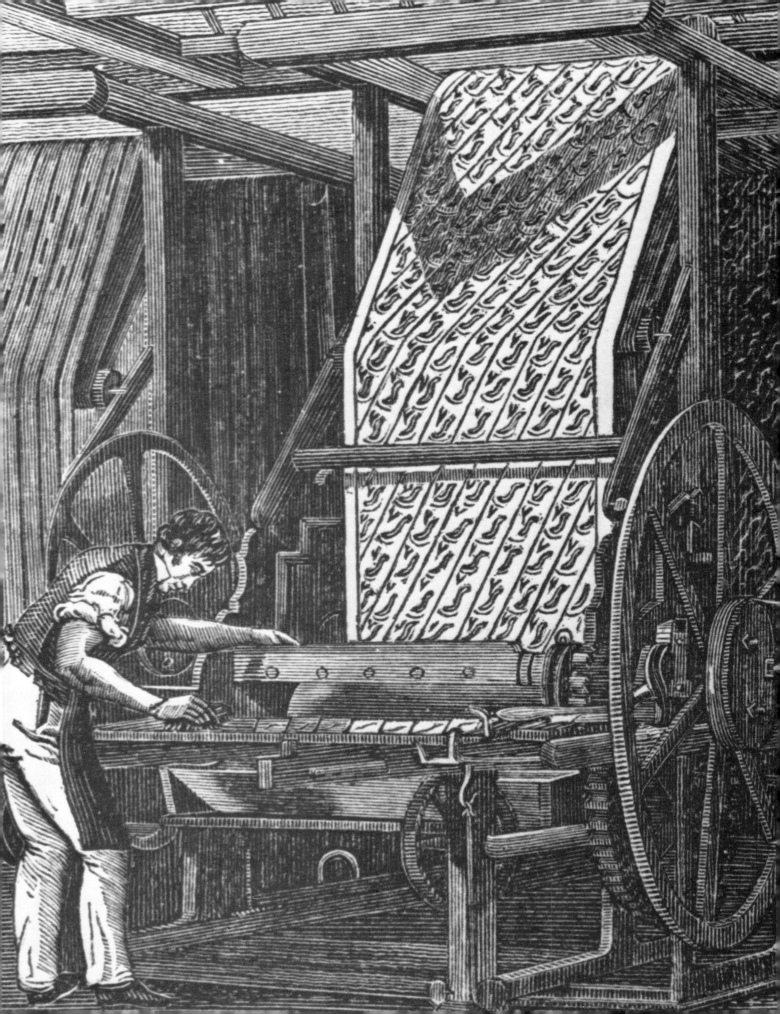

Chapter Five

FROM OCEAN TO INDUSTRY

I N THE 17TH AND 18TH CEN-turies, Narragansett Bay and the oceans beyond provided Rhode Island with its main opportunities and means of economic development, but in the first half of the 19th century the state's energy and ingenuity turned to industry. Even while the outcome of the Revolution was in doubt, mercantile houses prepared to reenter oceanic enterprise. However, the depression of the 1780s, British trade restrictions, wars, revolutions, the Embargo of 1807, and the closing of the slave trade all dictated new patterns of commerce. Some merchants found lucrative new opportunities, others succeeded by disobeying the law, and still others were ruined. Newport never fully recovered from the exodus of capital and resourceful merchants. Bristol and Warren succeeded for a few decades by slaving, privateering, and whaling. Providence, the most aggressive commercial town after the Revolution, actively engaged in coastal trade, European and Caribbean commerce, and the newer traffic with South America, Australia, and the Orient. These enterprises were the state's last significant efforts in oceanic commerce.

After the Revolution, most Rhode Island merchants experienced difficulties reestablishing trade with Europe and the Caribbean. The British Order in Council of July 2, 1783, closed the British West Indies to American ships, and Great Britain imposed a heavy import duty on goods Americans traditionally shipped to England. The first action closed an important part of the triangular trade, and the second made the price of American goods prohibitively expensive in England. The turmoil of the French Revolution and Napoleonic wars, extending through the War of 1812, made trans-Atlantic commerce unusually difficult. Rhode Island merchants, however, persisted and took advantage of the European demand for American goods by diverting trade to Baltic, German, and Mediterranean ports. Trade with Europe peaked between 1800 and 1807, when the number of ships entering Providence nearly tripled and the duties collected more than doubled. Embargo and war suppressed the European trade until 1815, after which it showed renewed vitality, although the volume was below prewar levels. By the mid-1820s trade with Europe was in decline, and a decade later it had virtually ended.

The political troubles of Europe spilled into the Caribbean, the traditional market of the slave trade and Rhode Island merchants. With the slave trade prohibited in 1787 by the state and then in 1808 by the federal government, most Narragansett Bay merchants abandoned traffic in human beings. Legitimate trading operations shifted from one Caribbean port to another to sidestep wars, revolutions, pirating, and commercial restrictions and managed to keep trade and profits high for a time. Caribbean trade emerged strong in the 1790s when commerce with Europe was depressed; but after 1800 it gradually fell as the slave trade closed and Europe again became important to the merchants.

Calico printing, introduced from England in the 1820s, was an inexpensive alternative to pattern weaving. The delicate machinery required skilled operators and engravers. Wood engraving from the Memoir of Samuel Slater by George S. White, 1836. RIHS (RHi x3 480)

Trade with Europe and the Caribbean was unquestionably the mainstay of Rhode Island's business, but the opening of markets in the Orient, South America, and to a lesser extent Australia infused new life into the mercantile community. These routes were opened by Providence merchants who desperately sought new opportunities. Although the least damaged of the state's ports, Providence felt the depression of the 1780s. Its merchants believed that Americans hungered for Brit-

aggressive enterprise.

Nicholas Brown returned to rum distillation and traded with Surinam for molasses. A number of firms tried slaving; but when the trade proved only marginally profitable and then illegal, most withdrew. In one ill-fated venture, the Browns constructed 15 schooners for codfishing; but the family's confidence in recovery was apparent as John Brown invested heavily in constructing wharfs in Providence. Almost simultaneously, Providence's lead-

ish products; so in 1783, 10 leading firms formed a cartel to purchase British goods and sell them at a fixed, high price. The venture backfired. They overbought, the market was depressed and glutted, and the traditional goods for payment (whale oil, spermaceti candles, and spirits) were unsalable because of high British tariffs. The merchants fell deeply in debt. For example, the firm of Brown & Benson owed their London supplier £26,000 sterling. In addition, Rhode Island traders were plagued by a further reduction of exportable commodities: agricultural products peaked and pig iron declined, the Hope Furnace lost money, the whaling industry on Nantucket had nearly collapsed, and spermaceti chandlers stood in ruins. Even rum, one of the more intoxicatingly profitable industries of maritime trade, stumbled and staggered. As a result, Providence experienced a postwar "paralysis of commerce more catastrophic" than elsewhere. Nevertheless, the town's merchants weathered the depression by

ing mercantile family began exploring new economic avenues. Moses Brown immersed himself in textile manufacturing; and in 1785 Nicholas Brown became the first Rhode Islander to trade with Brazil. John Brown opened the China trade in 1787 with the dispatch of the *General Washington,* and in 1792 he began trading with Australia. In both markets he was the first Rhode Islander and the second American. Soon, Brown & Ives, Clark & Nightingale, Joseph and William Russell, Edward Carrington & Company, Welcome Arnold, and other Providence concerns as well as the DeWolfs of Bristol and syndicates in Newport and elsewhere were involved in the China trade.

They learned the China trade through trial and error and found that it required huge capital commitments. It was not a business for the fainthearted or the underfinanced, but profits could be enormous. Since Rhode Island had virtually nothing that anyone in China wanted, an elaborate network developed: goods were traded in the Canary Islands, the Baltic, Bremen and Hamburg, the Caribbean, Mediterranean ports, and India in order to obtain a cargo for the Chinese market. Most commonly, cotton from India was sold in Canton for tea, silk, lacquer ware, and china. Brown & Benson dispatched the *Rising Sun* in 1792 with a load of beef, candles, wheat, and fish and whale oil to India to trade for cotton. The beef violated Hindu religious beliefs and was unsalable, and the rest of the cargo was inferior to Indian products. The voyage was saved by a consignment of 36,000 Spanish silver dollars, and the firm earned a meager profit of $6,000. By the mid-1790s successful China traders had learned their lessons and carried salable goods and increasing amounts of silver, sometimes in excess of 100,000 Spanish dollars. The China ships were larger than most other commercial vessels, cargoes generally ran between $40,000 and $90,000, and voyages lasted 18 months. Profits regularly exceeded $100,000, but one Brown & Ives Indiaman brought $430,000 in Amsterdam. Only the larger houses commanded the capital to conduct the trade, although smaller merchants often bought shares in such undertakings.

Despite the China trade's profitability, losses were sometimes staggering. Brown & Ives lost *Ann and Hope* off Block Island in 1806 with a cargo valued at $500,000, and the following year the *John Jay* splintered on a reef off Java, wiping out an additional $115,000. Carrington was forced to sell other assets in the early 1830s to cover over $300,000 in China-trade debts. Losses might have been even greater had it not been for the new structures and relationships among traders. Overseas agents, commission houses, captains, super-cargoes, and American consuls in China became important sources of trade information, credit, and skilled negotiators. The two American consuls at Canton between 1798 and 1811, Samuel Snow and Edward Carrington, were former employees of Providence firms.

By the 1830s the China trade was in decline, and ended for Providence in 1841 with the arrival of the *Lion*. Despite the glamor and fame of the China trade, during the peak years an average of only three

Edward Carrington (1775-1843), who served as U.S. Consul in Canton to 1811, was also a China trader, financier of internal improvements, promoter of the Blackstone Canal, and textile manufacturer. Carrington founded the firm of Edward Carrington & Company in 1815 and later owned 26 merchant ships. His career illustrates the transformation from ocean to industry and the accumulation of great wealth. RIHS (RHi x3 557)

ships returned to Rhode Island annually. Still, Providence was the third largest China-trade port in America, sizable fortunes were accumulated, and new trade routes were opened to the Pacific Northwest, Australia, and South America.

The Australian trade, supplying rum to quench the "unslackened thirst of the convict settlers," was over by 1812. The South American trade ran out of wind by 1831. The European and Caribbean commerce persisted but its volume was small. Customhouse duties fell from $400,000 in 1814 to $36,000 in 1860, while reexport trade declined from more than $1.5 million in 1805 to less than $10,000 by 1860. Brown & Ives sold their last ship, *Hanover*, in 1838, and joined other large mercantile houses in diversifying their economic activities. Oceanic commerce was nearly at an end.

Small merchants extended the maritime era by clinging tenaciously to a dying way of life. During the War of 1812 some Rhode Islanders, perhaps more greedy than patriotic, turned once more to privateering. After 1820, whaling rejuvenated ship-building, and both activities kept the towns of Bristol, Warren, and Newport in oceanic endeavors. But the whaling industry peaked in 1843, and by 1860 was finished. Freighting and coasting, the lifeblood of small traders, was strong in the 1840s and

Nantucket whalers supplied head matter for the spermaceti candle manufacturers of Massachusetts and Rhode Island until the industry collapsed in the 1770s and 1780s. Later, ships from Bristol went after the great whales, but the age of whaling was over for Rhode Island by the 1850s. Engraving from A System of School Geography by S. Griswold Goodrich, 1837. RIHS (RHi x3 4278)

remained fairly healthy until the Civil War. By this time, however, hauling coal and lumber from Canada, iron from Scotland and the Baltic, and cotton from the South had become a subsidiary part of Rhode Island's third economic phase—manufacturing.

Starting in the 1790s, some merchants began investing in industry and related enterprises. By the 1830s talent, capital, and power had shifted to manufacturing, especially textiles, metal trades and, to a lesser extent, jewelry. Merchants reoriented their interests and sought water rights, transportation facilities, banks, insurance companies, and a protective government. This economic transformation was nowhere more visible than in the northern towns of the state. There, Providence, Pawtucket, Woonsocket, and a host of mill villages gained supremacy and dictated the direction of the state for the next century.

Agriculture and maritime trade—Rhode Island's first two economic phases—had spawned lumber and gristmills, tanneries, slaughterhouses, cooperages, distilleries, iron shops, and forges. Mills appeared everywhere to harness waterpower; and where streams were unsuitable, as in Bristol, winds and tides were harnessed instead. By the 1790s the Providence Neck and the Moshassuck River were lined with such enterprises and their discharge polluted the water. But it was shipbuilding and its relationship to the iron industry that proved significant to Rhode Island's industrial transformation.

In the 18th century iron ore deposits were mined in Glocester, Cranston, Cumberland, and at Mineral Springs in North Providence and processed at Hope Furnace and elsewhere. The demand for cannon, shot, and ships during the Revolution triggered the growth of ironworks and attracted skilled mechanics. Pawtucket, site of a waterfall, close to iron deposits and at the head of a navigable waterway, became a shipbuilding and ironworking town. There, Stephen Jenks, Sylvanus Brown, Oziel Wilkinson, and others manufactured muskets, nails, hoops, shovels, scythes, and marine hardware. The town's reputation extended to Halifax, Canada, whose merchants hired Sylvanus Brown and 50 Pawtucket mechanics to fabricate and install power systems for grist- and sawmills. It was not by accident that Moses Brown looked to Pawtucket for skilled wood- and ironworkers for his textile experiments.

In the throes of the post-Revolutionary depression, Moses Brown thought that textiles had the potential to help America become economically independent of Great Britain. At the same time he hoped to create employment for fellow Quakers, who were restricted in their choice of occupations, and possibly to help his two brothers out of debt. During 1787 and 1789 Moses learned what he could about the textile industry and attempted unsuccessfully to begin cotton manufacturing. In partnership with his son-in-law William Almy, he purchased from three Quaker craftsmen a crude spinning jenny and carding machine and installed them in the Market House in Providence. The machines failed but Moses' interest in textiles had not diminished. He wrote his Philadelphia Quaker friends for the names of newly arrived British mechanics.

The answer came unsolicited from New York in December 1780 from Samuel Slater who wrote that he could "give the greatest satisfaction, in making machinery, making good yarn...." Without awaiting Moses' reply, Slater headed for Providence. Almy & Brown hired him to build the machinery on the Arkwright system and to manage

their factory in Pawtucket. The firm agreed to provide raw cotton and to make the yarn. Slater built new machines, but relied upon Quaker craftsmen, especially woodworker Sylvanus Brown and ironworker Oziel Wilkinson. On December 20, 1790, Slater successfully spun cotton yarn on his water-powered machinery in an old fulling mill in Pawtucket. Rhode Island had given birth to cotton manufacturing in America.

By 1791, Slater was spinning yarn that exceeded local demand, so Almy & Brown pioneered market distribution and expanded their operation. First they convinced American weavers and merchants to use American-made yarn; then in 1803, they used their Quaker connections in New York, Philadelphia, and Baltimore to open up the West. Hard work, liberal credit, and subsidized merchants sustained the markets, and by 1819, 82 percent of their yarn was being sold to Philadelphia wholesale houses. Almy & Brown continued to expand and in 1807 constructed Warwick Manufacturing Company at Centerville, one of nine new cotton spinning mills opened in Rhode Island between 1805 and 1807. The Pawtucket operation became a model for the cotton industry as its craftsmen moved to other mills in Rhode Island and to New York and New Jersey. While Slater continued to manage Brown's mills, he built another plant in Pawtucket, Massachusetts, in 1799, became a partner in the Slatersville complex in 1806, and established a mill in Webster, Massachusetts, in 1811.

The Embargo of 1807 and the War of 1812 encouraged merchants, especially in Providence, to invest in manufacturing; and by the 1820s cotton processing displaced maritime commerce as the economic backbone of the state. Brown & Ives, who complained of their "increasing embarrassment" in commerce, spent huge sums in 1808 to establish the Blackstone Manufacturing Company. Edward Carrington had shares in eight mills and a host of other investments in nonmaritime enterprises. Throughout the war, expansion was virtually unchecked: 25 mills stood in nine Rhode Island towns in 1809; 100 mills operated in 21 towns in 1815. Prices for land and water rights increased dramatically as saw and gristmills along the Blackstone, Branch, Woonasquatucket, Pawtuxet, and Pawcatuck rivers gave way to new factories. New place names appeared yearly. Between 1807 and 1822 the Woonasquatucket River spawned the mill villages of Georgiaville, Greystone, Centerdale, Allenville (now Esmond), Allendale, and Lymansville. The process repeated itself throughout the river-rich northern half of the state, less so in the southern half, and virtually not at all east of the Bay.

ABOVE: Samuel Slater (1768-1835) built the first successful cotton-spinning machine in America in 1790. He served his apprenticeship with Jedediah Strutt, a partner of Richard Arkwright, the inventor of the power spinning frame, and emigrated to America carrying the design in his mind. Slater became a successful textile and cotton machine manufacturer and by 1827 was worth $700,000. Engraving by W.G. Jackson, D. Appleton & Company, New York. RIHS (RHi x3 2064)

LEFT: Philanthropist, industrialist, reformer, and leading antislavery figure in Rhode Island, Moses Brown (1738-1836) established important ties with the Quakers of Philadelphia during the American Revolution. The "Quaker connection" later proved significant in the distribution and marketing of the textile products of Almy & Brown. Oil painting on canvas, attributed to Henry E. Kinney, circa 1898. RIHS (RHi x3 3128)

ABOVE: Zachariah Allen (1795-1882) was an inventor, scientist, philosopher, and manufacturer. He pioneered the water reservoir idea in 1823, lightweight shafting, mutual fire insurance for mills, and patented a governor for steam engines. He was also known for his philanthropy, dry-season employment for his workers, and writings on solar energy. He also created a model mill village at Allendale (now part of North Providence) that included a Thomas Tefft-designed stone church and Sunday school. Oil on canvas painting by James Sullivan Lincoln, 1882. RIHS (RHi x3 3213)

BELOW: Saunders Pitman (1732-1804) fashioned this silver teapot about 1790. It is an exquisite example of jewelry items handcrafted in Rhode Island into the 1820s. Courtesy, Rhode Island Historical Society Museum

Rapid expansion during the war contributed to an equally rapid contraction after it. Capital flowed back into maritime efforts, British textiles flooded the market, and the 1819 depression destroyed demand. Although nearly two fifths of the mills closed, these problems only temporarily halted the industry's expansion. Depression removed weak investors, fostered innovation, and led to the consolidation of small operations. Some firms adopted steam power, installed Gilmore power looms, diversified their range of goods, and moved most operations to one site. Millowners secured favorable legislation from the state to impound water and won protective tariffs from the federal government. When oceanic commerce began its decline in the 1820s, the textile industry once again expanded, with larger mills and newer companies dominating the field. By the Civil War, Rhode Island's cotton industry ranked second in the nation with a total of 176 mills, 15,739 employees, and an annual production valued at $20 million. Slater's experiment had become an industrial empire.

The woolen industry experienced patterns of cyclical growth and development similar to those of cotton. Prior to the 1830s, the woolen industry was marked by small mills, low capitalization, and an average labor force of fewer than 10. In 1804 Rowland Hazard of Peace Dale built a mill for carding and dyeing, but he used local farmers for spinning and weaving. Realizing that the farmers were undepend-

able, Hazard cautiously expanded his mill, adding the first power looms in the American woolen industry in 1814, and bringing farmers to his mill to weave. Hazard's operation was the model for others, and Washington County emerged as the center of the woolen industry in the state.

The northern area was not outdone. In 1812, Sullivan Dorr, Samuel Arnold, and others built the Providence Woolen Company. Although it later failed, the company's introduction of steam power greatly benefited all textiles and stimulated others to expand. Zachariah Allen also contributed, first, by establishing the Allendale mill in 1822 and later through his innovations in power mechanics, mill construction, and mill fire insurance. The leader of the woolen industry both state- and nationwide before the Civil War was Edward Harris, a man with no formal education but a genius for organization. After working for several mills, he purchased a factory in 1832 in Woonsocket, and by the 1850s operated five woolen mills that produced cassimeres and other specialty items. Harris' success made him Woonsocket's first millionaire and primary booster of the town's early growth.

By the Civil War, Rhode Island's woolen industry was dominated by Providence, Woonsocket, and Burrillville. The state's 57 mills had an invested capital of $3 million, 4,200 employees, and more than $7 million in annual products. It was the second largest industry in the state and produced a range of specialty items greater than that of the cotton industry.

Closely related to textiles were two branches of the metals industry, one producing textile machinery and the other a diversity of metal products. While Slater could be called the father of American textile machinery, the sons of Oziel Wilkinson, the descendants of Stephen Jenks, and the many English and Quaker mechanics actually placed Rhode Island among the leaders in textile-machinery production. Some worked in maintenance shops attached to mills; others emerged as inventors and opened their own shops. Although slow to mature, the textile machinery business prospered as textiles expanded and managers exploited the

home market for the equipment. Soon, the state boasted of such establishments as James S. Brown of Pawtucket, Fales & Jenks of Central Falls, and the Providence Machine Company. Their power looms, ring spinning frames, and braiding machines were installed locally and as far away as Georgia, Louisiana, and even Scotland. Supplementary companies manufactured bobbins, spools, leather belts, and various items vital to the industry.

Related, but more diverse, and thus less prone to the business fluctuations of the textile market, was the metal-trades industry. Although slower in developing than textile-machinery manufacture, diversified metal shops emerged in the 1830s with the establishment of Brown & Sharpe, Eagle Screw Company, Barstow Stove Company, New England Butt Company, Builders Iron Foundry, and a host of smaller shops. The industry accelerated thereafter, and the addition of stationary steam engines launched George H. Corliss' career and gave Providence the distinction of making the finest steam engines in America. By the Civil War, Providence County had three fourths of the 142 metalworking firms in the state, and the American Screw works was the largest metals employer with over 600 employees. In the second half of the 19th century, four of the base-metal firms were among the "Five Industrial Wonders of the World." The fifth, Gorham Silverware, belonged to the jewelry industry.

The jewelry industry in Rhode Island did not benefit as directly as did textiles and base metals from the decline in oceanic commerce, and thus took much longer to mature. Without substantial capital or foreign competition, the production of jewelry remained primarily a handicraft industry. In the recessions that followed the War of 1812, jewelry makers turned to cheap items, such as gold-filled and gold-plated chains, necklaces, and rings, thereby expanding costume jewelry production. A notable exception occurred in 1813, when Seril Dodge entered into a partnership with Jabez Gorham and four other journeymen to produce fine silver items. In 1831 Gorham formed a partnership with a Boston silversmith, and in 1847 his son traveled extensively in Europe and brought English silversmiths to Providence and installed steam power to drive the machinery. Other jewelers soon moved into Providence textile complexes that had surplus steam power which the artisans used to run their operations. While Providence became the jewelry center of the state with 57 of the 86 establishments, the industry had only eight firms with more than 25 employees before the Civil War. Nevertheless, a foundation for one of the state's leading industries had been laid.

The concentration of industry and population in the northern part of the state might be construed as the result of geography, especially the availability of waterpower. However, men with vision and money made it happen. Recognizing that the limited hinterland was unsuitable for extensive trade and seeing the potential of manufacturing, Providence men worked to extend their domain. They embarked on internal improvement projects and simultaneously developed banks, insurance companies, and other service institutions. In the 1790s, the town rebuilt the Weybosset Bridge, John and Moses Brown constructed competing Central

ABOVE: The Blackstone Canal opened July 1, 1828, with chief investor and commissioner Edward Carrington traveling the length from Providence to Worcester in regal procession. Irish laborers built the canal, which was engineered by Holmes Hutchinson of Rhode Island, and established communities from Providence to Woonsocket and Worcester. From Providence Patriot and Columbian Phoenix, November 11, 1829. RIHS (RHi x3 4305)

BELOW: Designed by Thomas A. Tefft and opened in 1848, this elegant Romanesque train station dominated Exchange Place and the center of Providence for the next half century. (Photo, 1872) RIHS (RHi x3 379)

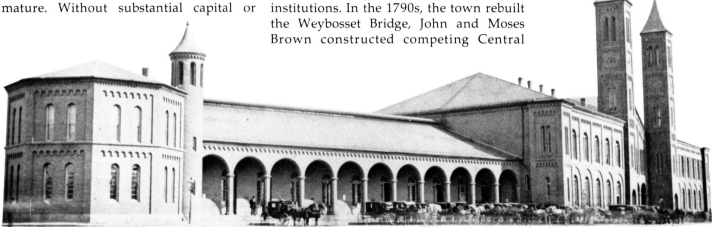

The H.L. Fairbrother & Company Leather Belting Manufactory, located in Pawtucket, is depicted here in 1819. It was an example of the secondary industries that grew up to supply a product to the new textile and machine tool industries. RIHS (RHi x3 1819)

(Red) and South (Washington) bridges, and merchants subscribed to the Providence-Norwich Turnpike, one of 46 such roads incorporated in the state by 1842. These turnpikes connected mill villages to each other, and turned Providence into the hub of an extensive transportation network.

Visions of draining commerce from western Massachusetts to Providence prompted John Brown in 1796 to apply for a charter to construct a canal from Providence to Worcester. Boston merchants opposed the idea; but in 1823 the Browns, Carrington, Dorr, and others renewed the plan, received charters from both states, and in 1828 opened the Blackstone Canal. The 45-mile canal was not an engineering marvel for it took barges all day to travel seven miles. Nevertheless, in its first few years it drained the hinterland and supplied mills with provisions and raw cotton. Competing water demands of mills, speedier overland freighting, and the opening of the Boston-Worcester Railroad in 1831 led to the canal's demise. The Blackstone Canal Company wanted to abandon operations as early as 1832, but millowners successfully fought the canal's closing until 1849. Although the waterway was a financial failure, it stimulated industrial growth in the Blackstone Valley and irreversibly tied that region to Providence.

Providence men turned to railroads at an early date and secured General Assembly support, but out-of-state companies were severely restricted. After several false starts and legislative restrictions which soured several Massachusetts companies on entering the city, the General Assembly granted Providence merchants a charter, without restrictions, to build a short line from a terminal at Fox Point across the Seekonk to connect with the Boston line. A horse-drawn car opened the Boston-Providence line in 1835, and two years later the Stonington Railroad terminated on the harbor in South Providence. In 1847 some of the merchants who had invested in the Blackstone Canal brought the Providence & Worcester Railroad to completion. Subsequent construction of the Providence, Warren & Bristol, and the Fall River, Warren & Providence railroads extended the city's hold on the eastern shores. Although Providence had only limited success in its attempts to expand its rail connections into upper New York and the West, the rail network made the city the undisputed transportation center of southern New England. To demonstrate its status Providence built the largest train station in America in 1848, and the Cove Basin was lined with stone and encircled by a fashionable, tree-lined promenade.

From slow beginnings, banking and insurance institutions soon became indispensable to the economic transformation of Rhode Island. As in other economic areas, the state's leading merchant family led the way: John Brown created the first bank in the state in 1791 with the Providence Bank, and in 1799 Brown & Ives founded the first insurance company with the Providence Insurance Company. The number of state banks in the first half of the 19th century fluctuated with business conditions and state regulation. Most bank directors were millowners; nevertheless, state banks generally followed sound practices, failures were few, and none occurred in the Panic of 1837. Part of this may be explained by the state regulatory policies. When in 1809 the Farmers Exchange Bank of Glocester became the first bank in America to fail, the General Assembly made bankers personally liable for losses. With the national rise of antibank sentiment in the 1830s, Rhode Island became the first state to enact a comprehensive banking statute. By 1860 Rhode Island had 91 banks and 21 savings institutions scattered in almost every mill village. Providence, however, had emerged as the financial center with two fifths of the banks and four fifths of the capital.

While banks provided an essential outlet for venture capital and financed economic growth, insurance companies protected the commercial community from loss. The Providence Insurance Company and the Newport Insurance Company, both started in 1799, met with competition when Richard Jackson organized the Washington Insurance Company in 1800. The Providence companies having survived the Providence fire of 1801, the flood of 1807, and the Great Gale of 1815, merged into the Providence Washington Insurance Company by 1820 and shifted from maritime to industrial insurance. Industrial fire insurance was expensive until Zachariah Allen established the Manufacturers Mutual Fire Insurance Company in 1835, organized specifically for mills. Within two years fire insurance rates fell 60 percent. By the Civil War, six underwriting companies operated in the state; and Providence, with four of them, nearly monopolized the business by issuing 92 percent of all fire insurance.

The economic transformation from maritime trade to manufacturing made Rhode Island the most industrialized state in the Union. In 1860, manufacturing engaged over 22,000, or 36 percent of all workers, while maritime trade employed less than 3 percent, and four fifths of the state's capital was invested in textiles and base metals. During the time the population of Rhode Island rose from 68,825 in 1790 to 174,619 in 1860, the industrialized northern towns had increased their share of that total from 30 to 66 percent. As chief contributors, Providence and the neighboring towns of North Providence, Smithfield, Cranston, and Warwick were also its principal benefactors. Between 1832 and 1861 Providence's population jumped from over 16,000 to 55,666 and her assessed valuation rose from $12 million to $61 million. Although hundreds of mill villages existed almost exclusively because of textiles, Providence had a more diversified economy; and it had emerged as the undisputed transportation, financial, and industrial capital of southern New England.

Banks proliferated all over the state of Rhode Island with each issuing its own paper currency which was supposed to be redeemable in gold or silver. The Farmers Exchange Bank of Glocester failed in 1809, and investigators found that it had $86.48 in specie in its vault against $500,000 in paper in circulation. The failure led to improved banking laws and closer supervision of banks in Rhode Island. RIHS (RHi x3 4308)

INDUSTRIAL WONDERS OF THE WORLD

S OME HISTORIANS HAVE argued that Rhode Island's heavy concentration in a few industrial fields was the result of a pervasive economic conservatism within the business community and an unwillingness to take risks and diversify. Historians cite the top-heavy investment in textiles, the continued reliance on the labor of women and children, and the slow adoption of technological innovations such as the power loom. In fact, Rhode Island was a center of innovation in other textile machines, and some nontextile firms grew to become the largest of their kind in the world. The fundamental question is not why Rhode Island failed to diversify, but why did the state become the most industrialized state in the nation? While economic conservatism did emerge in the second half of the 19th century in contrast to the innovativeness of earlier industrialists, it rested not so much with business leaders as with conditions which the state's limited resources imposed. Most early manufacturers creatively juggled the limited assets at their disposal to develop the state's industries.

Rhode Island was an unlikely center for industry. It had no *good* deposits of iron, coal, or other minerals. It had a limited land mass for continued market and population growth. Except for the Providence & Worcester Railroad, the transportation system gave it access only to the coastal and competing centers of New York and Boston. Waterpower sites had to be developed, suffered through summer droughts and winter freezes, and were

This label for Perry Davis' Vegetable Pain Killer, a patent medicine containing alcohol and opium, dates from 1854. RIHS (RHi x3 4297)

owned by a large number of settlers. The labor force before the 1830s was the same Yankee stock that sailed the oceans, farmed the land, or built the mills. Rhode Island's investment capital could not compare with that of other states and came from surplus profits of oceanic commerce. To industrialize, Rhode Islanders had to import cotton, wool, iron, capital, and labor, and then ship most finished products through New York and Boston to regional and national markets that required cultivation. No wonder that in the early years most mills were small, had limited capitalization, experienced frequent changes in ownership, and employed the cheapest local labor available—women and children.

The types of investors affected the scope of industralization. From the outset three groups emerged: sea traders, farmers and merchants, and mechanics (especially the English or those trained in Samuel Slater's mills). Traders appeared more willing to invest their surplus capital in industry; but great sums were tied up in oceanic commerce. Their capital became available mainly during periods of trade contraction, such as the Embargo or War of 1812. Most merchants and farmers were underfunded, retained small mills longer, and were wedded to the mill village concept. Many succumbed to their competitors and sold out. Of the three, the English and the mechanics were the most conservative and traditional group. Samuel Slater, his brother John, and others established the early mills, introduced woman and child labor, and resisted mechanization.

William Sprague (1830-1915), shown here as the dashing "war governor" who accompanied the Rhode Island 1st Regiment to Bull Run, served as Governor (1860-1863) and U.S. Senator (1863-1875). He married Kate Chase, daughter of U.S. Supreme Court Justice Salmon P. Chase. An extravagant and flamboyant man, he pyramided the A. & W. Sprague empire toward bankruptcy in 1873. Lithograph by J.H. Bufford, 1861. RIHS (RHi x3 4304)

A major problem was finding workers in a small population already employed in agriculture. Alexander Hamilton suggested in his "Report on Manufacturers" (1791) that only "idle" women and children might be spared from farm work, and the early mills depended upon them. It is not surprising that Slater employed nine children to tend his first machines or that he recruited large families. The industry by 1820 employed more children than women and twice as many women as men. Millowners used the "Rhode Island" system which brought entire families into mill complexes and created a dependent labor pool. It also kept down production costs and facilitated gradual plant expansion until later immigration created a larger labor pool. The transition from artisan and agricultural pursuits to factory work occasioned friction even where the millowners were most paternalistic.

Slater recognized the inefficiency of the "putting out" system and installed looms in his mill to bring weavers to the factory, but in 1802 a number of disgruntled weavers protested against the new regimentation. Almy & Brown prevented Slater from installing a power loom until 1823; but when he and other Pawtucket millowners attempted to cut wages to weavers paid by the yard, the workers, led by women, walked out. The first textile strike in American history lasted a week, during which time arsonists set fire to one mill and workers demonstrated in the streets. Generally, however, most millowners were viewed as benefactors by the community; and labor problems were, on the whole, minor. The owners' paternalism gradually ended in the era of expansion and greater mechanization after the 1840s.

Rhode Island's slow adoption of the power loom has been most frequently cited as an example of economic conservatism. While it is true that the development of a power loom at the Waltham mill of Francis Lowell in 1815 thrust Massachusetts ahead of Rhode Island in cotton textile manufacturing, Rhode Island probably adopted the new loom as fast as it could. One must recognize that Rhode Island's economy was overextended by 1815. During the War of 1812, investors pumped money into mills, banks, and turnpikes, but during the postwar depression, mills collapsed at an alarming rate, markets disappeared, and the textile-machine industry was in disarray. The supply of adult workers had not appreciably increased since the 1790s, nor had labor shown a willingness to accept the regimentation of factory life. It should also be recognized that the Waltham power loom was a complicated machine that sold for $125. Consequently, most Rhode Islanders who were caught in the postwar financial squeeze had really no choice than to await better economic conditions. Most bought the Gilmore power loom, which was simpler and cost only $70. By 1826, one third of the mills had power looms, and in the 1830s nearly 90 percent engaged in power weaving. Considering the state's limited resources, it was not economic conservatism that allowed it to keep abreast of the bigger neighboring state; it was sound business practices, frugal methods, and calculated risk-taking and daring. These same traits thrust Rhode Island's industries into national dominance in the second half of the century.

One could scarcely accuse the Spragues of timidity as they piled up an empire worth $19.4 million. They began modestly enough when in 1808 William Sprague converted his gristmill on the Pocasset River into a small mill for carding and spinning cotton yarn; but the real founder of the fortune was his son William, Jr., who pioneered the use of power machinery. At the death of the first William Sprague in 1836, his sons William and Amasa formed

the 1860s and beyond financial safety by the 1870s. By then they owned a series of vertically integrated textile plants that covered all operations from the purchase of raw cotton to the manufacture of finished cloth. They owned timber in Maine, water-power sites for textile mills in South Carolina, land in Kansas and Texas, a street railway in Providence, a steamship line, five banks, an iron foundry, a mowing-machine factory, a horseshoe and horse-shoe-nail factory, as well as mills at Quid-nick, Centreville, River Point, Crompton, and Arctic, and the Cranston Print Works. In the nearly self-contained mill villages their workers rented company-owned tenements and shopped at the company

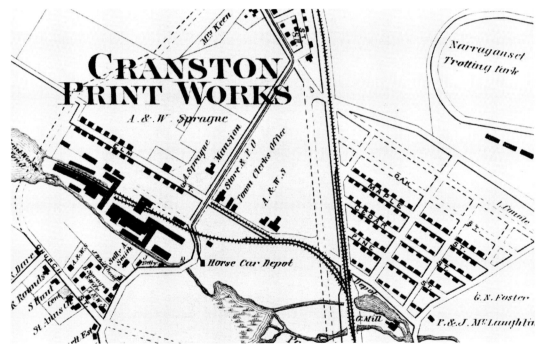

ABOVE: Robert Knight (1826-1912), top, and Benjamin B. Knight (1813-1893), BOTTOM, created the B.B. & R. Knight Company. At the Columbian Exposition of 1893 an enthusiastic description of their domain declared, "One corporation, the largest in the world, renders its dozen villages musical with the hum of 421,000 spindles and makes them beautiful by the happiness of more than 7,000 operatives." From Fruit of the Loom *(n.d.) RIHS (RHi x3 4294)*

LEFT: Beer's 1870 map of the Cranston Print Works of the A & W Sprague Manufacturing Company shows the layout of a mill village, complete with neat rows of company houses for workers, the company store and post office, church, and owners' homes. The Narragansett Trotting Park, another Sprague enterprise, was established in 1867. From Beer's Atlas, 1870. RIHS (RHi x3 4367)

the A.& W. Sprague Manufacturing Company and expanded the enterprise over the next 20 years. Not content with textiles, William was president of two banks and the Hartford, Providence & Fishkill Railroad. Economic power was translated into political power as he served as General Assemblyman, Congressman, Governor (1838-1839), and United States Senator (1842-1844). By the time William, Junior, died in 1856, the Spragues were the leading calico-printers in America.

Amasa's sons, also named William and Amasa, carried the company to its peak in

stores. Company farms raised cattle for slaughter for their stores and reared draft horses for their factories and street railway.

The Spragues used the political leverage of their 12,000 employees to dominate Providence politics, the state government, and even the Rhode Island Supreme Court. William III was elected Governor (1860-1863) and United States Senator (1863-1875). Despite his wealth, power, and ambition, William was unable to break the social and economic leadership of the Browns. When his speculation forced him to borrow from the banks, the Browns tried to stop his credit and encouraged his creditors to press him. The Panic of 1873 toppled the Spragues and forced their companies into bankruptcy.

By the end of the 19th century, cotton textiles in the state were dominated by four great combinations. Brown & Ives abandoned oceanic trade for textiles and owned the Blackstone Manufacturing Company, operating 300,000 spindles in Rhode Island and Massachusetts. The firm of B.B.&R. Knight, which was started in 1852, picked up portions of the crumbling Sprague empire, including six mills in Cranston in 1883 and the Cranston Print Works in 1888. Before World War I, B.B.&R. Knight owned 19 mills in Rhode Island and Massachusetts, including 15 mill villages in this state, and their trademark, "Fruit of the Loom," was world famous. The Lippitts, another great concentration, had begun in West Warwick in 1810. Each generation added to the company, but the greatest expansion came under Henry Lippitt, who took over in 1850. More the consolidator than the innovator, Lippitt acquired the Social, Harrison, and Globe mills in Woonsocket and the Manville Mill in Cumberland. He also acquired the Silver Springs Bleaching and Dyeing Company, and in 1865 he founded the Lippitt Woolen Company. Like the Spragues, the Lippitts entered politics. Henry Lippitt served as Governor (1875-1877) and his sons Charles and Henry F. were respectively Governor (1895-1897) and United States Senator (1911-1917).

Another giant, the W.F. & F.C. Sayles Company, dominated textile bleaching. Having started the company in 1847, William Sayles was joined by his brother Frederick in 1863 and together they owned the world's largest bleachery in Saylesville, the Moshassuck Railroad, the Lorraine Woolen Mills, and several other enterprises. Both attended to business, although Frederick became Pawtucket's first mayor in 1886, and William represented Pawtucket in the state senate for two years.

Although no one of them dominated textiles, the effect of these great concerns was to accelerate the consolidation of the industry. By 1900 the state had only half as many individual mills as in 1860, but they manufactured several times as much product with twice as many operatives employed in large plants. With the exception of the flurry caused by World War I, the era of the cotton textile industry had reached its zenith in Rhode Island and was passing. Investment and mill construction definitely slowed down and New England cotton textiles began to feel the competition from the South. In fact, a substantial part of the new investment in the second half of the 19th century was not in spinning and weaving but in bleaching, dyeing, and printing plants which processed increasing quantities of cotton cloth shipped for finishing from the South. More and more Rhode Island firms invested in southern mills. With capital going elsewhere, plants and equipment were not improved and modernized as needed. The *Providence Magazine,* voice of the Providence Board of Trade, warned in 1893: "Send all the surplus earnings away from our state for a decade, and you will have left general decay in business and bankruptcy staring you in the face."

As cotton declined and sent its capital to the South, the state's woolen industry matured and prospered with the infusion of foreign capital. By 1900 the value of woolen goods exceeded that of cotton. The industry was less prone to market fluctuations than cotton; and because it complemented rather than competed with cotton, it experienced growth during periods of cotton depression. For example, the industry leaped forward during the Civil War when the Wanskuck and Riverside mills were constructed, and boomed in the 1870s as the Atlantic and other large mill complexes turned the Providence Woolen Company into the state's leader. Providence became the center of the industry in Rhode Island and by 1900 was second in the nation in woolens and first in worsteds.

At the turn of the century, Aram Pothier encouraged French worsted manufacturers to invest in the state. Three French worsted mills were built in Woonsocket before World War I, and several more went up in the 1920s so that by the mid-1920s the so-called "French Mills" dominated Woonsocket. One of these, the Branch River

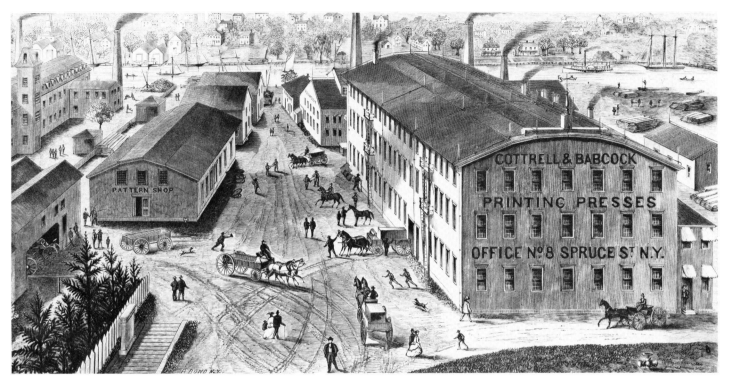

Wool Combing Company, was the largest of its kind in the world. Continuing investment in worsted mills meant that work remained there long after the last cotton mill had closed its doors. Other than jobs, however, these absentee French landlords contributed little to Woonsocket.

The future prosperity of the state depended on other forms of manufacturing and industry. Textiles arrived first and would continue to be Rhode Island's principal industry until the 1920s, but other enterprises grew alongside it. Most important were developments in base metals, jewelry, and rubber. Some companies became the largest of their kind, and by the 1890s Providence boasted of its "Five Industrial Wonders of the World." The city was the home of the largest tool factory (Brown & Sharpe), file factory (Nicholson File), steam engine factory (Corliss), screw factory (American Screw), and silverware factory (Gorham). The Hotchkiss Ordnance Company on Aborn Street manufactured the rapid-firing light cannon that massacred the Sioux at Wounded Knee in 1890; and later, local factories produced bicycles, automobiles, trucks, and airplane parts. Neighboring Pawtucket had a number of textile-related giants, including the

largest thread company (J. & P. Coats), hair cloth company, and wadding plant. Bristol and Woonsocket had big rubber factories, but an 1886 directory of Rhode Island's leading manufacturers and merchants did not list a single manufacturer in Newport.

Most of the large plants were in the metropolitan Providence area—where they were surrounded by a bewildering array of 1,500 other factories producing everything from buttons to blackboards, lightning rods to locomotives, hats to hydrants, and mirrors to monuments. At one time Providence ranked sixth among the nation's cities in her industrial production, and it was in the top 20 cities in population. It also had the highest per capita savings in the nation.

Most of the great businesses rested on some invention. The American Screw Company developed the first practical machine to make pointed screws in 1849 and, as a consolidated giant, nearly monopolized screw production in America. Brown & Sharpe grew from the 1833 partnership of David Brown and his son Joseph R. Brown making jewelry findings and repairing watches and clocks. Lucian Sharpe became a partner in 1853; and with a force of 14 employees, they manufactured

The C.B. Cottrell & Sons Company in Westerly, whose machines printed the nation's leading magazines in 1900—Scribner's, McClure's, Leslie's, Ladies Home Journal, and Saturday Evening Post—was the largest manufacturer of rotary printing presses. This engraving of an earlier plant of Cottrell & Babcock Works is by B. Bond of New York. RIHS (RHi x3 4361)

sewing machines, introducing mass production methods. The creation of accurate machines for standardizing parts led Joseph Brown to his invention of precision tools, including the Vernier Caliper (1851), the Tooth Rotary Milling Cutter (1864), and the Universal Grinding Machine (1874). Spurred by Brown's inventions and Sharpe's business acumen, by 1902 the company employed over 2,000 men in an enormous plant on Promenade Street.

William T. Nicholson transformed the file-making industry by inventing machinery in 1864 to mass-produce quality files. By 1900, the Nicholson File Company manufactured 60,000 files daily in 3,000 varieties and had begun to absorb its competitors. The company owned plants in seven states, marketed eight different

devised the first machine for making horseshoes in 1857 and prospered until electric trolleys and automobiles took over the streets. William Corliss invented a "burglar-proof" safe, and produced it for nearly 20 years before the Mosler Safe Company absorbed his business in 1895.

William's more famous brother was George Corliss, the inventor and manufacturer of the finest and most efficient steam engines. In 1849 he patented a new steam engine, and incorporated the Corliss Steam Engine Company in 1856. Using his inventions, he manufactured engines of the highest quality. By the Civil War the Corliss Company was the only factory capable of machining the turret washer and bearings for the revolutionary iron ship, the *Monitor*.

ABOVE: Inventor and manufacturer George Corliss (1817-1888) came to Providence in 1844 hoping to produce his newly invented harness sewing machine. After designing a perfected steam engine, he began the Corliss Steam Engine Company in 1856 on Charles Street. He held 68 patents and pioneered ideas in standardization and mass production, but died before he could put them into full effect. From the Life and Work of George H. Corliss, *1926. Courtesy, Providence Public Library*

LEFT: Browne & Sharpe employees pose for the camera in front of the plant on South Main Street in Providence in 1872. Even though the metal trades required skilled workers, children (note those sitting on the curb in front) were employed as well. RIHS (RHi x3 4340)

brands, and produced 80 percent of all files made in America.

Other innovators abounded. Frederick Grinnell invented a new automatic fire sprinkler in 1882, making his General Fire Extinguisher Company the leader in the field. Joseph Manton developed a ship's windlass in 1857, which became the standard for the United States Navy and most ships of American registry. Charles Perkins

His genius was limited only by a streak of inflexibility and the inability to delegate tasks to others. He was his own designer, architect, and builder; and he would not rely upon anyone to design his factories, machinery, or even his own home. His strong views about the Sabbath prevented the Centennial Exposition of 1876 from beginning on its scheduled Sunday opening date, despite President Grant's request for that day. Corliss had supplied the Exposition with a colossal steam engine. Symbolizing Rhode Island's industrial might, it was the center of attraction and the sole source of power for all of the 8,000 machines in Machinery Hall. So, he wrote, "Open these gates to desecrate the Sabbath and I will dismantle my engine and withdraw the power. You can do as you please with the Exhibition, but the engine will not run on Sunday."

Rhode Islanders used the popular international fairs and expositions to gain national recognition of the state's products. Corliss won the highest prize at the Paris Exposition of 1867, and Gorham silver was entered in every major exposition after 1879, winning top honors in all of them. For the Columbian Exposition of 1893, they cast a silver statue of Columbus, that fair's symbol, and won 47 awards. Caroline Hazard's poem for "Rhode Island Day" at the Exposition asked what Rhode Island's contribution might be:

Last of the thirteen, smallest of
    them all
What canst thou bring to this
    World's festival ... .
What can we bring? No outward
    show of gain,
No pomp of state; we bring the
    sons of men!

In fact, Rhode Island had plenty of gain to show: one hundred thirty exhibitors displayed products, causing one observer to say, "Scarcely another state in the Union furnished such a varied collection of interesting and important exhibits."

Energetic marketing and advertising advanced a number of products to national recognition: the underwear of "Fruit of the Loom," "Ban-Lon" sweaters, Clark and J.& P. Coats threads, Barstow stoves, Armington & Sims steam engines, C.B. Cottrell printing presses, and the streetcar bumper known as "Providence Fender." Rubber companies kept the nation's feet dry with the "Providence Shoe" and lessened laundry chores with the "Woonsocket Rubber Rollers" for washing machines. The nation's pain allegedly was relieved by "Yellow Dock," "Sarsaparilla," and Perry Davis' "Pain Killer," but the

The Corliss Steam Engine was the central attraction in Machinery Hall at the Centennial Exposition in Philadelphia in 1876. This gigantic machine supplied power to all the 8000 machines in Machinery Hall. Corliss' objections to the machine's running on Sunday forced the exposition to open on Wednesday, May 10, 1876, and his colossus was turned off every Sunday. Courtesy, Providence Public Library

medical and surgical supplies of Davol were a definite improvement. One could also bake a cake with Rumford Baking Powder, toss a salad with "Providence Salad Oil," fry up an egg from a "Rhode Island Red," delight in a Narragansett oyster or clam, and go sailing on a Herreshoff yacht. And if clothes and house needed whitening, one could always use Kendall's "Soapine" and Gutta Percha's "Barrelled Sunlight" paint.

Industrial diversity was a source of considerable pride to the state's boosters at the turn of the century; but more importantly, it allowed Rhode Island to survive the withdrawal of the textile industry in the 20th century. These things were especially true in the industrial heart in Providence. With the city's "Big Five" and its multitude of smaller establishments, its population, wealth, and influence grew significantly before World War I. One writer boasted, "Thus does Providence show an example which might well be emulated by the other cities of the country. With her glorious record in the past and her present assured, what may we not hope this city will have grown to be when her tricentennial comes around?" In fact, by the time of the tricentennial in 1936, one of the Big Five was gone, two more were slipping away, and the textile industry was rapidly disappearing. Two of the expanding industries that softened these blows were rubber and jewelry.

The manufacture of rubber goods had

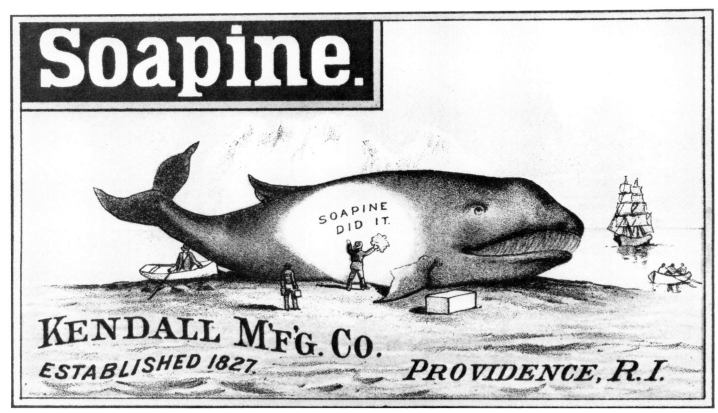

Soapine.

SOAPINE DID IT.

KENDALL M'F'G. CO.
ESTABLISHED 1827.   PROVIDENCE, R.I.

Reproduced here are the trademarks of B.B. & R. Knight Company's "Fruit of the Loom," (right), and the Kendall Manufacturing Company's "Soapine," (above), which was one of America's first soap powders. RIHS (RHi x3 4295, RHi x3 1744)

begun in Providence as early as the 1830s, and the "Providence rubber shoe" was being produced by 1837. The industry prospered, and a substantial number of companies appeared. In the 1870s and 1880s Joseph Banigan developed the Woonsocket Rubber Company into a large, prosperous concern, and by 1889 his Alice Mill was the largest rubber-shoe factory in the world. When the United States Rubber Company was formed, consolidating 15 independent firms, Banigan became its first president and general manager.

At least one Rhode Island governor, Augustus O. Bourn, was a wealthy rubber manufacturer. Founder of the National Rubber Company in 1864, Bourn entered politics as a state senator from Bristol in 1876. He served as governor from 1883 to 1885 and in 1888 authored the "Bourn Amendment" to the state constitution, which granted foreign-born citizens equal franchise rights in general elections. Other leading figures in the rubber industry were Joseph Davol, whose Davol Rubber Company specialized in medical and surgical wares, and Colonel Samuel P. Colt, whose

FRUIT OF THE LOOM

National India Rubber Company in Bristol produced rubber boots, clothing, and wire insulation. Colt was also president of United States Rubber from 1901 to 1919.

With a few notable exceptions—including Ostby & Barton, Uncas, T.W. Foster & Brother, and of course Gorham—the jewelry industry was marked by small, labor-intensive shops. Starting in the pre-Civil War era, when even Brown & Sharpe made jewelry findings, the industry boomed with the increasing popularity of costume jewelry, innovations in plating and chain-making, and the evolution of jobbing shops which manufactured specialty items or performed one process, such as stone-setting or chain-linking. When the government demonetized silver in 1873, jewelry manufacturers took advantage of the drop in silver prices to produce novelty items such as silver toilet articles.

The undisputed giant was Gorham Silverware. Building on its pre-Civil War strengths, the company incorporated in 1865 and expanded to 450 employees by 1872 by securing a contract to manufacture all of Tiffany's silverware. After Tiffany opened its own factory, the new head of Gorham, Edward Holbrook, aggressively sought to make a world reputation for his firm. He entered its products in all world fairs and traveled each year to Europe to buy machines, recruit skilled craftsmen, and learn new techniques of manufacturing and sales. He built the world's largest bronze-casting plant, which turned out statues for the Columbian Exposition and numerous parks, gardens, and squares throughout the nation. In 1890 Gorham constructed the largest silverware factory in the world on Elmwood Avenue and began buying up its competitors in other states. By 1920 the company had 1,820 employees.

From 86 plants in 1860 the jewelry industry grew to over 300 by 1922 and employed 14,500 workers. Providence became the nation's jewelry capital, employing as many jewelry workers as New York, Philadelphia, and Newark combined. While the proliferation of small shops made the industry relatively flexible and able to adjust to fads and fashion's trends, salaries, benefits, and job security remained among the lowest in the state.

Government in Rhode Island was traditionally dominated by the prevailing economic interests of the day. Even in the 18th century when Rhode Island was the most democratic state, it had a "democracy of indifference" and deference. Generally few of the enfranchised voted and when they did, they nearly always voted for wealthy landowners and merchants. Before the American Revolution, Newport merchants dominated Rhode Island politics on behalf of the commercial interests because they believed that what was good for Newport

Irish immigrant Joseph Banigan (1839-1898) rose to become the first president of the United States Rubber Company. After resigning in 1896, he established the Joseph Banigan Rubber Company, erected the Banigan Building in Providence (the tallest structure in the city at the time), and lived in a mansion on Wayland Avenue. From Richard H. Bayles, History of Providence County, *1891. RIHS (RHi x3 4226)*

was good for Rhode Island. When Providence became king of the Independent State in the 19th century, its merchants and industrialists felt that what was good for Providence was good for everyone. With a restricted franchise the sense of deference lasted until the end of the 19th century. Only with the rise of the ethnic Irish and the growth of the industrial working class was the democracy of deference seriously challenged. Until then, business and government had a close relationship, and the General Assembly created a friendly political and legal climate for industrial growth.

Businessmen and industrialists dominated all the high political offices for 90 years beginning with the election of William Sprague in 1838 and ending with the death of Aram Pothier in 1928. The 38 men who served as governor included 26 millowners, bankers, railroad owners, and manufacturers, 3 corporation lawyers, 2 physicians, and 2 newspaper publishers. A similar pattern was evident among Lieutenant Governors, United States Senators, and other important elected officials. Though city councils tended to be slightly more populist, the majority of their members came from the business community. The Providence Board of Trade, founded in 1868, exercised greater power than mayors

Marsden J. Perry (1850-1935), the "Utility King" of Rhode Island, came to Providence in 1871. He soon became a director of the Union Trust Company, owner of the Narragansett Electric Company, Providence's gas and water companies, and the Union Railway Company. Perry's downfall came shortly after the financial panic of 1907, which produced a run on the Union Trust Company and ruined his financial power base, but not his personal wealth. From Men of Providence in Cartoon, *1906. RIHS (RHi x3 4364)*

and enjoyed a close working relationship with the Board of Aldermen and the General Assembly.

After the death of the powerful and popular Providence mayor, Thomas Doyle, the powers of that office were clipped, leaving the city council and a proliferation of commissions and boards to conduct the city's business. As in other American cities, corruption in the assessor's office, the public works department, and in virtually all urban service projects surfaced yearly. By 1880, Providence had exceeded its statutory limit of indebtedness by 200 percent and had abandoned the popular referendum as a means of securing voter approval of its servants' actions.

The state's legal system stood behind the industrial and commercial leadership. When railroad interests sought to erect a new terminal on Cove lands, citizens formed the Public Park Association and elected a whole slate of candidates to city and state offices. A fight among the association, the legislature, the city council, and the railroad interests pushed the matter into the courts; but the railroads won. So, the Cove was filled, the terminal erected, and not a single claim of the city as to location and ownership was recognized.

As city councils desperately fought to retain local control, the higher stakes over corporate taxes and utility franchises between 1875 and 1910 shifted the center of power to the state legislature. In a series of moves which weakened the powers of city governments, the legislature passed laws exempting the stock of out-of-state corporations from local taxes, reducing the tax valuation on plant machinery by one half, and permitting cities to grant a 10-year tax exemption for new plants. Mature industrial cities, such as Providence and Pawtucket, lost as this "special" piece of legislation enticed Eugene Phillips from Providence to East Providence, where he developed the industrial town of Phillipsdale. But the greatest violation of local autonomy occurred over the franchising of transportation and utility companies.

Republican "Boss" Charles Brayton, United States Senator Nelson Aldrich, and Marsden J. Perry collaborated on a series of shrewd maneuvers that made Perry the utility king of Rhode Island. Perry became the veritable epitome of the rapacious traction magnate. He recognized electricity's potential and bought the small Fall River Lighting Company in 1882, the Narragansett Electric Lighting Company in 1884, and its only competitor, the R.I. Electric Company, in 1889. He also acquired waterworks, gas companies, and then the entire Union Railway Company. By 1890 Perry controlled 70 percent of the state's street railway lines and all electrical power in Providence. To electrify and extend his transportation holdings to all parts of the state, he needed money; and to overcome city control of utilities, he sought an exclusive franchise from the legislature. Aldrich secured the money from the Havemeyers, wealthy sugar barons of Philadelphia; and in 1891 Brayton manipulated the General Assembly to grant Perry "exclusive" franchises for 20 years for both his electric and streetcar systems. These franchises were made "perpetual" in 1895, cost Perry a meager 3 to 5 percent of his

TOP: In 1881 Nelson W. Aldrich (1841-1915) succeeded Ambrose Burnside as United States Senator and eventually became so powerful that he was called the "General Manager of the United States." He was, in fact, well connected with the barons of railroads, industry, public utilities, and finance and served them in various capacities. In 1901 his only daughter married John D. Rockefeller, Jr., merging those two names and fortunes. His home on Benevolent Street in Providence is now the Museum of Rhode Island History at the Aldrich House. RIHS (RHi x3 789)

ABOVE: Brigadier General Charles Ray Brayton (1840-1910) was the "Blind Boss" of the Republican Party. Although never elected to office, Brayton controlled patronage, managed campaigns, and exercised a major influence within the Rhode Island Republican organization. Lincoln Steffens denounced the Aldrich-Perry-Brayton trinity in his 1905 expose: "Rhode Island has been a state for sale because the Rhode Islanders were a people for sale." RIHS (RHi x3 545)

gross revenues, and, most importantly, rendered city government powerless to regulate the utilities.

The entire financial empire was incorporated in New Jersey as the United Traction and Electric Company: Aldrich was president, William Roelker, a state senator, was secretary and treasurer, Perry was a director, and Brayton acted as legal counsel for the railway company. Other companies, such as the Rhode Island Company, were also chartered by this group in New Jersey and their assets held by still more holding companies from whom various pieces of the empire were leased. Since Rhode Island did not tax corporate assets held outside the state, stockholders sheltered handsome profits and Perry emerged as one of the most powerful men in the state. As a symbol of his power, he bought the John Brown house on Power Street, present home of The Rhode Island Historical Society.

Perry also played a role in consolidating Rhode Island's railroads. Five years after the New Haven Railroad Company had negotiated an 89-year lease of the Providence & Worcester Railroad in 1889, Perry, acting as receiver, handed the bankrupt New York and New England Railroad over to the New Haven. Within New England, the New Haven faced only limited opposition, and within Rhode Island only Perry's interurban electric railroad offered short-haul freight competition. When the 1906-1907 depression left Perry's empire in financial difficulties, he was able to weather it by selling his interurban to the New Haven for four times its value. The New Haven now had complete control of all railroad and steamship transportation in Rhode Island.

Distressed by higher freight rates and monopolistic practices, the business community appealed to Governor Aram Pothier, who in turn enlisted the aid of Charles M. Hays, president of the Canadian Grand Trunk Railroad. Hays, previously prevented by J.P. Morgan from entering New York, planned to bring his line to Providence. This time the New Haven frustrated his plans by purchasing rights-of-way and short spur lines, driving up the cost. In 1912 Hays sailed to London

in pursuit of more capital. On his return trip aboard the Titanic, Hays and the Grand Trunk connection with Providence went down with the ship. Secret agreements with the New Haven made by the new president of the Grand Trunk so flagrantly violated the law that in 1914 federal authorities ruled that the Grand Trunk must resume its work. However, World War I and lack of money ended the scheme and attempts to revive it in the 1920s failed. Providence remained the largest city in America served by a single railroad, and Rhode Island industries were saddled with the highest freight rates of any city on the New Haven line.

Perry's power and arrogance provoked the 1902 streetcarmen's strike by his refusal to obey the 10-hour law passed by the legislature. Despite an occasional flash of militance, Rhode Island labor had traditionally been passive, weakly organized, and divided by the polyglot character of the population; but Perry's defiance of a popular law outraged the carmen's union. After a month-long strike Perry broke the union with the help of the Providence police, old-time carmen, strikebreakers from as far away as Philadelphia, and Governor Charles Kimball, who declared martial law and called out the militia for the first time since the Dorr War of 1842. When the state supreme court upheld the 10-hour law, Brayton and Kimball had it repealed in the legislature.

The friendly government-business alliance provoked opposition. Kimball was immediately succeeded in office by two reform governors, Lucius Garvin, a progressive Democrat and member of the Providence Radical Club, and George Utter, publisher of the Westerly Daily Sun, and by the first Roman Catholic Irish Democratic governor, James H. Higgins. As a result of the Brayton Bill of 1901, the office of governor had been reduced largely to a figurehead. Even so, the election of reformers and Irish Democrats symbolized the shifting of the political ground. The growing strength of the Democratic party, and the increasing power and militance of labor unions after World War I would end the cozy business-government relationship.

Chapter Seven

THE POLYGLOT STATE

THE EXPANSION OF Rhode Island's economy was accompanied by an equally significant transformation of the state's population from native to immigrant. Although about 4 percent of its population in the 1820s was black, the Independent State's inhabitants were mainly white, native-born, English-speaking Protestants. The arrival of many different immigrant groups during the next 100 years changed this. These newcomers settled mostly in the industrial towns and mill villages; few found their way to the remote rural areas of western and southern Rhode Island. Immigrants swelled the industrial work force, strove to achieve economic security, and influenced the fabric and tone of organized labor. Some lived in mill housing, but the majority flocked to the urban tenements. Each group developed organizations and institutions that cushioned the shock of alienation and perpetuated Old World patterns of thought and behavior. This isolation from the mainstream of Rhode Island affairs deepened Yankee distrust of immigrants and kept the newcomers disenfranchised throughout much of the 19th century. The divisions and interethnic conflict that developed were more significant for the state's history in the 19th and 20th centuries than religious differences were for Roger Williams' time. Nevertheless, immigrants kept coming. By the 1920s Rhode Island had the highest percentage of immigrants in the nation, Catholics outnumbered Protestants, a cacophony of foreign tongues drowned out English, and signs of ethnic diversity were everywhere. The "English Colony of Rhode Island and Providence Plantations" had become the "Polyglot State."

Before 1820, Rhode Island had well-defined black populations in Providence, Newport, and South County; some English and Scottish mechanics and weavers in mill communities; and a handful of French who had remained after the American Revolution. Over the years the number of blacks gradually increased and in 1980 stood at over 27,500. Despite this growth, blacks have declined to 3 percent of the total population while other ethnic groups have increased phenomenally. Rhode Island's economic transformation made the state attractive to immigrants. Textiles lured English weavers, loom-fixers, and skilled mechanics; and the expansion of the metal trades and the growth of fine-jewelry manufacturing brought many more. In 1865 the English accounted for 16 percent of the state's foreign-born inhabitants, and by 1905 more than 24,000 English lived here. So strong was this migration that only Irish, French-Canadians, and Italians outdistanced them in 1920.

In the 1820s and 1830s, work on the Blackstone Canal and railroads drew Irish immigrants to southern New England. Many also found work in the mills and on the waterfront. Their number, however, was small until the potato failure literally meant death for starving Irish peasants between 1845-1846. Nearly a million Irish fled from certain poverty to an uncertain

Most turn-of-the-century immigrants arrived with skills unsuited for industrialized society. Many, such as this unidentified Italian laborer photographed around 1910, built up the cities, tended the textile machines, cast jewelry items, and fabricated metal products. Courtesy, Providence Journal Company

future in America. Because most arrived penniless, many were trapped in coastal cities. Some fanned out into neighboring states in search of work and relatives, creating a chain that brought thousands of Irish to the state. By 1865, a whopping 68 percent of all immigrants in Rhode Island were Irish. Thereafter, Irish immigration remained steady, but their proportion of the total population slipped to 21 percent by 1905 because of other arrivals.

Although a few French-Canadians had immigrated to Rhode Island decades before the Civil War, they totaled only 3,687 by 1875. However, over the next 30 years they increased substantially, and by 1905 the percentage of foreign-born French-Canadians nearly equaled that of foreign-born Irish. Acute agricultural difficulties in the province of Quebec pushed about 700,000 to America; 500,000 of them settled in New England. In the early years of the migration, some French-Canadian males crossed the border to work in mills during winter and returned home for spring planting. Soon, entire families made the trek. When the agricultural depression deepened and the recruitment of these families by millowners was in full force, seasonal migrants became permanent settlers. By 1910, Rhode Island had 34,087 foreign-born French-Canadians, the third largest such community in New England. Although the Quebec government offered families free transportation, 100 acres of land, and grants up to $1,000 for clearing it if they returned to Canada, the vast majority preferred the meager rewards of mill work.

Between 1875 and World War I, as modernization of western Europe swept eastward, wars, economic crisis, land consolidation, political unrest, natural disasters, and the persecution of Jews by Russia and Armenians by Turkey sent millions of uprooted people seeking opportunity and sanctuary all over the world. Most came to America. In Rhode Island, the Italians outnumbered all the rest. Barely present in 1885, they began arriving in larger numbers in the 1890s; and by 1905 over 18,000 foreign-born Italians lived in the state. The peak years for Italian immigration were yet to follow. In 1911 a

RIGHT: In May 1911 the ship Madonna *of the Fabre Line opened direct connections between Providence and Mediterranean ports. By 1913 state officials had constructed adequate docking facilities and the arrival of the* Venezia *was used to dedicate the new State Pier. The Fabre Line continued to operate until it officially terminated service in 1934, but the flow of immigrants into the Port of Providence dwindled after 1921 and federal authorities removed Providence's official port-of-entry status. Photo by William Mills & Son, 1913. RIHS (RHi x3 4354)*

FACING PAGE: Italian immigrant women await immigration official inspection and documentation at the Providence Municipal Pier in July 1921. Problems with documentation at the Port and in the community prompted the creation of the Providence Legal Aid Society that same year. Immigrants suspected of carrying contagious diseases were detained aboard the ship Newark, *a makeshift quarantine station in the Providence harbor. Courtesy, Providence Journal Company*

French steamship company, the Fabre Line, established direct connections between Mediterranean ports and Providence. It brought thousands of Italians and smaller numbers of Portuguese, Greeks, Armenians, and Russian Jews. In 1914 over 18,000 immigrants disembarked at Providence, making the city the fifth largest port-of-entry in the United States. World War I halted the flow, but in 1919 it resumed with a rush as the Port of Providence welcomed more than 15,000 new arrivals. By 1920, of the state's 173,499 foreign-born residents, 19 percent were Italian. The federal immigration restriction legislation of 1921 brought the era of mass immigration to a close. The low quotas assigned to the Port of Providence forced the Fabre Line to suspend operation,

stripped Providence of its official port-of-entry status, and slowed the influx of newcomers for the next 40 years. Still, in 1950, as in 1920, Rhode Island ranked first in the nation in its percentage of foreign-born and native-born of foreign and mixed parentage.

In the past 30 years Rhode Island has lost that distinction but still attracts new immigrants. The majority of recent arrivals have come from the Orient and from Latin America. American involvement in Vietnam and that war's impact on surrounding countries left thousands homeless. With federal funding the International Institute of Rhode Island brought hundreds of Vietnamese, Cambodians, Laotians, and Hmongs to the state, raising the total Oriental population to over 10,000 by 1980. The largest number of recent arrivals, however, has come from Latin American countries. Some have been "freeway" or "spillover" immigrants from the huge Hispanic communities of New York City and New Jersey, others have been recruited by local textile firms, and still others have fled political turmoil or immigrated to join relatives. By 1980, preliminary federal census figures indicated 19,707 Hispanics lived here, although social agencies have estimated that their total might be 30,000.

Recent arrivals have state and federally funded social service agencies assisting them in finding work and housing, attending to legal matters, and in some cases providing job training. In education their children benefit from mandated bilingual and bicultural programs. Mutual self-help agencies, such as Acción Hispania, find themselves caught in the position of being a social protest group and of meeting the needs of an ethnically divided Hispanic community.

Nineteenth- and early-20th-century immigrants had little aid from such sources. Instead, they relied almost exclusively upon relatives, friends, religious and charitable institutions, and immigrant aid societies founded by the respective ethnic groups. Organized efforts invariably were handicapped by a lack of funds, insufficient knowledge of opportunities, and native resistance. Consequently, jobs, housing, legal services, and education tended to become a word-of-mouth experience. Occasionally, an enterprising immigrant would establish his own intelligence office or employment agency to place his countrymen, sometimes for a fee. Davide Senerchia went even further: he created his own immigration bureau and steamship company and brought hundreds of other Italians to the mill village of Natick from his hometown of Fornelli, Campobasso, Italy.

The opening of the Port of Providence in 1911 by the United States Immigration Bureau brought thousands each year and required better facilities. The city and state were slow in erecting a new pier, in heating it, in setting up satisfactory detention quarters, and in providing a quarantine station for those suspected of carrying a communicable disease. Local officials acted only after repeated threats by the Fabre Line to withdraw service and by the federal government to close the port. Perhaps the two most effective nonethnic relief organizations were the Immigrant Education Bureau and the Legal Aid Society. The Union of Christian Work established the

Bureau to relieve the "acute suffering of women and children" at the dock, in the home, and in the schools. This effort at Christian charity was soon tainted with the jingoism of the "Americanization Movement" which dominated the public and private institutions of the nation and Rhode Island during and after World War I.

Few immigrants who came to Rhode Island had a choice of settlement because employment opportunities, relatives, and friends acted as population distributors. Since industry concentrated most heavily in the northern section of the state, that area attracted a disproportionate share of the state's newcomers. The Irish concentrated in mill villages along the Blackstone and Pawtuxet rivers and along the waterfronts in Newport and Providence, in the latter at Fox Point, known as "Corky Hill." The least concentrated were the English and Scottish textile workers who flocked to Pawtucket, Central Falls, and Providence, although many others tended looms and carding machines in rural mill villages. Before the Civil War, blacks were

Jewish immigrants congregated in three areas of Providence. This photograph depicts the lower end of Charles Street in 1899, a part of the Charles-Orms section that included Poles, Armenians, Lithuanians, Greeks, Irish, and several other nationalities. Nearby stood the Sons of David synagogue. RIHS (RHi x3 4006)

A St. John the Baptist parade took place on Clinton Street in Woonsocket in 1906. Parades were popular forms of expression among all ethnic groups; and the various clubs, organizations, and institutions that ethnic communities generated added to both their vitality and their internal disunity. RIHS (RHi x3 4397)

found in Newport and Bristol and lived in two segregated areas of Providence, while a declining number lived in rural South County. This pattern of forced and voluntary segregation continued in the second half of the 19th century as industries expanded and new arrivals intensified the competition for housing. By 1910, the combined total foreign-born and native-born children of foreign or mixed parentage made up 80 percent of the population of Woonsocket and Central Falls: 70 percent in Providence, Pawtucket, and Cumberland; and more than 50 percent in Burrillville, Johnston, Cranston, Warwick, East Providence, Smithfield, North Smithfield, Bristol, Warren, Portsmouth, and Tiverton. These communities had become a microcosm of the world's nationalities, while the remote rural areas of western and southern Rhode Island had remained Yankee.

Some ethnic groups dominated specific neighborhoods and, occasionally, entire cities or towns. Warren, Bristol, and Portsmouth had heavy concentrations of Portuguese; and by 1930 over 5,500 Portuguese lived in East Providence, the largest concentration in the state. Central Falls retained its multiethnic mix, but shared most of Rhode Island's Poles with

the Olneyville section of Providence. French-Canadians turned Woonsocket into "French City" so that by 1920 nearly 75 percent of the population was of that nationality. It was said that natives were forced to learn French to survive. In northern Rhode Island the villages of Oakland, Mapleville, Harrisville, and others in the Pawtuxet Valley were also heavily French. The English were scattered, except for the mill village of Greystone in North Providence which was solidly English.

Within larger cities, ethnic neighborhoods often developed. For example, Cranston was once an ethnic mosaic: the Welsh settled around the pumping station in Pettaconett, Germans thrived by the breweries in Arlington, Swedes were isolated near Budlong Farms, Irish dominated the Cranston Print Works, and Italians occupied Knightsville. Within Providence, immigrants of all nationalities surrounded river valleys where mills and factories stood, while old-line Yankees preserved their domain on the East Side. By 1920, the 19,239 foreign-born Italians, the largest ethnic group in the city, had displaced the Irish on Federal Hill, taken up flats in the North End and Eagle Park, and congregated in Silver Lake. Jews clustered near Broad Street in South Providence, on

North Main Street, and in the Charles-Orms section, the most ethnically diverse neighborhood of the city. With the crowding from new arrivals and some degree of economic mobility, the Irish abandoned Fox Point in favor of suburban Cranston and Warwick, stayed in South Providence or moved to the middle-class Elmhurst section. The process was repeated with other groups: Italians left the Hill after World War II for garden plots in North Providence and Johnston.

Despite the exodus, Providence, Pawtucket, and Central Falls continue to be multiethnic, while East Providence, Bristol, and Warren became more Portuguese, and Woonsocket struggled to retain its French heritage. In 1980 Providence's residential segregation was largely confined to blacks, Jews, Italians, and Portuguese; and the vitality of ethnic neighborhoods such as Fox Point and Federal Hill depended heavily on federal funds for urban renewal and neighborhood rejuvenation. Hispanics and Orientals have congregated in cheap and low-income housing in South Providence, Pawtucket, Central Falls, and in various towns of the Blackstone Valley. While some have suggested that the presence of these new groups has driven population from the city, one could argue with greater persuasion that they have stabilized the housing market in blighted areas.

Throughout much of the 19th and first half of the 20th centuries, housing for immigrants was rarely adequate but generally sufficient for their pocketbooks. Although substandard by today's measures, mill villages and urban tenements were suitable housing for their time. Most Rhode Island immigrants, like the Irish, came from crofter cottages and shanties with earthen floors sometimes shared with farm animals. The majority were poor upon arrival, possessed little or no mechanical skills, and earned meager wages. Since 27 percent of all foreign-born were illiterate in 1880, Rhode Island ranked number one in New England in that category. These conditions created a captive, economically dependent population whose housing needs were met by millowners and tenement developers.

Nevertheless, adequate housing remained an acute problem. Immigrants managed to survive, however, by doubling up families, taking in boarders, and jamming as many people into the two- and three-deckers as was possible. Consequently, Rhode Island became the most urbanized, densely settled state in the nation.

Although Providence never experienced the crowding of New York City or Boston, immigrants and their descendants were slowed in their quest of the American dream of homeownership. For example, in 1920 more than 70 percent of all dwelling units in Providence, Central Falls, and Woonsocket were rentals; and by 1950 of the three, only Providence had dipped below this percentage. Today, second- and third-generation ethnic landlords live in their own suburban homes and rent their former tenement flats to blacks, Hispanics, and Orientals. Consequently, Rhode Island still has the lowest percentages of homeownership in the nation.

Ethnically segregated neighborhoods preserved Old World customs and manners and nurtured a network of organizations, institutions, and businesses that catered almost exclusively to their own kind. Crowding brought out intraethnic tensions and conflicts which both divided and enriched immigrant communities. Northern Italians continued their longstanding feud with southern Italians, splitting them into separate churches, social clubs, fraternal, and benevolent associations. Portuguese remain divided by place of origin and color of skin among the mainlanders, Cape Verdeans, and Azoreans. Jews separated by nationality and then into Orthodox, Reform, and Conservative synagogues. Since the majority of immigrants were Roman Catholic, that religion most dictated the shape of institutional development and interethnic animosity.

The early arrival of the Irish made them the king of American Catholicism, and Rhode Island was no exception. Their pattern of establishing parishes and securing them with parochial schools, benevolent and mutual aid societies, and fraternal societies and clubs made the church indispensable for the retention of Irish

The three Santoro brothers, left to right: Giuseppe, Carmelo, and Sebastiano, and their families pose for their portrait in 1922, just prior to Carmelo's first visit to his native village. The brothers had immigrated in 1907, settled in the Italian North End of Providence, and together established a macaroni factory. They lived near each other, worked together, celebrated all holidays together, and their children grew up as brothers and sisters. Today Grazia Santoro (holding baby on the right) is the only one still living of that generation, but their offspring are still very close. Photo by J.M. Petrucci. Courtesy, Carmela Santoro

shaped most of their organizations. The resulting clubs, benevolent associations, and even their press, the *Italian Echo*, were more secular than religious, more particular than community-oriented, and generally weaker than those of other groups. Instead of establishing parochial schools, they sent their children to public schools. They failed to become a united political group, and some Italians converted to Protestantism. While 20th-century suburbanization has destroyed the old Irish neighborhoods, their suburban churches have perpetuated much of their institutional network. Suburban Italians, on the other hand, retain a deep loyalty to the old neighborhoods based on birthplace and family.

In contrast to the Italians, French-Canadians looked to their church for their institutional structure; and in contrast to the Irish, French *habitants* vested decision-making in a parish council which was headed by a *curé*, or pastor, instead of a bishop and church hierarchy. And while Irish clergy tried to overcome nativism by preaching assimilation, the French doggedly clung to *survivance*—the preservation of faith, language, and customs. From the outset, these two groups clashed over the establishment of national parishes, but by the 1870s four had been established and later 12 more were built in the state. Woonsocket was the center of this network. Here, parishes became neighborhood community centers; they erected parochial schools, built orphanages, supported clubs, generated social agencies, chartered insurance companies, and even sponsored their own athletic teams. In time, French-Canadian colonies all over New England were tied to each other and to the homeland by federations of these agencies and by frequent visits to nearby Quebec. The French-Canadian newspaper, *La Tribune*, became the organ of *survivance* when it editorialized that a woman's place was in the home, rearing and bearing children, and that young women should center their lives around the church and the home.

Survivance was reluctantly tolerated by Irish bishops until the "Sentinellist" controversy of the 1920s. The seeds of the crisis, however, were not exclusively

identity. In addition, Catholic high schools and colleges gave the Irish the educational institutions needed for upward economic mobility. But Polish, Italian, and French-Canadian Catholics had other loyalties and assigned different roles to their religion; thus, interethnic strife ensued.

Four Polish parishes left the Roman Catholic Church and affiliated with the Pennsylvania-based Polish National Catholic Church. Although the Irish church hierarchy under Bishop Matthew Harkins granted Italians the right to establish 12 national parishes, the appointment of northern Italian Scalabrini priests angered southern Italians. Southerners sought to oust the priests, stayed away from church services, and eventually created their own church in St. Ann on Federal Hill. Italian fidelity to family, place of birth, and social class rather than devotion to the church

religious as a combination of factors converged to trigger it. The French-Canadian community was hit hard by the postwar conditions: recession and the textile strike of 1922 put thousands out of work; the state's 1919 "Americanization Law" forced hundreds of adult immigrants into Americanization classes; the 1922 Peck Education Act mandated that English be the language of instruction in all nonpublic schools; and the authoritarian Bishop William A. Hickey, who wanted to centralize control of parish education in the diocese, announced in June 1922 a million-dollar high school fund drive with quotas for every parish. The Franco-American community's fear that the Bishop's assimilationist policy was designed to destroy *survivance* had come true.

Bishop Hickey had distributed "100 percent Americanism" pastoral letters, and he was a close friend of Democratic party leaders. Democrats could elect an Irish governor if the French-Canadians were alienated from the Republican party. The Bishop's assimilationist position and his friendship with Democrats led him to secretly work with the Republican-dominated Peck Commission. When the Act passed, French-Canadians blamed Republicans for attacking their schools, and William Flynn, a Democrat, was elected governor in 1922. The Republicans brought the popular French-Canadian, Aram Pothier, out of retirement in 1924 to regain the State House.

Initially, French-Canadians demonstrated widespread resistance to the fund drive and to Bishop Hickey. Militants unsuccessfully petitioned Pope Pius XI and brought suit in the state's courts. When the Pope excommunicated 63 petitioners in 1928, the movement had come to a bitter end. *Survivance* emerged scarred, but perhaps "more pliable" and moderate. Preservation of religion and some customs continued, but French instruction in their parochial schools began to decline; and by the late 1960s it was dead. While the Peck Act and the Sentinellist crisis played a role, the decline in French-Canadian immigration after 1930 stripped *survivance* of its traditional source of strength. Today, older Franco-Americans struggle to preserve a fading heritage among the young.

Ethnic communities were more than oases for religious, social, and cultural activities. In part, they became self-sufficient economic units. The larger and more densely settled groups, such as Italian, French-Canadians, and Portuguese, generated economic opportunities ranging from grocers to undertakers. Such enterprises advanced the economic worth and self-esteem of individuals, who often rose to leadership positions within their communities. The more resourceful were able to expand beyond exclusively ethnic patronage and local markets, thereby generating additional employment opportunities for their countrymen. In the 20th century Columbus National Bank, Gilbane Construction, Uncas Manufacturing, De Blois Oil, and Fain's Carpets have become important statewide enterprises.

For the vast majority of immigrants, from the Irish to the Hispanics, "American opportunity" meant working in textile mills, factories, jewelry shops, and on construction gangs. Most had no trade suitable for industrial Rhode Island and little or no education. They had, however, what the Yankee establishment wanted: hunger for work, muscle, pride of family, and respect for authority. As a consequence, unskilled factory work became their chief means of survival. In 1910, for example, 48 percent of the French-Canadian, 37 percent of the English, 32 percent of the Italian, 24 percent of the Irish, and 22 percent of the German industrial labor force worked in textiles. Most labored as machine operators under English and Scottish weavers and loom-fixers, who from the start had served as the "trained nurses of an infant industry." More striking was the concentration of immigrants in other unskilled categories: 64 percent of all Portuguese wage earners toiled as agricultural workers, domestics, laborers, and in transportation; 35 percent of the Italian workers were classified as agriculturalists, domestics, and laborers; and even among the Irish who had arrived much earlier, 20 percent earned a living as domestics and laborers, although the Irish tended to be fairly well distributed among a wider range of job classifications. The blacks of Providence on the other hand, were almost exclusively confined to laborer, servant, teamster, stevedore, and janitor. Only the English, Scots, and Germans demonstrated significant occupational diversity, but even they had fewer than 10 percent of their respective labor force in the professional and white-collar fields. These areas and the control of industry were with few exceptions in the hands of the Yankees. More than 70 percent of this elite had middle- and upper-class backgrounds and old-stock parents. A bastion of Protestantism, this elite had no Jews and only one Catholic. Over 90 percent had completed secondary school, and more than 90 percent belonged to the Republican Party. Rhode Island was a state of ''haves'' and ''have nots.''

The ''have nots'' toiled for low wages and found advancement to skilled positions slow. In the early years of industrialization, relatively uncongested communities and millowner paternalism, which provided mill housing, libraries, churches, and other amenities, partially offset the long working hours and low pay. However, rapid industrial expansion and mass immigration ended paternalism, and in its wake came housing congestion, an abundant supply of labor, and industrial poverty. For example, in the 1870s, Edward Harris' mills in Woonsocket paid workers

$6.54 for a 12-hour, six-day work week. By 1919, despite wartime pay scales, the average take-home pay for all immigrant workers was just $14 per week, and 40 percent of the Italian work force received less than $10. In the 1980s some Hispanics and Portuguese work in jewelry shops that pay less than minimum wage and offer almost no benefits.

Such conditions confined the foreign-born to industrial poverty and led to an increase in the employment of women and children. Formerly, the Rhode Island System employed entire families; in later years, economic necessity and immigrant value systems sustained the practice. Millowners recruited French-Canadians because they supposedly were not averse to having the entire family employed and because they had greater respect for authority than the Irish. Some immigrant groups also placed more value on experiential learning and work than on formal education so that child labor was not a phenomenon alien to their culture. As a consequence, immigrant employment in industry reproduced the pattern of the Old World agrarian environment: entire families labored long hours at meager rewards. Understandably, in 1905 in Rhode Island 7,457 French-Canadians and 6,902 Italians over the age of 10 were illiterate, school attendance among most

ABOVE: Unlike most blacks throughout the 19th and much of the 20th centuries, restaurant or tavern owner Thomas Howland gained a little economic independence. Though he became the warden of the Third Ward in 1856, making him the first black elected to any office in Providence, the following year he emigrated to Liberia. From an oil on wood by John Blanchard, circa 1850-1857. RIHS (RHi x3 3106)

BELOW LEFT: Employees of Providence's Nicholson File Company tend file cutting machines around 1900. Dark, congested, and occupationally dangerous working conditions were a part of the industrial scene. Because on-the-job accidents increased as immigrants augmented native labor, to offset the language barrier many companies painted red those machine parts causing the most accidents. RIHS (RHi x3 2905)

foreign-born children was notoriously low, and 5.8 percent of the labor force consisted of children. The General Assembly enacted various laws to curb child labor, but work permits were readily granted.

Immigrant women played a significant role in the state's labor force. According to an 1892 directory, an estimated 21,000 were engaged in domestic service, but manufacturers employed significant numbers of them. Women comprised the majority of workers in 42 of 181 cotton and woolen mills, in 11 of 12 twine and thread factories, and in other textile-related plants. One of the largest employers of women was the Atlantic Mills with 1,037. Costume jewelry attracted many women, some as "homeworkers," but Ostby & Barton, with 53, was the largest employer of women in this industry. Although few metal firms hired women, those engaged in lighter and highly mechanized metal fabrication employed the most; for example, the American Screw Company had over 750 women in 1892. By 1908, observers noted a "significant increase" in female telephone operators, stenographers, typists, schoolteachers, bookkeepers, and clerks. Also recorded were 13 female dentists, 32 "physicians" (only one had an M.D.), 3 ministers, 1 advertising agent, 1 lawyer, 1 architect, 1 lighthouse keeper, 3 undertakers, and 51 hucksters and peddlers. The *Providence Magazine*'s claim that women had "apparently invaded every industrial class in Rhode Island" came close to truth, but trailblazing in nonindustrials was done by middle- and upper-class women of native stock who were also involved in social reform and women's rights. For a vast number of immigrant women and their daughters, the chief workplace was still the factory, so that by 1936 over 23,000 women operatives almost equaled the number of men.

The employment of large numbers of women and children and low wages were obstacles immigrants encountered in moving up the economic ladder. Those who did advance did so primarily outside of industry: the self-employed, the ethnic merchant, the construction worker turned contractor, and those who entered state and local government. Occupational succession, in which a new immigrant group pushes an earlier one into higher positions, seems to have worked badly throughout the 19th century. In the 20th, a mature economy, a rapid decline in the textile and textile-machinery industry, and the Great Depression wrecked the aspirations of many. Additionally, the slow rate of upward mobility was partially caused by the cultural baggage of some immigrant groups and the disenfranchisement of naturalized citizens with less than $134 worth of property.

Slowed in their advancement through legitimate means, some immigrants turned to marginal criminal activity. In time, gaming, black-marketing, and racketeering fell under Mafia control, and Rhode Island became the headquarters of organized crime in New England.

The French-Canadians' tenacious attachment to *survivance*, their respect for authority, and their large families imprisoned them in mill communities and hindered their geographic and occupational mobility. Italians, too, experienced problems because of their strong loyalty to family, their rootedness in neighborhood, and their commitment to experiential learning. Those groups which valued formal education, remained away from the mills, and encouraged their children to exceed their fathers' station tended to rise more rapidly. For example, Providence's Jews began as impoverished as any group, but by the 1950s they led all others in achievement: 90 percent had white-collar jobs and 40 percent had attended college, compared to 40 percent and 13 percent respectively for the population at large. While it is difficult to establish how many were economically hurt without the vote, the state's Irish were denied one avenue of upward mobility that they used with great skill elsewhere. Not until late in the 19th century could Irish politicians dispense patronage on the local level, and not until the 1930s could they do so on the state level. Once in control of the state government, Democrats secured economic advantages for the working class which organized labor had failed to achieve for a century.

Before then, organized labor in Rhode

With the introduction of the telephone, large department stores, expanded commercial offices, and other enterprises, the number of women in the work force increased substantially. These telephone operators monitored the Providence station and routed calls to all parts of the state. From Providence Magazine, *November 1921. RIHS (RHi x3 4349)*

Island was weak, split between rural and urban workers, factionalized by ethnic competition, troubled over tactics, and thus successfully opposed by management, the press, and even the general public. The major issues of the 19th century, the 10-hour day and effective child labor laws, were never resolved. Only among the skilled trades, such as carpenters, brewers, plasterers, weavers, loom-fixers, and mule-spinners, were small craft unions successful in improving conditions of work and in raising wages. These workers formed the Central Trades and Labor Union in 1884 and two years later affiliated with the American Federation of Labor. The textile portion of the A. F. of L. formed the United Textile Workers of America from a series of locals composed of skilled workers.

Despite this effort, by 1900 only about 10 percent of the state's textile workers were unionized. The first major attempt to include the unskilled operators occurred in 1882 when the Knights of Labor founded an assembly in Olneyville. Four years later, the Knights boasted a membership of 12,000 and issued a weekly paper, *The People.* By the early 1890s, however, only a few hundred belonged, and women ran the union. Elizabeth A. Hunt had become head of the Knights in the state, and the executive committee had at least seven women. The demise of the Knights resulted from its inability to enlist skilled craftsmen and because its membership was composed primarily of the curious, of politicians, and of laborers expecting miracles, revenge on the bosses, or continuous strikes. Another major drawback was its Irish leadership which alienated the French-Canadians and other ethnic groups.

Although carmen demonstrated some solidarity in 1902, organized labor was unable to gain statewide acceptance until the post-World War I years. Management could always rely on police and troops, immigrant strikebreakers, and disunity within labor. Radical labor organizations, such as the Industrial Workers of the World, had little success; workers in Pawtucket even asked city officials to throw the "radical and violent" IWW out of town. The city willingly complied. Labor

National Guard troops protect the property of the B.B. & R. Knight mill in Pawtucket in 1922. The United Textile Workers of America, composed of locals of skilled workers, called the strike with AF of L approval. It marked the first time that organized labor won any considerable public support after years of "yellow dog" contracts, blacklisting, labor spies, and strike breaking. Courtesy, Providence Journal Company

gained appreciable public support only after textile firms announced a 22.5 percent wage cut in 1921, followed by another 20 percent reduction in 1922. The United Textile Workers Union struck, millowners summoned the police, violence erupted on picket lines, and Governor Emery J. San Souci sent the National Guard. They failed to break the strike, which lasted through the summer; finally in September management agreed to withdraw the second pay cut and restore the former hours. Twenty thousand strikers had made their point: labor could win if it held out long enough. Unfortunately, while labor won some desperately needed benefits, the victory accelerated the destruction of a major source of its livelihood—the textile industry. Plagued by southern competition, unfavorable freight rates, and the failure to modernize, plants closed at an alarming rate in the 1920s and 1930s. The more organized labor succeeded, the fewer the mills remained in which labor could harvest the fruits of victory. When the bloody strike of 1934 erupted, one era ended and a new one began. Gone were most of the old-stock Yankee capitalists, their mills, and their Republican Party. Here were the Irish and other ethnic workers, the Great Depression, and their Democratic party. The alliance of labor and the Democratic party could not escape the past: it sought gratification, forged political machines, and struggled to dominate a polyglot population.

Chapter Eight

THE PLAYGROUND OF
NEW ENGLAND

RHODE ISLAND HAS long been a place of recreation, rest, and sport; it could be called the "Playground of New England." Recreation became available for everyone from the super-rich to the urban middle class and the factory or mill operative. The ocean and Narragansett Bay have been permanent features even when the principal industries and the state's economy ignored them. In the 19th century, as oceanic commerce retreated, the Bay increasingly became a playground. Far more people fished or sailed for sport than for a living, and Presidents Chester Arthur and Grover Cleveland joined thousands in fishing Rhode Island's waters. In the last quarter of the 20th century, the state has reemphasized its connection with the sea and stressed its attractions by calling itself the "Ocean State."

Cleveland Amory, describing the decline and fall of the playgrounds and spas of the rich in *The Last Resorts*, included Newport as one of those last resorts. In truth, Newport was the first resort of America's wealthy. As early as the 1720s, health-seeking southerners came to escape the heat and disease of southern climes. First came planters from the British West Indies, then the stream widened to include the well-born from Georgia, the Carolinas, Virginia, and Philadelphia. In 1765 Robert Melville, Governor of Grenada, wrote: "The climate is the most salubrious of any port of his Majesty's possessions in America. ... It is made the resort every summer of numerous wealthy inhabitants of the Southern Colonies and the West Indies,

seeking health and pleasure." The *Newport Mercury* recorded 452 summer visitors between 1767 and 1775. The mixture of people made the seaport a lively, sophisticated place. Compared to Boston or Philadelphia, Newport was an open town that welcomed theatrical troupes and other entertainments and pleasures banned elsewhere.

The American Revolution interrupted the summer traffic, but it resumed in the 1780s with southerners from Savannah and Charleston. Even George Washington sent his nephew to Newport in 1783 for a rest cure. By the 1780s so many were coming that it became a business to provide for the annual increase in the town's population. The maritime and natural disasters of embargo, war, and hurricane between 1807 and 1815 set back Newport's recovery; but from 1815 to the 1840s its resort industry expanded rapidly. Formerly most vacationers stayed in rooms or rented houses, then a number of luxury hotels were erected, and a few visitors began to build summer homes. The famed Atlantic and Ocean houses were both raised in the 1840s on Bellevue Avenue. George Noble Jones of Savannah constructed "Kingscote" in 1839, and Ralph Izard, Henry Middleton, and the Balls of South Carolina built homes nearby. In the 1850s real-estate promoters Alfred Smith and Joseph Bailey developed the section along Bellevue Avenue and Ocean Drive. The right to build a bathhouse on Bailey's Beach went with the deed to each property.

After the appearance of grand hotels and as summer cottages were multiplying,

The beach at Narragansett Pier appears quite crowded in this 1890 photograph. While some aspects of Narragansett Pier rivaled the elegance and exclusiveness of Newport, many more middle-class people flocked to the hotels and summer cottages along the South County coast. Courtesy, Providence Public Library

the *Newport Mercury* editorialized in 1850: "While we would throw no obstacles in the way of summer business ... we are firm in our belief, that the greatest calamity which has ever befallen Newport is making it a fashionable resort in the summer." If closing its doors to industry was a calamity, the editor was right; but Newport's future was as a watering place for High Society. It and the Navy kept the town from fading into just another Bay village. The *Mercury* soon joined the celebration and in 1864 began publishing annual "cottage lists" of

Julia Ward Howe (1819-1910), author of the "Battle Hymn of the Republic" and suffragist, summered in Newport with others of the intellectual and social elite. These included her husband Samuel Gridley Howe, philanthropist and abolitionist, Thomas Wentworth Higginson, author, abolitionist, and later commander of black soldiers in the Civil War, Henry Wadsworth Longfellow, both Henry James's, the historian George Bancroft, and artists John Singer Sargeant, John LaFarge, and William Morris Hunt. Courtesy, Newport Historical Society

owners and locations, including a rental list. These served the social purpose of announcing one's presence as well as the business intent of making property available.

In the two decades before the Civil War, some of Boston's Brahmins and an increasing number of New York and Philadelphia wealthy began summering in Newport and transforming it into a posh resort. Some were outspoken abolitionists who clashed with the slave-owning aristocrats. As a result, the Izards and other southerners ceased coming to Newport, and the Civil War left only northerners. Thereafter, the focus of the resort shifted from the hotels to the big houses and palaces, which the wealthy described as "cottages." As cottage construction accelerated Newport witnessed the lavish display of wealth.

America's dollar aristocracy con-spicuously patterned themselves after the European nobility, built copies of chateaux, palaces, and castles, spent lavishly, and tried to snare a title or two. It is estimated that by 1909 more than 500 American heiresses had married titled Europeans with dowries totaling $220 million. The ninth Duke of Marlborough in 1895 married the beautiful but unwilling Consuelo Vanderbilt, who was forced into the union by her domineering, social-climbing mother, Mrs. William K. Vanderbilt. The dowry was $10 million. President Ulysses Grant frequently visited Newport in the 1870s, and his niece married the Russian Prince Michael Cantacuzene, Count Speransky at Newport in September 1899.

While being rich was a prerequisite, just having money was not enough to gain admission to High Society. One had to do the right things, go to the right places, and be accepted by the right people. New York's elite was compelled to summer in Newport because Mrs. William Backhouse Astor did. She was convinced by her confidant, Ward McAllister, that Newport was the place to go for summer. He drew up the list of the Four Hundred so Mrs. Astor could be certain to invite only the right people to her balls and parties. The competition to gain entrance into the Four Hundred became intense, and having a cottage in Newport was one test. Between 1890 and 1914 it was a Newport boast that "the eligible newcomer needed at least four seasons to get in." While money enabled Society figures to buy nearly anything, the social patterns were quite regimented. *Metropolitan Magazine* in 1897 observed: "Newport is a place where everyone does the same thing at the same time—like soldiers in a camp. ... The mess hall of this camp is called the Casino. Whenever a soldier gives a dinner, the fact is telegraphed all over the United States during the serving of the entrees."

When Mrs. Astor's reign ended, a mighty struggle for dominance ensued between Mrs. Hermann "Tessie" Oelrichs, Mrs. Stuyvesant "Mamie" Fish, and Mrs. O.H.P. "Alva" Belmont (formerly Mrs. William Vanderbilt, who scandalized High Society by being the first of that set to divorce). Society was a female-dominated sphere in which the drive and intellect that built industrial empires in the man's world found an outlet. Husbands tended to be weekend participants and bored bystanders in the whirl of Society, and they retreated to their New York offices or yachts as quickly as good manners would allow. Their reward was the prestige of being able to afford all of this costly ornamentation as a testimony to their wealth and success. And it cost a lot. In the depression days of the 1890s, America's worst economic crisis before the 20th century, some of the grand-

by shopping centers and apartment houses, others chopped into condominiums or occupied by schools and colleges. Mrs. Astor had received only the *right* people, but now her mansion is a tourist attraction and its ballroom used for wedding receptions.

All of this is not to suggest that Newport has been abandoned by the wealthy. Many of the cottages are still privately owned and occupied, and Bailey's Beach is still exclusive. The gaping crowd is no longer treated to grand carriage parades, osten-

Newport's Bellevue Avenue is depicted here in the 1870s. The correspondent for Harper's Weekly (August 1874) wrote: "The afternoon drive, usually down Bellevue to Ocean Avenue, and so back to town, is a superb pageant of carriages, handsome women, elegant men, and graceful children." Courtesy, J. Stanley Lemons

est cottages were built, including Ocher Court (1892), Marble House (1892), Belcourt Castle (1894), The Breakers (1893-1895), and Cross Ways (1899). Parties costing $200,000 gave little pause; and a banquet on horseback, a dinner party for dogs, or a party with diamonds and sapphires as favors only enlivened the round of balls, picnics, galas, and gatherings.

The opulent era ended in the 20th century because of new income and inheritance taxes, shifting sensibilities about the display of wealth, the disappearance of the servant class, and the ravages of death and depression. Some mark its end with the discontinuance of the Newport *Social Register* in 1936. One after another the great cottages have fallen, some replaced

tatious balls, and liveried butlers and footmen. Wealth abounds, but is displayed differently or discreetly. Newport is still a resort town with a substantial number of wealthy summer residents, but it also depends on the automobile tourist trade.

Newport was not the state's only recreational resort. No other was as lavish; but Jamestown, the West Island Club in Little Compton, Narragansett Pier and Casino, and Watch Hill in Westerly were worthy competitors. Surrounding these exclusive beaches, hotels, and clubs were more modest establishments which catered to the upper middle class. Along the upper Bay, between the 1840s and World War I, a series of beaches and amusement parks rivaled New York's Coney Island. Shore

RIGHT: *Professional photographers were not permitted at the exclusive Bailey's Beach, but young Henry O. Havemeyer, nephew of the founder of the American Sugar Refining Company, snapped this picture of Mrs. William K. Vanderbilt, Jr., wading in the ocean in 1894. She is dressed in her bathing suit. Courtesy, Newport Historical Society*

BOTTOM: *The* Vue De L'Eau *of the Shore Transportation Company takes on excursion passengers at the east side of Crawford Street Bridge in Providence about 1895 for the Narragansett Bay playgrounds listed. Boat companies competed with each other for passengers and contracts with resorts. The company also operated two other boats, the* Ponham *and the* Squantum. *Courtesy, Providence Public Library*

resorts were developed at Oakland Beach, Buttonwood Beach, Mark Rock, Horn Spring, Rocky Point, Field's Point, Silver Spring, Golden Spring, Nayatt Point, Ocean Cottage, Boyden Heights, Bullock's Point, Crescent Park, Cedar Grove, Walnut Grove, Cherry Grove, Camp White, Kirwin's Beach, Pleasant Bluff, Hauterive, and Vanity Fair. The most popular were Rocky Point and Crescent Park, but Field's Point and Silver Spring gained international reputations for excellent clambakes and shore dinners.

Steamships and excursion boats were crucial to the development of shore resorts and parks. Even Newport depended upon the Fall River Line's daily runs between New York, Newport, and Fall River. The line's first overnight steamship sailed in 1847, and in the post-Civil War era it provided luxurious accommodations on magnificent vessels. Some of the beaches and resorts catering to the lesser folk also began in the 1840s, but their flowering awaited the excursion boats in the 1870s and 1880s. Many resorts maintained contracts with steamer companies to dock at their piers. In 1900 the excursion boats carried 1,250,000 passengers on the Bay, but they went into a decline after the building of the electric trolley lines to Crescent Park and Rocky Point. The automobile finished them off later. Even the mighty Fall River Line died in 1937, a victim of depression, labor

difficulties, and dwindling passenger traffic.

Rocky Point had its beginnings in 1847 when Captain William Winslow of the *Argo* began taking Sunday School groups there. Winslow expanded slowly, then sold the park to Byron Sprague who spent

lavishly until he, too, sold out in 1869 to the American Steamboat Company. Under the expert management of Louis H. Humphreys, former proprietor of the City Hotel and then the luxurious Narragansett Hotel in Providence, Rocky Point became a major resort and excursion park. Humphreys hired his good friend, D.W. Reeves, leader of the famous American Band, to play for several seasons. Until Rocky Point passed into the hands of Colonel Randall A. Harrington in 1888, it had a genteel, Sunday School clientele. It was closed on Sundays and prohibited alcoholic beverages, dancing, and gambling, effectively excluding the typical millworker who labored six days a week. Harrington added a dance hall, opened on Sundays, and "made the place perhaps the best known shore resort in New England."

For a time Harrington was Rhode Island's amusement czar. He owned Rocky Point, its chief competitor, Crescent Park, and the amusement concession at Roger Williams Park. George Boyden had opened Crescent Park in 1886, then sold it to Harrington. In 1894 Harrington leased Cres-

cent Park to Charles I.D. Looff, a New York woodcarver who built the first steam-powered carousel for Coney Island. Looff moved to Riverside and established a factory to build merry-go-rounds. One of his most fabulous carousels, an elaborately carved 66-horse wonder, was installed at Crescent Park in 1895, and he developed the park into one of the finest in the East. The Filene Cooperative Association of Boston came by train for their annual company picnics. Their brochure touted it, say-

Servants of a Newport house pose in the late 19th century. At some "cottages" the servants were made up of many nationalities: the butlers and valets were often English; the housekeeper would be English, German, or Swedish; the maids, gardeners, groundskeepers, and groomsmen were usually Irish; and everyone wanted a French cook. Courtesy, Newport Historical Society

ing, "Crescent Park holds more opportunities for a good time for you and all your family and friends than any other place on the map."

When some Boston businessmen announced their plans for an expensive and elaborate amusement park in Rhode Island called Vanity Fair, the *Providence Magazine* was unrestrained in its praise: "You fill the mind with brightness and pleasure and you destroy at once much of the baser material composing it. Clean amusement is a positive antidote for crime and immorality, and the men who project such enterprises are public benefactors." Vanity Fair opened in May 1907, with the mayors of Providence, Woonsocket,

Pawtucket, and Fall River, accompanied by a throng of 25,000 people who came to see its boardwalk, water toboggan, roller coaster, Ferris wheel, Wild West show, Japanese village, circus and wild animals, children's theater, vaudeville, scenic railway, and midway. The most popular attraction was an act called "Fighting the Flames," in which fire fighters rescued pretty maidens from a burning five-story structure. The crowds loved it. Despite the brilliant opening, Vanity Fair did not pay enough, and it went into receivership at the end of its first season. An accidental fire in 1912 destroyed a substantial portion of

the park, and in 1915 Standard Oil bought the site for an oil tank farm.

Vanity Fair was a latecomer in a declining business, and its brief life warned of evil days for the Bay's amusement industry. Today, only Rocky Point is left. After Colonel Harrington died in 1918, it too entered three decades of decline and destruction. The Sprague Mansion House burned in 1919, and most of the park was leveled by the Hurricane of 1938. Before the site was rescued in the late 1940s and rebuilt in its present incarnation, it was eyed by real-estate developers and then by an oil company as a tank farm. Crescent Park died a lingering death, and the carousel closed in the late 1970s. The future use of the park grounds was a heated political issue in East Providence, and the beautiful carousel became the object of worry and vandalism.

The steamships, ferries, and trolley lines and the resorts they served all fell victim to changes in popular tastes. The "go-anywhere vehicle"—the automobile—dispersed their customers, and pollution destroyed shellfishing and swimming in the upper Bay. The water flowing from the Providence and Seekonk rivers had been polluted since the 1790s, but Providence drank the water from the Pawtuxet River unfiltered until the early 20th century. However, the waste and sewage of a rapidly expanding population and industrialization soon made the river unfit for any living thing. Field's Point, despite its highly praised shore dinners and beach, fell to progress, pollution, and patriotism. In 1912 the Point was literally sliced away, the shoreline straightened for a seawall 3,000 feet long, and new piers for deepwater ships erected. Pollution made bathing unsafe, and the beach that remained became part of the Rheem shipyard in 1942 for the construction of "Liberty" ships.

One did not have to go to the Bay for sports and recreation because the cities provided such things all year round. In winter one had indoor recreation such as hockey and boxing, dancing at Rhodes-on-the-Pawtuxet or the Biltmore Ballroom, singing societies and recitals, and live theater and the movies. In summer, parks and gardens resounded with band music,

RIGHT: A crowd of handsome gentlemen and elegant ladies watch a game of lawn tennis at the Newport Casino circa 1890-1895. The United States Lawn Tennis Association held its championships there from 1881 until 1914. Professional tennis still comes to Rhode Island annually for the National Tennis Hall of Fame tournament. One year the Davis Cup tournament was played on the grass courts at the Agawam Hunt in East Providence. RIHS (RHi x3 2433)

FACING PAGE: This typical clambake probably took place in Providence. All of the shore resorts served a clambake, but some became widely noted for the size and quality of their shore dinners. Silver Spring advertised that all dinners were served by "colored waiters." Crescent Park could serve 5,000 at a regular Rhode Island shore dinner and 1,000 could be served "in the magnificent dining pavilion, overlooking Narragansett Bay, where the famous 'Six o'clock Bake' is the feature from 4 to 8 p.m." For 75 cents (including orchestra) one got cream clam chowder, blue fish, salmon, squiteague, eels, clam fritters, swordfish, lobster, soft shell crabs plus many vegetables, bread, watermelon, ice cream, coffee, and one bottle of claret. RIHS (RHi x3 2327)

streets saw parades, and sports arenas filled with cheering crowds. By 1917 Providence had become an important theatrical city with 27 theaters. Over the years they presented minstrels, vaudeville, burlesque, stage plays, operas, musicals, symphonies, ballet, movies, and lectures. Minstrels and vaudeville became so popular that the larger amusement parks presented them to attract crowds. For example, Rocky Point had an outdoor theater called the Forest Circle which featured minstrels including the Forrest Amazons, the first troupe of female minstrels seen in New England.

Providence was once a major league city and home of championship teams. The Providence Grays won the National League pennant in baseball in 1879 and 1884, and the world championship in 1884. The National Football League, organized in 1916, was a struggling organization when the Providence Steam Rollers joined in 1925. They won the NFL championship in 1928, but financial hard times forced the owners to surrender the franchise in 1931. The Steam Rollers played in the Cyclodrome on North Main Street.

Cycling came to Rhode Island in the 1870s with the founding of the Providence Bicycle Club, and it got the bicycle officially classified as a vehicle with road rights. Similar clubs sprang up all over America. They converged on Newport in May 1880 for the first national meet of American bicyclists and formed the League of American Wheelmen. In 1886, as part of the state's 250th anniversary celebration, more than 1,500 league members wheeled in the bicycle parade. Inevitably, the bicycle craze led to the construction of the Cyclodrome for professional cycle racing. Eventually bicycling and the Cyclodrome were casualties to the automobile; and the structure was replaced by a drive-in movie theater in 1937. Bicycling has made a partial comeback today, and the Narragansett Bay Wheelmen regularly sponsor weekend excursions.

As professional sports have become truly national and heavily televised, Rhode Island has become part of the Boston market. Most Rhode Islanders consider the Boston Celtics, Red Sox, and Bruins, and the New England Patriots their home teams. The Rhode Island Reds hockey team folded in 1977 after 51 years and moved to Binghamton, New York, despite the opening of a larger arena, the Providence Civic Center. Various efforts at minor league basketball and soccer have all ended in failure. The principal local sporting attractions are now major college competition in basketball, hockey, and soccer.

In Rhode Island the "sport of kings" has disappeared or "gone to the dogs." Amasa Sprague established the fashionable Narragansett Trotting Park in Cranston in 1867. It hosted such notables as Cornelius Vanderbilt and J.P. Morgan and inspired William Sayles to buy and raise world-class horses. By 1925, the site was sold and platted. Thoroughbred racing began in 1934 at Narragansett Park, which the *Baltimore Sun* praised as "the showplace of the North, one of the finest tracks in the country." However, it, too, closed permanently in 1978 and the land is scheduled for industrial and residential development.

RIGHT: Matilda Sisseretta Joyner Jones (1869-1933), popularly known as Black Patti, sang as a soloist with various concert companies, the Levy and Gilmore bands, and other performing groups from 1888 until 1896. She sang at the Pittsburgh Exposition, the World's Columbian Exposition in Chicago in 1893, and all around the nation. From 1896 to 1916 she was the central figure in the Black Patti Troubadours. She retired to her home in Providence where she lived until 1933. Her funeral took place at the Congdon Street Baptist Church and she was buried in Grace Church Cemetery. Courtesy, Rhode Island Black Heritage Society

FAR RIGHT: The Strand Theater, shown here about 1919, was built in 1915 on Washington Street at Union Street in Providence. The Providence "theater district" had 17 theaters by 1920 that catered to nearly every level and taste in stage and screen entertainment. RIHS (RHi x3 2758)

The state's other track, Lincoln Downs, opened in 1947, but was converted to dog racing in 1977.

Newport has been home to several sports of the rich: polo, tennis, golf, and yachting. James Gordon Bennett, Jr., owner of the *New York Herald*, introduced polo to America in Newport in 1876 and frequently entertained leading polo players as guests. One such was an Englishman, Captain Candy, who rode his horse into the clubhouse of the exclusive Reading Room.

Candy was expelled and Bennett forced to resign. In retaliation, Bennett founded a rival club, the Casino, and in 1879 built his clubhouse, the famous Newport Casino. There, the United States Lawn Tennis Association held its first championship in 1881. From then until 1914, the Casino hosted the USLTA championships, and Tennis Week at the end of August became a highlight of the "Season." The USLTA moved to Forest Hills, New York, in 1917; but the National Tennis Hall of Fame

opened in the Casino in 1952 and is celebrated annually with a professional tournament. Rhode Island's first golf course was constructed in Newport, and the first amateur and open championships of the United States Golf Association were played there in 1895. Once golf and tennis were games of the rich, but today Rhode Island has nearly 50 golf courses, and almost everyone who can swing a racquet plays tennis.

Yachting still remains a sport of the con-siderably wealthy, and Newport is home to the most celebrated yachting competition, the America's Cup Race. The first race occurred off the Isle of Wight in England in 1851, and the trophy has remained in America since then. The New York Yacht Club, which sponsors the race, moved the competition to Rhode Island in 1930. The state had a reputation for having master builders of Cup racers, as the Herreshoffs of Bristol built every winner from 1893 to 1937. The biennial Bermuda Yacht Race

13 weeks to see this spectacular production. In the 1890s the American Band played each evening to thousands during the season in Roger Williams Park. A rival venture, the Sans Souci Gardens of William E. White and the National Band, which also opened in the summer of 1878, staged operettas and featured band concerts and singers. One soloist in 1887 was Matilda Sisseretta Joyner, soon to become internationally famous as Black Patti. Although she was compared to the legendary Adelina Patti, Black Patti found her career shunted into singing in the Cakewalk Jubilee, musical variety shows, and the Black Patti Troubadours, which was essentially a minstrel show with an opera star.

The minstrel show was America's first mass entertainment form, and Providence became a major source of minstrel troupes and a thoroughly minstrel-mad city. In the 1870s and 1880s virtually every theater in Providence and Pawtucket featured minstrels, and shows often ran for 10 months. Ashcroft Street is named for Billy Ashcroft, leading endman in the late 19th century; he and Dick Sands, also of Rhode Island, shared the title of "Champion Clog Dancers of the World." The endmen were the stars. Jerry Cohan, father of George M. Cohan, was a minstrel endman as early as 1867. As minstrels declined, Cohan switched to vaudeville; and it was as part of the Four Cohans that George M. first appeared in the theater. The Four Cohans were featured at the grand opening of the Imperial Theater in 1902, and when the Albee Theater opened on April 21, 1919, George M. was the headliner. Born in Providence, he was a great favorite, even if he later declared that he hated the place. Vaudeville in turn faded before the movies, and Providence's largest theaters were built essentially to be movie palaces. The Strand opened in June 1915 and seated 2,500; the 3,000-seat Majestic began with movies and vaudeville in April 1917; and the 3,200-seat Loew's State was dedicated in October 1928. Nearly all theaters accommodated a variety of entertainments from girlie shows and Victor Herbert's operettas to the Boston Symphony Orchestra (since 1882), and legitimate theater.

New England's first theatrical perfor-

moved to Newport in 1936, and now the Transatlantic Yacht Race also sails out of the "Yachting Capital of the World." The newest ideas are a round-the-world yacht race beginning and ending in Newport, and an invitational "Hall of Fame" race for the top 20 yachtsmen.

For more ordinary folks, band concerts, parades, and theaters added gaiety to life. In the late 19th century Providence supported one of America's greatest wind bands, Reeves' American Band. Begun in 1837, the band came under the directorship of D.W. Reeves in 1866, and he expanded it into a full-time occupation. Nearly every significant occasion included the American Band. In June 1878 Reeves opened the Park Garden, near Roger Williams Park. The following summer he staged an awesome version of Gilbert and Sullivan's H.M.S. *Pinafore*, complete with a full-sized ship, a chorus of 100, and orchestra of 28. Audiences of over 4,000 came nightly for

mances occurred in Newport in the summer of 1761 when Hallam's Virginia Players appeared successfully. But when they played in Providence the next summer, over 400 citizens petitioned the General Assembly, saying that theatricals "not only occasion great and unnecessary expenses, and discourage industry and frugality, but likewise tend generally to increase immorality, impiety and contempt for religion." The General Assembly complied. Some determined opponents wanted to destroy the little theater on Meeting Street even before then, but John Brown and friends dragged a cannon from a nearby armory and threatened to fire on the mob. Theater returned to Providence in December 1792 when Joseph Harper's company played at the courthouse. A real theater was erected in 1795 on the present site of Grace Church with funds from that same John Brown and friends, and the statute against theatricals was repealed. As Providence grew to become New England's second largest city, it became a major stop on the touring circuit for minstrels, vaudeville, and individual performers such as Jenny Lind, whose triumphant appearance in 1850 was held in Howard Hall.

Over the years one could see nearly any sort of stage entertainment that the American theater industry provided. Occasionally the spirit of 1762 will arise and close a show. For example, Eugene O'Neill's Pulitzer prize-winning play, *Strange Interlude*, was banned in 1930 for being "too lewd"; and in 1940 the Providence police denied a license to present John Steinbeck's *Of Mice and Men*. But tastes change, and in 1981 the highly praised Trinity Square Repertory Company staged *Of Mice and Men* and took it on an international tour. Through the 1930s and 1940s the theaters of Providence and movie houses of any town could count on patronage for almost anything that Hollywood wanted to dish out. In the 1950s suburbanization and television radically transformed the theater business and the grand "temples of illusion" fell to wreckers and porno shows. The Majestic was rescued in 1971 by the Trinity Square Repertory Company; and Loew's State has been reprieved as the Ocean State Center for the Performing Arts.

Newport has sought to establish itself as a music and performing arts center during summer seasons. It began with the Jazz Festival in 1954, which occasioned "an uproar among the old guard that almost drowned out the music itself." But, the festival succeeded financially and featured many of America's famous jazz artists. Despite its great music, its troubled history forced the festival to close after the 1971 disorders. That year the billing included top performers, but the festival attracted thousands of the floating population of the youth culture. During Dionne Warwick's performance, a mob of young people, high on drugs and alcohol, abandoned their jugs of wine and tree-top hammocks and stormed the festival fence. In minutes they smashed the fence and rushed the stage. Audience and performers fled in fear, and the police had to restore order. For true jazz lovers, the evening was a sad occasion; jazz at Newport was abandoned in favor of New York City where it billed itself as the "Newport Jazz Festival in New York City." In 1981 festival promoter George Wein returned to Newport with a limited version held in old Fort Adams. Other efforts, such as the Folk Music Festival, the Newport Opera Festival, and a dance festival have all come and gone. The Newport Music Festival, the most elegant and elite, stages concerts in the mansions and has remained afloat with the support of wealthy patrons.

America's first resort and New England's playground are now fully committed to promoting their assets. The literal heart of enterprise in Newport is tourism and resort business. The city rebuilt most of its waterfront, added new hotels, and expanded moorings for pleasure craft. The state itself is contributing to these developments as officials promote Rhode Island nationally as the "biggest little state" with "something for everyone." The Bay teems with an estimated 30,000 vessels, and a true excursion boat returned in 1978 with the appearance of the *Bay Queen*. The opportunities for recreation are far more numerous than at any time, if not so spectacular as in the old days of the amusement parks.

FACING PAGE, TOP: Joe Williams sang with Count Basie and his band in the Newport Jazz Festival in the later 1950s. RIHS (RHi x3 4369)

BOTTOM: The Trinity Square Repertory Company presented Of Mice and Men *in 1981. Trinity Square Repertory Company, which began in 1964, was first housed in the Trinity United Methodist Church located at Trinity Square in Providence. In 1968 the company was the first American regional theater to perform at the Edinburgh Festival in Scotland. Artistic Director Adrian Hall led the company to national exposure on the Public Broadcasting Service's "Theater in America" in 1974, to a new home in the old Majestic Theater in 1973, and a Tony Award in 1981. Courtesy, Trinity Square Repertory Company*

1764   1914

150TH ANNIVERSARY
OF THE FOUNDING OF
BROWN UNIVERSITY
OCTOBER 11-15

Chapter Nine

THE STATE OF THE HEART, SOUL, AND MIND

RHODE ISLAND'S RICH religious and ethnic diversity has produced a varied and sometimes contradictory experience. The state takes pride in being first in America to conduct the "lively experiment" in religious freedom which has become part of the American system. The private, voluntary congregation became a model for other institutions as well. Private agencies generally preceded public ones, and a number of those that are publicly supported today had their beginnings as private or philanthropic endeavors. In time the increase in population and social complexity meant that private means were unable to accommodate all who needed services. Art and culture remain privately supported but social services have generally been assumed by the state.

To the horror and disgust of its neighbors, colonial Rhode Island admitted all the rejected consciences of New England and the New World, including, as Cotton Mather disapprovingly noted, "Antinomians, Familists, Anabaptists, Anti-sabbatarians, Arminians, Socinians, Quakers, Ranters, everything in the world but Roman Catholics and true Christians." In the beginning, religious toleration was almost the only thing that independent-minded Rhode Islanders could agree upon: and for them church and state were to be separate. Such principles have not, however, kept various religious majorities over the centuries from seeking to impose their morality upon everyone.

For Yankee Protestants, Sunday was a day of church-going and rest; but this clashed with the European notion that Sunday was a day of recreation. As a result, sabbatarianism produced "blue laws" which sought to limit Sunday activities. Various church groups fought the secularization of the Sabbath by trying to prevent Sunday baseball or the showing of movies. In recent years the Sunday sales laws crumbled in the face of the determination of the shopping malls and supermarkets to remain open. The crusade to prohibit alcoholic beverages became highly political, complete with party and officeseekers. The state's first temperance meeting was held at the First Baptist Meeting House in Providence in 1827, and the effort culminated in the statewide prohibition by 1852. While this law was repealed during the Civil War, prohibitionists' concern about the alleged affinity of the immigrants for ardent spirits drove them to amend the state constitution in 1886 to prohibit the manufacture and sale of alcoholic beverages. This, too, was repealed in 1889 in the first election after the Bourn Amendment had enfranchised naturalized citizens. So, by the time the national prohibition amendment arrived in 1919, Rhode Island refused to ratify it and unsuccessfully challenged its constitutionality in the United States Supreme Court.

Presently Rhode Island is the most Catholic state in the nation; Roman Catholics constitute nearly 70 percent of the population and 90 percent of the legislators. This Catholic majority, like its Protestant predecessors, uses its political power to legislate its morality, as for instance on the issues of

This postcard from 1914 announced the 150th anniversary of the founding of Brown University. RIHS (RHi x3 4330)

abortion or the survival of parochial schools.

Contrary to Roger Williams' principles, during most of the 18th century Roman Catholics were barred from the franchise when the colony's laws were first codified in 1719. No evidence exists to indicate that this prohibition was actually enacted before being slipped into the code; but, once in, it was not repealed until 1783. Rhode Island had only a few Catholics during the colonial period, but by the mid-1850s Providence alone had almost 10,000, and Rhode Island counted 19 Roman Catholic churches, 6 parochial schools, and an orphanage. With the creation of the Catholic parochial school system in the 1840s came an issue that has not been resolved to the present. Catholics made parochial schools a high priority; unfortunately, the drive to gain public funding for these schools began at the same time and has served to perpetuate the divisions between Catholics and Protestants.

The rise of parochial schools strengthened the effort to create a statewide public school system; and industrialization and immigration spurred educational reformers. In this respect, Rhode Island shared the national perception that the public school was the most effective, efficient instrument for bringing the children of immigrants into the mainstream of American life. Inasmuch as Rhode Island was America's first urban, industrial state, it is not surprising that she led the way in certain aspects of public education.

The impetus for a free public school system was led by John Howland of the Providence Association of Mechanics and Manufacturers, who asserted that "education is the common right of every child." As a result, in 1800 Rhode Island enacted America's first public school law to create a statewide system of free education. Unfortunately, except for Providence and Smithfield, the towns refused to implement the act, and it was repealed in 1803. Only Providence regularly maintained public schools for the next two decades, but even these educated only a fraction of the children because parents still had to pay for fuel and books. A new state law in 1828

established independent school committees and a permanent state fund for education. Thereafter, no town was without a school; but because many charged for books, the poor could not afford to attend. The wealthier people simply provided a private education for their children, as they always had.

One ignored problem was segregation of blacks. While the law did not mandate segregation, Providence, Newport, and Bristol, where most blacks lived, maintained segregated schools. In 1828 Providence had opened a school for black children, but the teacher was paid 20 percent less than teachers of whites. George T. Downing, a successful caterer and hotel proprietor in Providence and Newport, began his attack on school segregation in 1855, a campaign that lasted until his victory in 1866.

Thomas Dorr ought to be remembered for his educational reforms. As a member of the Providence school committee from 1838 to 1842, he helped to improve the schools substantially, and he was instrumental in Providence's appointing a superintendent in 1839, the first in the nation. He also sought to bring free public schools to the entire state through the People's Constitution, but it was defeated. However, the new Constitution of 1842 declared that "it shall be the duty of the General Assembly to promote public schools. ..." The legislature commissioned Henry Barnard to conduct a comprehensive survey of the schools, the first of its kind in the nation. Like similar investigations in Connecticut, Massachusetts, and New York, it revealed appalling conditions and provoked a general reorganization of education in the state. As a consequence of one recommendation, in 1854 the state began a teacher training school which by 1957 had evolved into Rhode Island College, a general-purpose institution of higher education.

Despite various reforms, the public schools were still poorly attended because of fees and textbook costs and because the Rhode Island System of hiring entire families for mill work kept large numbers of children away. The 1880 Census revealed that the illiteracy rate among

BELOW: The driving force to abolish segregated schools in Rhode Island, George T. Downing (1819-1903), was the son of a successful New York caterer and oyster house owner. In 1846 George opened a summer branch of his father's restaurant in Newport. Four years later he started a catering business in Providence, and finally he built a luxury hotel in Newport called the Sea Girt House. He began his attack on segregated schools in 1855 and finally won in 1866. Courtesy, Rhode Island Black Heritage Society

native-born whites (not to mention the foreign-born) was four times as great as neighboring Massachusetts, and that almost 22 percent of all school-aged children did not attend a single day of school. These shocking figures led to a free textbook law in 1893, higher requirements for attendance, a truancy law, and the lengthening of the school year.

Still, public education remained in a deplorable condition. It was underfunded and its curriculum unsuited to the ethnic and industrialized character of the state. The largest school district had only one truant officer until 1926, its administrators were Yankees, its teachers nearly all Irish, and its students polyglot. Manual training and commercial education were not introduced until late and were still unavailable in most places. In 1919 "Americanization" became a major thrust as a result of nativist fears, and a state measure forced public schools to assume the Americanization classes that had formerly been conducted by groups such as the YMCA.

Just as Yankee attitudes, financial restraints, and inadequate facilities sometimes alienated immigrant students, immigrant attitudes often precluded school success. Many ethnic groups did not identify with the public schools. The Irish and French preferred parochial schools, while a large number of children of the industrial working class left school at an early age. Woonsocket, with a population of 24,000 in 1890, graduated only 11 students from high school. In the first decades of the 20th century, Rhode Island had the lowest percentage of children attending any level of school in New England, and attendance after the age of 14 declined sharply since many obtained work permits. For example, in 1920 Providence handled 7,266 work certificates. Not surprisingly, juvenile delinquency rates were "higher than in any state in the Union except the District of Columbia and Delaware." With the exception of Nevada, Rhode Island had the highest illiteracy rate of all northern and western states. Only the South was worse off. The result of these factors was to create a weak educational system and a general state of mind which gave public education a lower priority. Even today, Rhode Island

ranks near the bottom in educational achievement as fewer than half of the adults have graduated from high school; and it is 34th in literacy, lowest in New England.

In sharp contrast, Rhode Island's wealthier classes have high educational achievement and schools to serve their aspirations. Upwardly mobile ethnics and professionals have created in their suburban communities, such as Barrington, Cumberland, and Lincoln, some of the best public schools in the state. Affluent Yankees send their children to Protestant academies or private schools. Such institutions antedate public schools as wealthier colonists educated their children with tutors, dame schools, Latin schools, and proprietary and private academies. Dr. James Manning, for instance, started a Latin preparatory school in connection with Rhode Island College (Brown) in 1764. The Quakers established a denominational school in 1784, today known as Moses Brown School. Over the years a host of academies and seminaries sprang up in every corner of the state.

The state's only institution of higher education until the mid-19th century was Brown University. While it was named for Nicholas Brown, Jr., in 1804, the name recognizes the crucial part played by the

ABOVE: Because of inadequate schools and direct costs to poor parents for the schooling of their children, the likelihood was that children such as these would grow up undereducated or virtually illiterate. This photo entitled "Along the Tracks: A Playground Badly Needed," probably by Lewis Hine, appeared in Child Welfare Conference and Exhibit, *January 6-12, 1913. Courtesy, Newport Historical Society*

FACING PAGE, BOTTOM: As a state legislator in Connecticut, lawyer, writer, and educator Henry Barnard (1811-1900) helped to establish a state board of education and served as its first secretary. He then became Rhode Island's first commissioner of education (1845-1849) before going on to become Connecticut State Superintendent of Education (1850-1854), chancellor of the University of Wisconsin (1858-1860), president of St. John's College, Annapolis, Maryland, (1866-1877), and the first U.S. Commissioner of Education (1867-1870). James Sullivan Lincoln painted this oil on canvas portrait of Barnard in 1857. RIHS (RHi x3 3110)

family, especially Moses, John, and Joseph, in the location and early development of the college. The family has continued its close association and benefactions over the years. Brown probably passed up a chance to become the state university because it did not wish to open an agricultural department after the General Assembly assigned to it the state's share of the federal land grant under the Morrill Act of 1862.

Woonsocket's Precious Blood Grammar School (left) and St. Clare High School (right) at the corner of Park and Hamlet streets are pictured as they looked about 1920. The French-Canadians, like the Irish, expanded their institutional network by building an entire parochial school system throughout their settlements in the state. With the decline in new immigrants, coupled with gradual assimilation and escalating costs, many of these institutions collapsed. The grammar school closed in the early 1970s, and the high school was converted to Chateau Clare, housing for the elderly. RIHS (RHi x3 2285)

city." Brown could enrich its programs by "effecting a constantly widening affiliation with the cultural and scientific agencies of the state and of the metropolitan district." Subsequently, the university did institute several new programs, and in the 1970s developed the state's only medical school. Sometimes, however, the needs of the university brought it into conflict with local concerns. Brown's callous destruction

Brown surrendered the aid; and in 1892 the legislature created Rhode Island College of Agricultural and Mechanic Arts, which in 1951 became the University of Rhode Island.

Under president Benjamin Andrews in the 1890s, Brown assembled a distinguished faculty, founded the Women's College (Pembroke), and began a limited graduate program. Although Brown was proud to maintain the atmosphere of a "typical New England college of arts and sciences," a 1930 external study criticized it for remaining aloof from the metropolitan context. They declared that Brown "has the possibility of a more distinguished service," but it would have to alter its "national state of mind" and accept that the university is "conditioned by a great

of several blocks of 18th- and 19th-century houses caused the historic preservation movement on College Hill to spring to life in the mid-1950s. Since then, Brown has been more careful that its internal needs are not destructive to the surrounding areas. While various local politicians continue to maintain that Brown ought to be wide open to local applicants, the school still sees itself as having a national constituency.

The Roman Catholic educational system reached maturity with the opening of Providence College in 1919. Founded by Matthew Harkins, Bishop of the Diocese of Providence, it has traditionally served the Irish and is the alma mater of a large number of the state's political leaders. A women's college, Salve Regina, began operation in 1947. The system underwent a transformation in the 1970s when Salve Regina expanded to a four-year institution, the unaccredited College of Mount St. Joseph closed, and Providence College went co-educational.

The late 1960s and early 1970s were flush times for higher education in the nation, and most of the state's colleges and universities expanded and developed. Rhode Island's public junior college, begun in 1964 with 250 students in temporary quarters in Providence, expanded by 1980 into the Community College of Rhode Island with 12,000 students on two permanent campuses in Warwick and Lincoln. Roger Williams College, founded in 1948, became a four-year institution and moved to a new campus in Bristol in 1969. Likewise, Bryant College, opened as a business college in 1863, moved to its new location in Smithfield in 1971. Into the vacuum created by the exodus of these colleges from Providence to the suburbs came Johnson & Wales, which has gone from a junior college in 1963 to offering graduate degrees by 1981. In the 1980s, with the rising costs of private education and the shrinking student pool, privately educated legislators have been seeking legislation to shore up their institutions. While this may guarantee the survival of Rhode Island's educational diversity, it comes, as it did with secondary education, at the expense of public higher education.

Just as private education predated the public school system, so did many other services begin in the private sphere; and many of the institutions that are now regarded as public had their origin in philanthropy. The earliest libraries, such as the Redwood Library in Newport and the Athenaeum in Providence, were private, or were philanthropic projects for the benefit of the public, as in the case of Edward Harris' establishment of a library and cultural center for Woonsocket in 1856. Dozens of private subscription libraries appeared and disappeared before a public system developed in the late 19th century. In 1875 the Free Library Act provided for matching state funds to any library that was free to the public. With this, library doors opened in virtually every town. The Pawtucket

Public Library illustrated the transformation. It began as a private subscription library in 1852 but was assumed by the town in 1876. It was the only Rhode Island library in the late 19th century wholly owned and supported by a municipality. However, it also benefited from philanthropy as Frederick Clark Sayles donated the land and building in 1899. A progressive institution, the Pawtucket Library was one of the first in the nation to adopt the open-shelf system, a Sunday reading room, a children's program, and a librarian to serve high-school students.

In the pre-Civil War years, the healing of the body was mostly a matter of luck because medical practices were premodern and health-care facilities were virtually nonexistent. From today's perspective, all of the competing medical theories of that age were quackery, whether it was the heroic medicine of the "regular" physicians or the unorthodox ideas of the homeopaths, hydropaths, heliopaths, mesmerists, phrenologists, or spiritualists. The era was one of great experimentation because it was clear that orthodox medical practice was simply dangerous to the patient. For example, Elizabeth Buffam Chace, a leader in abolitionism, women's rights, and poor relief, became deeply involved in spiritual healing, hydropathy, and "animal magnetism" after losing five children under the care of "regular" physicians. The *Providence Journal* supported dietary reform, specifically, the "Graham Cracker" crusade. Some local members of the Transcendentalist movement established a utopian community called Holly House near Providence in 1841 and sought to preserve their health by abolishing all coercion and private possessions and by abstaining from tobacco, alcohol, and sex.

Until the start of Butler Hospital for the Insane in 1847, Rhode Island had no hospitals. Butler resulted from the philanthropy of the Browns, Goddards, Hazards, and Cyrus Butler; and it was the state's only asylum until the public institutions were opened at Howard in 1870. Butler remains a private mental health facility, but Rhode Island Hospital became the first general hospital in 1868. It, too, had its beginnings in philanthropy with generous donations

Elizabeth Buffum Chace (1806-1899), an antislavery and suffrage leader, was reared a Quaker and an abolitionist by her father, who founded the New England Anti-Slavery Society. After her first five children died, Elizabeth devoted her life to the antislavery cause. Her husband was a successful industrialist who supported her reform activities. Though the couple had five more children, Elizabeth plunged into the suffrage crusade after the Civil War as well as working for penal reform, education, temperance, peace, and care of orphans. Portrait from Elizabeth Buffum Chace, Her Life & Its Environment, *1914. RIHS (RHi x3 2388)*

Homeopathic medical practice put great store upon science and public health, with the result being that as medical science advanced, homeopathy converged with orthodox medical practice. In 1878 the Rhode Island Homeopathic Hospital opened and evolved into Roger Williams Hospital on Chalkstone Avenue in Providence in 1947. Pictured here is a nursing class at the Homeopathic Hospital in the 1920s. Courtesy, Roger Williams Hospital

Mary Ann Balch Lippitt (1823-1889), shown here at age 20, saw three of her children die and a fourth left deaf from an 1856 scarlet fever epidemic. Because no school for the deaf existed, she set about teaching her daughter to speak. This work led her to found the Clarke School for the Deaf in 1876. From a portrait owned by the Lippitt family. RIHS (RHI x3 4360)

from the Ives family. Although the hospital is publicly supported, the Goddards, Metcalfs, Sharpes, Chafees, Browns, and others have underwritten major development in the 20th century. Philanthropy launched Woonsocket's hospital in 1888, and Pawtucket Memorial Hospital (1910) resulted from nearly $500,000 in contributions from the Sayles and Goff families. Similarly, the Hazards were the principal founders of the South County Hospital in 1919. The Rhode Island School for the Deaf, started by Mrs. Henry Lippitt in 1876, assumed by the state in 1891, provided complete care and training for the children free of charge.

Rhode Island's parks reflect this same philanthropic impulse: Colt Park in Bristol, Goddard Park in East Greenwich, Wilcox Park in Westerly, Roger Williams, Metcalf, and Davis parks in Providence, and Jenks Park in Central Falls. The state park system grew out of a private organization, the Public Park Association. Begun in 1883, it labored to save the Providence Cove and Promenade from railroad development. While it failed in that, its petition to the General Assembly produced the Metropolitan Park Commission in 1904. The Commission developed a grand plan of parks, and began by opening Lincoln Woods in 1909. The Metropolitan Park Commission was absorbed in 1935 by the newly formed Department of Agriculture and Conservation, which in turn led to the Department of Environmental Management. The era of the magnificent donors is gone, and today most of the municipal and state parks, such as the new Bay Islands Park system, have to be purchased.

With the exception of prisons and poorhouses, most of the institutions in this state began as benefactions of the great industrialist families, and these same people pressed government to assume new responsibilities. The trend in the past has been to denounce such people as "robber barons"; but this ignores the many libraries, hospitals, asylums, boys clubs, museums, and parks that they gave. Whatever motivated these people, whether Christian stewardship, guilt, paternalism, or quest for recognition, it remains that they made a commitment to improve the quality of life in their communities and state. They gave more to the general welfare than all other groups combined.

The role of philanthropy diminished and the reform impulse quickened as soaring populations pressed municipalities for far more services. However, getting government to accept changes and responsibilities was an arduous task. One major force for reform was the Rhode Island Council of Women, which coordinated the activities of women's clubs, charity organizations, and church groups that represented the growing activity of middle-class women. The council secured the appointment of a woman factory inspector in 1894 and made Rhode Island the first state to require every town to hire police matrons. It worked successfully from 1892 to 1910 to raise the minimum age for child labor from 10 to 14 years, but was totally rebuffed on prohibition. Its strong support for Charles V. Chapin, Providence's outstanding commissioner of public health, helped put the city in the forefront of public health. As the reform effort waned after World War I, cities and towns were unable to meet needs; consequently, general

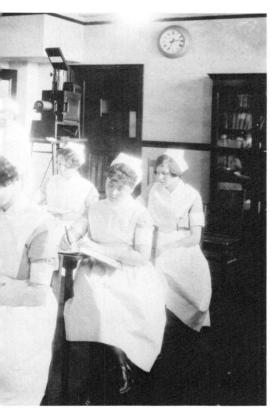

survive. The Providence Symphony Orchestra was first heard in 1890, was revived in 1911, and again in 1932, but succumbed to the Depression. The present Rhode Island Philharmonic Orchestra began in 1945 and has persisted only because of patrons and annual fund drives.

The state's artistic backwardness stemmed from at least two factors. Until the late 19th century Rhode Island lacked an urban middle class of sufficient size to support institutions of fine arts. In addition, the heavy presence of Quakers and Baptists had discouraged ornamentation and "impractical" arts. For example, the Newport Quakers remodeled their Meeting House to remove its interesting cupola because Philadelphia Quakers criticized it as being "too Popish." Half of the members of the Providence First Baptist Church seceded in 1771 because congregational singing had been introduced. It was not the poor musical quality that offended; music itself was a "desecration of the worship." Had they still been members, they would have strenuously opposed the form of the new building which was erected in 1774-1775. A radical departure from the plain meeting-house style, it was the first Baptist meeting house in New England to have a steeple and bell. But then, the leading figures in the Providence church were the Brown brothers, who were patrons of the arts and who dreamed of a greater Providence.

solicitations and religious charities tried to fill the gap. The *Providence Journal* started its Santa Fund in 1924, and the Community Chest (United Way) came to Rhode Island in 1926. Local and charitable resources failed in the Great Depression, but from the crisis came the urban-federal partnership which created a new dependency on the part of municipalities to maintain services.

Without philanthropic support, artistic institutions would have had little place in Rhode Island's life. Although artists had flocked to Newport in the 18th and 19th centuries seeking commissions from the rich, no art school or club appeared until after the Civil War. Newport had music teachers in its golden age, but the only long-lived musical organization in the state was the American Band, a military band. Eben Tourjee, born in Warwick, established a music conservatory in Providence in 1865, but found better opportunities in Boston, where he established the New England Conservatory of Music in 1867. The Boston Symphony Orchestra has regularly played in Providence since 1882, but local symphonies have struggled to

The Reverend Anna Garland Spencer (1851-1931) stands in the pulpit of the Bell Street Chapel, Providence, where she served as minister from 1891 to 1902. She led the Rhode Island Council of Women as president from 1896 to 1902 during its most reformist stage and served on the National Council of Women for years. She declined to accept the presidency of the National Council, but became a professor of sociology and ethics at Meadville Theological School in Pennsylvania, and then special lecturer in social science at Teachers College, Columbia, University. Courtesy, Religious Society of the Bell Street Chapel

ABOVE, LEFT: Thomas Robinson Hazard (1797-1886), "Shepard Tom," was one of five sons of the founder of the Peace Dale Woolen Mills. He sold his part of the property in 1838 and retired to a life of philanthropy, reform, and literary pursuits. From History of Washington and Kent Counties, R.I., 1889. *Courtesy, Rhode Island College/Special Collections*

ABOVE, RIGHT: Caroline Hazard (1856-1945) was the daughter of Rowland Hazard, superintendent of the Peace Dale Woolen Mills. She became Wellesley College's fifth president (1899-1910) and published 20 books of poetry, local and family history, and educational philosophy. RIHS (RHi x3 1678)

Providence became Rhode Island's cultural center as it expanded in the next century. A growing city required buildings; and talented local architects, such as John Holden Greene, Thomas Tefft, and James Bucklin, created notable structures. In the late 19th century, the leading architectural firm was Stone, Carpenter and Willson which designed buildings in styles as diverse as the old Providence County Courthouse (1877), the Baker House on Hope Street (1883), and the Providence Public Library (1900). Still, when the state erected a new capitol building, the commission went to the New York firm of McKim, Mead, and White.

With the exception of an occasional portraitist, such as Gilbert Stuart, or the miniaturist Edward Greene Malbone (both of whom left Rhode Island to pursue their careers), the state could not boast of distinguished artists until the Gilded Age. The stimulus which led to an art school and the Art Club was the Centennial Exposition of 1876. Rhode Island's imagination, talent, and toil had largely gone into commerce and industry, and its industrial products compared favorably with those of other states at the Exposition; but it was obviously deficient in art. Rhode Island School of Design had its origins in this discovery.

The *Providence Magazine* declared: "To a few public-spirited, far-sighted women the city owes this ornament; one that will stand for ages as a monument to the Sex." Mrs. Jesse Metcalf and a small group of women, who had acted as a committee on the Rhode Island exhibit for the Exposition, began RISD in 1877. While its principal sources of support were philanthropic, the state began appropriations for scholarships in 1882. For many years RISD's principal role was to serve the textile and jewelry industries. Nevertheless, fine arts were taught, an art museum established, and cooperative arrangements made with Rhode Island Normal School for the training of art teachers.

Discussions in the spring of 1878 led to the founding of the Providence Art Club in 1880. Subsequently came Brown's first art professorship, the Water Color, Handicraft, and Ceramics clubs, and the Ann Mary Brown Memorial art museum. Providence became a regional center for professional artists, and RISD is now recognized as one of America's leading art schools. The state has a burgeoning artistic community which exhibits its work on many levels from the professional art schools to the local summer art festivals at Wickford, Burrillville, and Scituate.

Similarly, creative literature was fairly rare until late in the century as most writers had been scribblers of little stories of limited interest or consequence. Even ''Shepard Tom,'' Thomas Robinson Hazard, who is frequently cited as a major figure in the state's literary gallery of the last century, was a writer on local South County topics in books such as *The Jonny-Cake Papers* (1882). Shepard Tom was part of a prolific family noted for its industrialists, philanthropists, and literary figures. The first Rowland Hazard began the Peace Dale Woolen Mills and established a paternalistic mill village for his workers. His sons expanded the business, engaged in philanthropy and community improvement, and started a literary tradition that extended through several generations. The 20th century has seen a substantial increase in Rhode Island's literary output, including Pulitzer Prize winners Oliver LaFarge and Leonard Bacon, and the eccentric, misanthropic H.P. Lovecraft, one of the developers of the horror story and science fiction. However, Rhode Island still awaits the appearance of a school of literature or an author of the stature of a William Faulkner or Robert Frost.

The heart, soul, and mind of the state continues to reflect the independent nature of Rhode Islanders. A recurring theme of observers of its cultural scene has been that the varieties of cultures and the various artistic and intellectual interests have tended to act independently of each other. The elite cultural institutions have only a limited impact on the predominantly ethnic culture which is expressed in the fraternal societies, the saints' festivals, and the home. Rhode Island has several autonomous cultural centers. Newport tends to be a summer center with its music festivals (classics for the rich, jazz for the young), seaside activities, and night spots. A second area is in the rural region with its more traditional activities, such as May breakfasts, Grange, family reunions, and fairs. Metropolitan Providence, the third center, is home to most of the state's permanent cultural institutions. Although a small state, Rhode Island strives for cultural and intellectual excellence. It has the Trinity Square Repertory Company, which won a Tony Award in 1981, a professional symphony orchestra, two opera companies, a nationally recognized school of art with one of America's great small museums, a ballet company, a Shakespeare troupe, civic choruses, libraries, a zoo, and the rich cultural product of ethnic festivals, colleges, and universities.

ABOVE, LEFT: Leonard Bacon (1887-1954) was the son of industrialist Nathaniel Terry Bacon and Helen Hazard, a sister to Caroline Hazard. Reared in Peace Dale, he wrote 19 volumes of poetry, criticism, and essays, and won the Pulitzer Prize for poetry in 1940. Courtesy, Rhode Island College/Special Collections

ABOVE, RIGHT: Martha Bacon Ballinger (1917-1981), the daughter of Leonard Bacon, published nearly a dozen volumes of poetry, fiction, historical essays, and translations in addition to teaching English and literature at Rhode Island College. Her friend is Boz (1967-). Courtesy, Rhode Island College/Special Collections

Chapter Ten

THE PROVIDENCE CITY-STATE

I
N THE MID-17TH CENTURY, a Newport man named the colony "Rhode Island and Providence Plantations," thereby relegating Providence to second place. Two hundred years later, the reverse had become true: Providence dominated Rhode Island and all of southern New England. The city was the focus of business and commerce, manufacturing and industry, education and culture, population and politics. While Newport still set the pace for High Society, Providence led everything else. In the years before the First World War, the city assumed a truly metropolitan character and its leaders' boosterism could hardly be contained. By the 1920s the city's hyperurbanization caught up with it and people began to seek a better quality of life in the outlying plantations.

After the Civil War, Providence's 5.4 square miles could no longer absorb industrial and residential growth. Mills and factories followed river valleys to the north and west, and platted residential settlements erupted to the south. Civic leaders could not readily accept this external growth; consequently, the city annexed eight separate adjacent areas between 1868 and 1919 for various reasons. For example, the Republicans engineered the 1868 annexation of the eastern half of Cranston so the party could retain the General Assembly seat from the town; and the industrialist George Corliss petitioned the legislature in 1873 for the annexation of the eastern half of North Providence. The industrialist-studded Assembly readily

obliged because the area was "simply a continuation of the compact part of the city of Providence. ... The needs, the activity, the course of trade, the intercourse of the population in matters of business are in and with the city." By 1919, when Providence annexed a portion of Johnston, the real-estate grabbing had come to an end. Through annexation Providence nearly tripled its area to 18.5 square miles and almost doubled its population. Expansion gave the city the potential for further growth, elevated it into the top 20 cities in the nation, and conditioned its leadership to think in terms of "Greater Metropolitan Providence."

As Providence increased its limits, it also expanded public services. Although slow to accept the new responsibilities, Providence later set the standard for southern New England in providing utilities and urban services. In the 1850s the city lacked nearly all essentials to attract additional population. Thomas A. Doyle, who was elected mayor 19 times between 1864 and 1888, vigorously attacked the lack of most urban services. Under his administration the police department went from a night watch to a professional force with expanded powers; the fire department improved dramatically and a modern system of electric fire alarms was installed; a municipal water system was built, and work began on adequate sewers. A new city hall went up in Exchange Place, and new streetcar lines extended from the city's center in all directions.

The need for an adequate water supply

Avery Lord took this aerial view of the downtown area of Providence about 1930. The construction of the 1910s and 1920s dramatically transformed the skyline. RIHS (RHi x3 4231)

109

FAR RIGHT: Thomas A. Doyle (1827-1886) was elected mayor of Providence for the first of his 19 terms in 1864. He launched a vigorous effort to improve and professionalize Providence's city services. At the dedication of the Doyle monument, a reporter said of Doyle: "He has been opposed at one time by Democrats, and by Republicans, then by Independents, then by the chief tax payers, then by every department of the city government... He has been opposed by every journal published in Providence." Portrait by Moses Russell, circa 1855-1860. RIHS (RHi x3 3109)

RIGHT: The annexation movement captured the imagination of the city's boosters in the second half of the 19th century. As the Board of Trade Journal proclaimed in 1900: "We have not annexed vast areas of territory solely for the sake of making the city bigger and more populous." But the city did grow— by more than three times its original pre-Civil War size. Adapted by G.H. Kellner from J.J. Cady, Civic and Architectural Development of Providence, 1957

led Providence in 1866 to draw it from the Pawtuxet River. The city embarked on a five-year, $5-million project that built dams and reservoirs, pumping stations, and water mains. On Thanksgiving Day 1871, an exhibition fountain ceremoniously shot a jet of water from the new system higher than the buildings in Exchange Place; unfortunately, it froze into icy sludge in the subzero winds and rained down on some spectators, nearly freezing them to death before it was shut off. The Pawtuxet system proved inadequate for the city's continued growth, so in 1910 Providence began acquiring land in Scituate for a new reservoir. Work started in 1915 and would cost $12 million before completion. A vast area was graded, and small towns

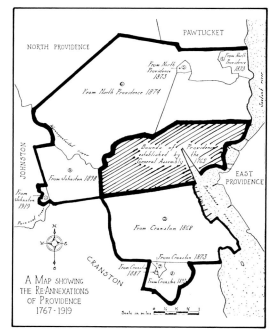

A MAP SHOWING THE RE-ANNEXATIONS OF PROVIDENCE 1767-1919

and factories were moved or demolished. The Scituate Reservoir, the "largest artificially created body of water in New England," was Providence's greatest public project. It became fully operational in 1928, and over the years other municipalities have tied into the system.

Unfortunately, no provision had been made for sewering the city so that the effluvia flowed into the Cove Basin, turning it into a big, open sewer. The "fearful odors" and "robust smell" of the Cove, especially in hot weather, and the periodic cholera outbreaks among people living along the Woonasquatucket and Moshassuck rivers so alarmed the public that the Cove was filled, sewers installed, and the Field's Point treatment plant constructed by 1900. As a result of the efforts of Commissioner of Health Charles V. Chapin, the city built a model secondary sewage treatment facility.

During his years in office, Chapin made many contributions to the city's health. Between 1856 and 1932, he and Edwin M. Snow placed Providence in the forefront of municipal health in America. Providence had the first medical examinations for the entire school population, first systematic medical care for the poor, and was first to abandon fumigation for the control of contagious disease. Providence City Hospital,

Providence traffic control policemen stand in front of the 1895 Fountain Street Station in the 1920s. Rapid growth and increased urban disturbances led cities to professionalize their police forces and assign them to ever more specialized duties, such as detective work, vice squads, and traffic control. Courtesy, Providence Public Library

opened in 1910, pioneered the use of aseptic nursing, and the city kept the most complete vital statistics of any municipality in the nation. Chapin even had the city post hundreds of signs against spitting on the sidewalks in an effort to combat the spread of tuberculosis.

Tuberculosis was so prevalent that it was called the White Plague; and as the city school system grew, "fresh air schools" were provided for tuberculosis-prone children. Rapid urban growth and the influx of immigrants forced Providence to build a large number of schools. Between the 1890s and 1920 the number of high schools went from one to four, and regular elementary schools rose to 96 plus five fresh air schools, one trade school, and 20 for "backward" (mostly non-English-speaking) children. The great influenza epidemic of 1919 left so many children with impairments that the city opened a special school for handicapped children and bused them to it.

By the 1920s school lighting had changed from gas to electricity, and all of the urban areas were linked by telephones. While Newport's Thames Street was the first American street illuminated by gas, Providence embarked on a large-scale lighting program before the Civil War. During the gaslight era, the Providence Gas Company supplied light, heat, and hot-flame fuel for towns, homes, and factories in three Rhode Island counties. The telephone and the telegraph emerged after the Civil War and in 1880 the Providence Telephone Company, born of the merger of two competing companies, began extending its lines to cover all of Rhode Island and parts of southeastern Massachusetts. With the telephone no longer a curio, by 1919 the company counted 60,594 subscribers in Providence alone.

As the technology of electricity advanced, the new industry began displacing gas companies. In 1884 Marsden Perry's Narragansett Electric Lighting Company was incorporated and received its first contract with Providence to replace 75 gaslights with electric streetlights. A generation later, when Exchange Place was lighted by modern arc lamps in August 1913, the *Providence Magazine* exulted: "As if by magic the great civic center and main business thoroughfares were transformed from inky darkness to brilliancy challenging almost the King of Day." Not everyone thought the new lights a good idea. When the city proposed to replace four old lights in Market Square with the new arc lights, one citizen protested that "if this were done it would make the square so brilliant at night that people would want lights burning all over the place."

Market Square and Exchange Place were the terminal points of the transportation network of the entire state. All roads, rails, and lines ran to Providence. By the 1880s, Thomas Tefft's elegant Romanesque railroad terminal was deemed insufficient and soon fell victim to progress and vandalism. The odorous Cove was filled and given to railroad expansion and the new Union Station erected on the site in 1894. The old station, where Abraham Lincoln had once spoken, conveniently burned one night in a fire of mysterious origin.

The street railway system and electric interurban lines radiated from this same center in all directions. Marsden Perry forged his monopoly in the 1890s and then extended the tendrils of the Rhode Island Company through the interurban trolleys west to Pascoag, north to Woonsocket, south to Cranston and Warwick, and east to East Providence, Barrington, Warren, and Bristol. The interurban lines became crucial to the economic health of shore resorts such as Rocky Point and Crescent Park.

The growth and prosperity of the streetcar company coincided with the heyday of Roger Williams Park. When Betsy Williams donated the land in 1871, the city accepted reluctantly because it was "so far out in the wilderness." Not until the late 1880s did the Providence park commissioners hire H.W.S. Cleveland to design and develop Roger Williams Park into one of the finest in New England. In the 1890s the park attracted throngs of people, and the trolley company subsidized the American Band to play nightly during the summer. The park commissioners reported in 1899 that 750,000 people attended the free band concerts, averaging 10,000 per night. Most people rode the trolleys to the park.

The Rhode Island Company had over 313 miles of track by 1909 and carried 80 million riders a year, but new competition had already begun. The city's streets not only echoed with the clang and roar of trolleys and the clatter of horse-drawn wagons and buggies, but also with the putt-putt and purr of horseless carriages. The *Providence Board of Trade Journal* in 1905 predicted, "The great number of automobiles now being used for pleasure only presages the use of trucks for business purposes in the near future; and the dray horse, in a few years, will be as uncommon a sight as is a horse car today."

In a few years automobiles and trucks added to the traffic congestion, and the streetcar company proposed in 1914 that the city build a subway system to solve the problem. In its grandest form, the subway would have connected with the interurban lines and extended from Taunton to Pascoag, Woonsocket to Bristol. However, the company was in no position to build it and the city was unwilling to risk such a venture. The Rhode Island Company, which had been operating at a heavy loss for several years, went into receivership in 1919. The United Electric Railways Company purchased the streetcar lines from the bankrupt company and began eliminating unprofitable services. From a peak of 138 million fares in 1923, ridership declined steeply so that by 1940 most of the electric trolleys were gone. Adopting the policy, "If you can't lick em, join em," the United Electric Railways Company put gasoline-powered buses on the streets and created a subsidiary which acquired 90 percent of the taxicabs in service.

Buses and automobiles had a tremendous advantage over electric trolleys in that they did not have to purchase rights-of-way or construct and repair their own tracks and roads. Streets and highways were built and maintained at the public expense. The paving of roads had begun as a result of demands from the bicycle interests in the 1890s and the state ordered the first sample macadam roads in 1895. The State Board of Public Roads was created in 1902 and highway construction advanced steadily thereafter, aided after 1916 by the federal government. At first

ABOVE: *Dr. Charles V. Chapin (1856-1941), who served as superintendent of public health in Providence from 1884 to 1931, brought the city to the forefront of public health in America. While critics referred to him as a "harmless sanitary crank," he brought improvements in everything from clean milk to waste removal. His principal support in the period from the 1890s to the 1910s came from the Rhode Island Federation of Women's Clubs. He published extensively and lectured on public health throughout the nation. RIHS (RHi x3 1578)*

RIGHT: *This 1899 Providence scene shows the rear of tenement houses on lower Charles Street and the West River, a tributary of the Moshassuck River. Despite the installation of sewers, water pollution was a constant source of irritation for public health officials, with the outhouses on the banks of the river adding to their despair. RIHS (RHi x3 4345)*

automobiles were toys of the rich, who showed them off and raced them; but assembly-line production soon brought the car to the masses. In 1904 Rhode Island had 767 automobiles; in 1921 it counted 43,662 automobiles, 64,118 licensed operators, 3,450 traffic accidents, and 98 highway fatalities. Throughout the 1920s the improvement of roads and highways brought every corner of the state within speedy reach of Providence, the focus of the system. However, the roads that led to Providence also ran the other way; and the movement to the suburbs was greatly increased by the "Go-Anywhere Vehicle."

This extensive transportation network terminated at Exchange Place, Providence's public square and outdoor community center. It also anchored a thriving downtown which contained the region's shopping, banking, commercial, entertainment, and cultural centers. But the hub of the city

Public concern about tuberculosis among schoolchildren caused Providence to open five "fresh air" schools by 1920. Children prone to tuberculosis attended these schools where the windows were kept open all the time, even during the New England winter. Though fresh air was supposed to control TB, one wonders about the incidence of pneumonia! From Providence Magazine, *April 1915. RIHS (RHi x3 4348)*

ABOVE: Trolley cars belonging to the Rhode Island Company are lined up on Westminster Street in the rain about 1905. Despite ridership in the millions, the Rhode Island Company was bankrupt by 1919 and was succeeded by the United Electric Railways Company. Peak ridership came in 1923 when the company collected 138 million fares; but even this was insufficient to save the trolley system. It soon gave way to buses and taxis. RIHS (RHi x3 1905)

RIGHT: The Crawford Street Bridge was heavily congested with traffic when this photo was made in 1927. Increases in the number of cars and trucks competed with pedestrians and trolleys. The Rhode Island Company paid $315,000 in accident claims in 1913, and it was reported "downright hazardous to be a pedestrian." Although some streets were repeatedly widened, the majority remained in their narrow colonial state, and traffic control devices were yet to be adopted. Consequently, during June and July 1923, 1,103 traffic accidents were recorded. Courtesy, Providence Journal Company

the state, western Connecticut, and southeastern Massachusetts came there to watch parades, participate in festivals, and welcome visiting dignitaries. They also came to shop, bank, and be entertained.

By the turn of the century, the shopping district and banking houses had abandoned North and South Main streets in favor of Westminster and Weybosset streets just south of Exchange Place. The area became a shoppers' paradise as the Boston Store, Diamond's, Gladding's, Shepard's, and the Outlet competed for trade. To accommodate mill workers, merchants stayed open until 11:30 on Saturday night. Diamond's advertised itself as "Rhode Island's Fastest Growing Store," and Gladding's held the distinction of being the oldest department store in New England, but the retailing showpiece was clearly Shepard's. It was the largest department store in New England, employed over 1,400, and contained 66 separate departments selling everything from groceries to furniture. In addition, the area's theater row, restaurants, and hotels attracted even more people.

Located nearby was the region's financial and commercial institutions. When Joseph Banigan erected the Banigan Building in 1896, the first steel-framed building in the city, he ushered in the era of highrise commercial architecture. Within two decades Providence's skyline had been dramatically altered as the Union Trust, Hospital Trust, and Turk's Head buildings all soared upward. The crowning achievement, however, was the construction of the 28-story Industrial National Bank building on the site of the old Butler Exchange on the south side of Exchange Place. When it opened in 1928, this building was the tallest in New England and symbolized the city's financial and commercial hold over the region. In addition to housing various banks, these buildings contained the greatest concentration of law offices, brokerage firms, insurance companies, and headquarters of factories and mills in all of southeastern New England.

Providence's leadership, not content with these gains, pressed private interests and municipal and state governments for additional civic improvements. The Cham-

had not always been west of the Providence River nor had Exchange Place been the showpiece of a booming city. Before the area was developed in the 1890s as the new train station and Exchange Place, it had been the Cove Basin. As the summer stinkpot, the Cove was bordered on the north by what the Providence Magazine described as the "grey, grim frowning State Prison, an ugly foundry, [and] a row of very disreputable tenement houses filled with undesirables. ..." But the businessmen's vision triumphed; instead of allowing the land to be used for "cheap restaurants, fishmarkets, and garages," they created what contemporaries called "a superb square and splendid garden, and a railroad entrance that is at present unsurpassed in America." People from all over

ber of Commerce spearheaded the fund raising for a new hotel; and when the Biltmore opened with the usual hoopla on the west end of Exchange Place in 1922, local enthusiasts dubbed it the "most luxurious hotel" between Boston and New York. The new hotel excited the Chamber, which immediately championed a convention center with an eye to hosting a national political convention. In 1926 the Rhode Island Auditorium opened, but instead of a national political convention it attracted the Providence Reds professional hockey team. The theater district was enhanced when lovers of the "silver screen" flocked to the lavishly appointed, 3,200-seat Loew's State Theater after it opened in 1928. The state government, too, augmented the city's domination over the plantations by centralizing formerly scattered state offices in the new State Office Building erected across from the capitol and by moving the judiciary into a new courthouse next to the financial district. In addition, state funds built the new Washington Bridge across the Seekonk River and created the first state-owned airport in America at Hillsgrove.

These decades of growth pulled all of Rhode Island under the domination of Providence. The city had annexed sizable chunks of the surrounding towns, making these communities into support towns for its reservoirs, prisons, reformatory, insane asylum, recreation facilities, and truck farms. It acquired a large part of Scituate and flooded it with water for the city, established a park system that extended into the towns of Lincoln, Cranston, and East Providence, and set the capitol on Smith Hill. It dominated the political, economic, educational, and cultural life of the entire state. All of Rhode Island's main roads terminated in or ran through the center of Providence; and most of the state received its telephone and electricity, gas and gasoline, coal and oil, and lumber and steel from the city. The state's first radio stations, beginning with WJAR in 1922, broadcast from Providence. Providence leadership tied the state together with highways, airways, trolleys, and transmission lines.

Little wonder then that city leaders both celebrated their achievements and looked for more progress. Combining boosterism with self-interest, they engaged in promotional activities and initiated plans for a better city. Central to these enterprises was the Providence Chamber of Commerce, which by 1914 called itself the Chamber of Commerce of Southern New England, and advertised Providence alternately as the "Gateway to Southern New England" and the "City of Fascination." After federal census officials assigned metropolitan status to Providence in 1920, the Greater Providence Chamber of Commerce was born, and within a year a promotional film on the city was distributed nationally.

Although these efforts were strictly promotional, civic leaders also pushed for urban planning and improvement in the quality of life. In 1909 they secured passage of a comprehensive building code, and in 1923 successfully lobbied for a citywide zoning ordinance. Another concern was the fouling of the Woonasquatucket and Moshassuck rivers and the polluted upper portions of Narragansett Bay. "If we are to act," warned the *Providence Magazine* in 1919, "we must act promptly." Two years later the General Assembly voted $1.5 million for water purification and sewer improvement.

One of the most noteworthy civic achievements was the creation of a City Plan Commission in 1914. Although other cities had adopted similar legislation earlier, Providence's commission, supported by business leaders and politicians and led throughout the 1920s by Henry Ames Barker, was lauded as one of the best in the nation. The commission spearheaded studies and surveys of the entire metropolitan region, including such areas for improvement as schools, traffic, public health, and industry; and it advanced a Plan for Greater Providence (1930). In addition, the commission proposed other projects, among them a plan to relocate the railroad terminal and remove the elevated tracks, called the "Chinese Wall." Although most of these plans were never realized, they document Providence's quest to improve itself and to dominate the surrounding communities. But underneath the boosterism and civic pride Providence

The business leadership of the Providence area worked to bind the entire southern New England region to Providence. This cartoon entitled "Pulling Together" is from the Providence Board of Trade Journal, March 1913. RIHS (RHi x3 4350)

was a mature and slowly weakening industrial city facing prosperous and assertive suburban communities.

Collectively, these 1920s studies painted a drab picture of Providence's situation and prospects. The Strayer School Report (1924) found the system glaringly understaffed and underfunded, and the schools mostly ungraded, overcrowded, badly equipped, lacking playgrounds, and unable to attract over 4,000 truants. The Public Health Survey (1928) noted that the city had lost its preeminence in the field with inadequate sanitary sewers, overcrowded housing, and expanding slums in the Wickenden, North Main, and South Main Street areas. Expenditure for public health was only one half that of comparable cities. The Whitten Thorofare Plan (1926) described the nightmare of traveling from one part of the metropolitan area to another because of narrow streets, lack of traffic control devices, and intersections with peculiar angles.

Most alarming, however, was the Metropolitan Providence Industrial Survey (1926-1928). Commissioned by the Chamber of Commerce of Providence and Pawtucket and conducted by a team of experts from the Massachusetts Institute of Technology, the report presented a grim story. Decaying plants, outmoded equipment, uneasy labor, high transportation costs, scarcity of liquid capital, and insuffi-

cient diversity placed the city in the backwater of industrial America. Despite an increase in white-collar employment and the rise of some new industries—electrical components, rubber goods, printing, and automobile-related enterprises—only 10 percent of the city's firms produced 63 percent of all goods and employed 51 percent of all workers. Equally disquieting was the finding that between 1900 and 1930, the city's population rose 31 percent, but the industrial work force increased by only 5 percent, the smallest gain of any American city. In addition, the survey concluded that Providence would have difficulty attracting new industries because, as the most densely settled of the nation's 29 metropolitan areas, Providence lacked adequate housing and had "no extensive areas ... for industrial development." Clearly, by 1925, Providence had reached its zenith of growth in population, industry, and land mass.

Nevertheless, the vision of a "Greater Providence" did not readily die. Most solutions to the problems, however, were handicapped by a steadily declining tax base, politics, divisiveness, and neighboring communities. The flurry of municipal projects before the First World War had saddled the city with one of the highest per capita rates of indebtedness in the nation. The state legislature, concerned about the fiscal solvency of all cities, imposed an indebtedness ceiling of 3 percent of assessed valuation in 1923. Providence's rate was already 4.7 percent, or over $30 million; and by the end of the decade it had risen to $41 million, nearly twice the debt of the entire state. Compounding the problem was a real decline in tax revenues despite an inflationary cycle throughout the decade. Between 1922 and 1926 tax revenues rose by $4 million, but this was only one fourth of the national increase. Providence was losing revenues as slum housing was abandoned, properties

city. Before World War I, the commission undertook appropriate projects and conducted its business with enthusiasm. By the 1920s, however, the annual reports chronicled its ineffectiveness. The commission's budget fluctuated between a meager $2,000 and $3,000; it had no monies to hire professional planners; its recommendations went unheeded by other municipal agencies; and it was forced to retreat to a survival philosophy that called for work only to "improve upon features already established, to correct mistakes due to earlier

ABOVE: This booster poster-stamp from the Providence Board of Trade Journal of February 1915 spoke more of hope than reality. Harbor improvement has been a continual desire at least from the time Mayor Doyle unveiled his grand harbor design in the 1880s down to the efforts of Mayor Vincent Cianci in the 1980s to make the Port of Providence the New England container cargo center. The reality has been that the port was mainly a place to land immigrants, fuel, and lumber. RIHS (RHi x3 4227)

LEFT: Following Boston's example, Providence business leaders sponsored Old Home Week. They decked the city with bunting, turned Exchange Place (now Kennedy Plaza) into a "Court of Honor," erected a triumphal arch on Weybosset Street, and threw a week-long party. This view of Weybosset Street was made in the summer of 1907 during Old Home Week. RIHS (RHi x3 292)

depreciated, mills and factories closed, and central-city structures were demolished for parking lots. City officials, however, caught between the Republican and Democratic parties' fight for control of the city and the state governments, and wanting to keep both population and industry from fleeing the city, kept the tax rate at a relatively constant $23 per $1,000 valuation. Appropriations for public health, schools, police, fire, and other departments suffered accordingly.

The fate of the City Plan Commission and the Whitten Thorofare Plan show clearly the impact of these problems on the

lack of vision, and to make provision to better meet modern conditions." The commission had no impact on enforcing the zoning ordinance and variances were granted at "alarming rates." By 1928 the annual report declared that "this Commission has postponed active operations during the year," and would be of "little public usefulness until conditions existed for effective cooperation in a complete and comprehensive enterprise."

Part of the commission's inactivity stemmed from its difficulties in helping implement the Whitten Thorofare Plan. This scheme was intended to relieve traffic congestion in the entire metropolitan area. It called for two 140-foot-wide boulevards, one running east-west and the other north-south, a belt parkway circling the city, and radial arteries extending from downtown Providence to the beltway. In 1927 the plan had the endorsement of Democratic Mayor Joseph Gainer, the Republican Board of Aldermen, and the business community. But the following year the plan was killed by partisan politics. A Republican city council asked the state legislature to repeal the enabling statute that would have created a Providence Thorofare Plan Board to oversee between $40 million and $80 million in expenditures. The request was purely political. Mayor James E. Dunne, elected by a plurality of a mere 171 votes and lacking the education and business connections of his predecessor, selected four fellow Democrats for the proposed board. This was a clear challenge to Republicans who controlled the city council and the state legislature for the last time in this century. The General Assembly honored their fellow Republicans' request, effectively killing the thoroughfare plan. But Providence's business leadership was unwilling to abandon its dimming vision. Its new approach called for regional planning, regional industrial development, and a renewed interest in annexing the Edgewood section of Cranston.

With the endorsement of Mayor Gainer, the annexation forces had pushed ahead in 1926, but his successor, Mayor Dunne, strongly opposed the idea. Nevertheless, a Greater Providence Planning Committee that included representatives from North Providence, Cranston, East Providence, Johnston, and Pawtucket met on July 24, 1930, and heard the committee's chairman, Alderman Sol S. Bromson declare: "The small town is like the small business. It cannot have the conveniences and advantages of the larger communities. ... The word annexation ... is an unhappy one. ... What is proposed is rather a merger of interests to work under one central head of government." The suburban leaders disagreed. A *Cranston News* editorial on November 14, 1930, clearly presented that city's case. "Cranston is about to come into

Joseph Gainer (1878-1945) was mayor of Providence from 1913 to 1927. Despite being a Democrat, he worked closely with the Republican-controlled Board of Aldermen to advance a whole series of civic improvements. In 1918 the Republicans also nominated him for mayor, a distinction shared only with the legendary Thomas A. Doyle. During his term Providence created the City Planning Commission, adopted zoning, widened streets, and completed the Scituate Reservoir project. From Providence City Manual, 1915-1916. *RIHS (RHi x3 4336)*

its own," it proclaimed. "Manufacturing plants and new homes must be built here as Providence is overcrowded. Why give this plum to another city ... ?"

Cranston and other adjacent communities could well afford an independent attitude and thwart all further efforts at metropolitan cooperation. Suburbanization had become so pronounced by 1900 that Rhode Island was the most urbanized state in the Union. Although many communities gained in population, the most significant gains were scored in the industrialized northern section of the state. As Providence grew by 28 percent between 1900 and 1910, the surrounding towns expanded by nearly 40 percent. Between 1915 and 1925 Providence increased its population only 8.1 percent while East Providence gained 40.3 percent, North Providence 33 percent, Johnston 29.5 percent, and Cranston 27.9 percent. These communities grew even faster after this time as Providence stabilized and then rapidly declined, making Providence one of the first large American cities to experience a drop in population. Equally important as the automobile and new roads in bringing about the change was the contrast between the quality of housing in the city and in the suburbs.

Early real-estate developers in Providence built primarily for the exploding population of immigrants and industrial workers. Between 1883 and 1910, a total of 24,377 two- and three-decker tenements were constructed, and just before the First World War, 9 out of every 10 new dwellings were tenements. Consequently, by 1926 nearly 80 percent of all dwelling units in the city were tenements; by 1933, nearly 90 percent of all housing was over 20 years old; half of the houses were still heated with a wood or coal stove, and only 32 per-

had incorporated as cities, and their charters granted them sufficient home-rule provisions to embark on their own ambitious urban improvements. In the period between 1922 and 1927, Cranston more than doubled its budget, and worked diligently to provide all essential urban services without drastically increasing taxes. Despite the town's failure to hold the line, its taxes rose by only half of the national average. Cranston also took steps to preserve the quality of suburban life by adopting a zoning ordinance in 1924 and

When Lewis Hine photographed this Olneyville (Providence) tenement dwelling in 1912, he noted that it had "eight persons, three rooms." Nearly 20 percent of Providence's families lived in tenements of less than one room per person. Between 1915 and 1921 housing starts declined so that the city entered the 1920s with a substantial housing shortage. From Child Welfare Conference and Exhibit, *January 6-12, 1913. Courtesy, Newport Historical Society*

cent were owner occupied. In contrast, suburban communities contained predominantly single-family homes, with well over half of them owner occupied.

Besides giving their residents better housing, cleaner air, and a more agreeable life-style, some communities could offer other advantages. Because East Providence and Cranston had legislative authorization to exempt new businesses from taxes, both towns lured industrial companies out of Providence. For example, East Providence developed the industrial village of Phillipsdale and Cranston attracted United Wire & Supply Company and Universal Winding Company in 1914. While East Providence, North Providence, and Johnston retained the town-meeting form of government, Cranston and Pawtucket

by inaugurating city planning in 1934; North Providence enacted zoning laws and a building code in 1930.

Although these steps would not protect suburbanites from paying higher taxes in the years to come, they did create a favorable climate for continued growth. Between 1900 and 1930, the population of Cranston rose from 13,343 to 42,911, North Providence from 3,016 to 11,101, Johnston from 4,305 to 9,357, and East Providence from 12,138 to 29,995. Providence's plans for a "Greater Providence" metropolitan government had crumbled, and with the setback came a gradual erosion of her domination over the plantations. Having experienced the pains of growth, socialization, and accommodation, the city now faced the Great Depression.

Chapter Eleven

EIGHTY GRAVEDIGGERS AND ONE TAPDANCER

Thousands of Rhode Islanders waited in lines throughout the Depression for food, fuel, medical aid, and jobs. This photo shows the unemployment line in front of the Cranston Street Armory, Providence, in January 1938. That year, despite massive public work projects, Rhode Island had the highest per capita unemployment rate in the nation with 121,394 people receiving some form of unemployment compensation. Although 1939 was slightly better, the state's economy did not improve until defense contracts stimulated production. Courtesy, Providence Journal Company

THE GREAT DEPRESSION shook Rhode Island's economic and political structure and forced it to depend increasingly upon a new federal-urban partnership. The national collapse exaggerated pre-Depression trends in Rhode Island because industrial growth was already declining in the 1920s. The Depression closed more factories and produced increased unemployment, but this, too, had been a common experience in Rhode Island. In 1935 the Democratic party capped its slow rise to power with the "Bloodless Revolution," ending nearly eight decades of Republican domination. State Democrats used New Deal programs to dispense jobs, construct public works, and hand out patronage. However, the resulting political corruption produced the "War of the Wild Irish Roses," handicapped relief efforts, and demanded reform. By the end of the 1930s state and municipal indebtedness had doubled, factories stood empty, and morale drooped. But the winds of nature and war soon halted the slide and cleared the way for revival.

The economic depression began for Rhode Island years before the Great Crash of 1929. Like other mature industrial centers, the state had gradually slid deeper into an economic crisis. Back in 1913 Brown University President William H. Faunce warned the business community: "We cannot browse upon the past and become fat. We cannot live on inherited wealth, inherited traditions, inherited memories when we should be getting together to create new wealth, to establish new traditions, and memories which posterity may cherish." Complacency, the First World War, and momentary prosperity blunted the message. Not even the crumbling of the state's textile empire in the 1920s created more than temporary efforts at relief.

War-inflated wages, falling prices for goods, transportation rates that were as much as 113 percent higher than other places on the New Haven Railroad line, and foreign cotton imports that rose from $10 million to $67 million crippled Rhode Island's industry. Some companies such as the huge B.B. & R. Knight "Fruit of the Loom" textile empire were sold at a loss. Other companies instituted steep wage cuts of 42 percent between 1921 and 1922, enforced work "speed-ups" and "stretch-outs," and reduced their work force. Instead of modernizing plants or converting to synthetic fabrics, many owners continued investing in southern mills. These policies drove Rhode Island's generally docile textile workers to the brink of economic despair. They turned to labor organizations and the Democratic party for help. But the violent textile strikes of 1922 and 1924 benefited no one. The *Providence Magazine* in 1923 charged that the state's industries clung to outdated management and sales methods and failed to grasp the idea of the "new competition." Unfortunately, industry failed to heed the message and did not develop a collective course or follow the examples of other communities.

Some New England states and cities

actively pursued new industrial development. They launched the New England Council of Economic Development, but Rhode Island tried an independent path, and by 1926 had assembled the Rhode Island Development Conference. As little came of it, the state decided to join the New England Council in 1929. However, one of Rhode Island's most illustrious and conservative industrialists, Henry D. Sharpe, president of Brown & Sharpe, cooled their interest. He asserted that 81.8 percent of all

"No Man's Land" during the September 1926 strike at the Jenckes Company mill in Manville. For the nation the 1920s was a period in which management and government cooperated to reverse gains made by labor during World War I; and Rhode Island was quick to employ force through local and state police and national guard troops to break strikes. Rhode Island's failing textile industry was hard hit by strikes as the formerly docile workers tried to prevent the repeated wage reductions. Courtesy, Providence Journal Company

new industries had come from within the state's industrial base and that it was a waste of time and money "seeking to induce industries to locate in Providence." The new competitors could be beaten by following the proven methods of the past. The industrial-credit fund of Lowell, Massachusetts, attracted 23 new industries with 3,200 new jobs in 1928; but Sharpe and other business leaders opposed a similar agency for Rhode Island as being too costly. By 1931 these same industrialists begged the state to create a publicly funded economic development commission with broad powers to extend low-interest credit to new industries locating in the state. Unfortunately, the state did not establish a professional economic development council until the 1950s. Instead, Rhode Island was preoccupied with the Great Depression.

Between 1923 and 1937 nearly 80 percent of the state's cotton mills closed and

the work force declined from 34,000 to about 12,000. In the first two years of the Great Depression all industries struggled to survive, and 40 percent of all textile workers, 47.1 percent of the jewelry workers, and 38 percent of the iron and steel workers lost their jobs. Those still employed worked from one-half to one-quarter time, and textile workers averaged less than $9 a week. By 1933 wages for all workers had fallen by 33.4 percent but those of industrial workers had fallen by 49 percent. Investment income dropped by more than one third, and building permits for new construction plummeted from $57 million in 1926 to $9 million in 1932. While all segments of the state were hit hard, urban areas felt the pain the most. Providence's retail stores lost more than 50 percent of their annual sales revenues, and over 20 percent of the stores closed. The city budget was reduced by $1.5 million, wages cut by 10 percent, and projects for civic improvement halted. In Woonsocket, French-Canadians looked longingly at their homeland, as 9 out of 10 cotton mills stood idle, including the gigantic Social Mills which had closed in 1927. The "French Mills," heralded only a few years earlier as saving the city, either operated at reduced capacity, converted from wool, or closed. In single-industry towns such as Harrisville, Greystone, and Slatersville, factory shutdowns meant near total collapse of the economic lifeline of the community. By 1932, from the beaches of South County to the hills of Cumberland, from the Connecticut border to Little Compton, 115,000 Rhode Islanders were out of work. Hard times and soup lines were here.

But as deep as the Depression cut into Rhode Island's economy, it did not affect all citizens alike. The old-line Yankees could afford to hold onto their mansions on the East Side of Providence, sail out of Squantum in summers, and winter at Palm Beach. In Newport, chauffeured limousines daily carried children enrolled in private schools. People along coastal waters lived on seafood, and one Jamestown resident remembered her grandmother eating so many lobsters during the Depression that she refused ever to eat another. In rural areas, such as Glocester,

where people had abandoned their farms for the factory in the 1920s, land was brought under the plow or sold. Perhaps some of the least affected during the Depression were municipal employees, especially teachers. In 1933 Providence tallied a record enrollment of 45,189 public school students. A substantial increase occurred in high schools, as youths who would normally drop out to work continued their education. Although teachers throughout the state experienced pay cuts and overcrowded classes, their employment was steady. Some, like Elmer C. Wilbur, chairman of the commercial department of Providence's Central High School, took their income and invested it in abandoned farms in northwestern Rhode Island. Industrial workers, however, depended on others for work or relief.

Care of the unemployed and revitalization of industry had been traditionally in the hands of private charities and business, but private relief soon proved to be inadequate and charity organizations were overburdened. Exhortations from citizens and from political officials generated some donations. With such help the Salvation Army provided 76,092 meals and rooms for over 22,000 in the first eight months of 1932. Neighborhood grocery stores extended credit, landlords postponed rents, and barter became a common way of doing business. Governor Norman Case and part of the business community subscribed to President Herbert Hoover's "trickle down" philosophy to pump new life into the

economy, but they also called upon industries to employ more workers. Swan Point Cemetery responded by hiring 80 gravediggers in 1933, far above the normal number. The state's banking community was examined in 1930 and judged extremely secure with $328 million on deposit, fifth highest per capita savings in the nation. With so much money on deposit, People's Savings Bank called on people to save less and spend more to stimulate the economy. The state government, however, did little. Governor Case established a credit fund from which municipalities could borrow money to avoid bankruptcy, but critics accused him of being more concerned about his proposed bridge across Narragansett Bay. In the midst of personal and economic despair, Rhode Islanders did not resort to violence. Instead, they turned to the ballot box and elected Theodore Francis Green their Governor and Franklin Delano Roosevelt their President.

Throughout his campaign, Green promised that he would place "humanity first" and bridges last. On January 1, 1933, he announced a $6-million relief fund for the unemployed; and when the bill reached the General Assembly, over 700 of the jobless came to give their support. But Green's program needed more than the state could provide, so additional relief came from the federal government in the form of the New Deal. Green was the primary conduit for federal relief funds for Rhode Island. By the fall of 1933 Roosevelt's fireside talks and recovery programs had given hope to many Rhode Islanders, and they showed their approval by staging the state's largest parade in downtown Providence. On October 2, a procession of 70,000 marchers, ticker tape, flags, and a profusion of blue eagle emblems snaked through the streets of the city. Out in mill villages and towns, similar parades took place, and one had a float showing the slaying of "Old Man Depression." Unfortunately for Rhode Islanders, the entire 1933 relief effort removed only about 7,000 from the unemployment lines. This all changed with the subsequent New Deal relief and recovery measures which altered the physical, cultural, and economic contours of the state.

The Providence Housewife League (1912-1946) became the Providence Homemakers League and affiliated with American Homemakers Inc. after World War I. Among other activities, it operated a clothing salvage store at 136 North Main Street in Providence, pictured here about 1922. The store expanded its operations during the Depression; and in addition to those responsibilities, the organization labored to find work for the unemployed. Ida S. Harrington and Eleanor K. Dearborn even gave weekly radio talks in the 1930s on aspects of homemaking. RIHS (RHi x3 4351)

Although a host of agencies operated within Rhode Island, the work of the Civilian Conservation Corps (CCC), Works Progress Administration (WPA), and Public Works Administration (PWA) had the greatest impact on the unemployed and on the environment. Inner-city youths were packed off to the forests and parks throughout the state, where they prevented soil erosion, cleared paths, improved forest stands, and drained swamps. The CCC camps were phased out in 1942 when youths marched off to war and defense plants. The WPA gave work to over 60,000 before it was disbanded in 1943. In Providence, WPA funds paid for the labor to build a new police station and firehouse, a municipal dock, a sediment treatment facility at Field's Point, and Mt. Pleasant and Hope high schools. In East Providence they helped construct a new city hall, Pierce Memorial Field, and Arthur E. Platt Elementary School. In Newport, the Cliff Walk, sidewalks, and harbor improvements took shape. For the state, WPA cemented the runways, installed lights, built a hangar, and upgraded the weather station at the airport, developed Goddard Park in East Greenwich, and built the harbor at Point Judith and Scarborough Beach at Narragansett. Writers published *Ships Documents of Rhode Island* and *Rhode Island: A Guide to the Smallest State*, among others. Planners completed a careful lot-by-lot survey of the entire city of Providence between 1932 and 1934; and repeated it in

1935. Musicians played concerts before large audiences, actors staged plays, and artists painted murals in the State House cafeteria and in the Providence Public Library. And one unemployed tap dancer was hired to tap dance her way through the public playgrounds of Providence.

Housing conditions in the state's industrial centers were inadequate, and a variety of New Deal programs helped finance mortgages, guaranteed rents, and supported new housing construction. Blighted areas long scheduled for removal were razed and the first public housing projects, such as the Chad Brown and Roger Williams complexes in Providence, were constructed. The Federal Housing Administration produced hundreds of real-estate surveys for American cities, and Providence was no exception. There, the lot-surveys were employed to designate neighborhoods according to property value retention: desirable neighborhood, declining neighborhood, blighted neighborhood, and stable neighborhood were some of the designations. FHA officials used those plat maps in granting mortgage loan-guarantees, but most of the money went to the desirable areas. What started as a plan to stabilize urban housing (Providence had over 13,000 vacant units) turned out to favor new construction. As a consequence, thousands of people left the inner city for the undeveloped area of northwest Providence or moved to suburbs and built new homes. Inner-city housing gave way to parking lots, arson, and vandalism. As late as the 1970s, banks still used the 1930s neighborhood designations in granting mortgages and for red-lining. Instead of saving the cities, the New Deal urban programs inadvertently helped destroy them.

As municipal and state agencies sought to respond to the myriad federal programs and requirements, some misused the funds and others worked at cross-purposes. The federal government wanted to purchase the old fire station on Providence's Exchange Place and erect a new post office. The State Planning Commission, headed by John Nicholas Brown, gave its approval, but the city council delayed three years before selling the station. The first state WPA administrator took a very frugal

WPA workers are shown on Mineral Springs Avenue, North Providence, in March 1936. After nearly three years of debate and foot dragging, most communities had advanced public works projects for approval to the State Planning Board. WPA financed the labor costs for thousands of projects in the state, including the resurfacing or construction of over 500 miles of roads. Courtesy, Providence Journal Company

The Chad Brown Housing Project Between Brown and Berkshire streets in Providence is pictured under construction in November 1941. The removal of slum housing and the rehabilitation of structures was the chief responsibility of the City Housing Authority during the Depression and thereafter. By 1982 Chad Brown, Roger Williams, Admiral Terrace, and other public housing projects were nearly all abandoned, boarded up, and ready to be razed. Courtesy, Providence Journal Company

approach to spending the taxpayers' money, which made him expendable to the Democrats. After his resignation, his only public comment was, "I'm going fishing." Projects got started, nevertheless, and the WPA payrolls swelled shortly before election time. Conservatives, who saw the New Deal as being revolutionary, called these actions boondoggles and made them into great political capital.

Some of the greatest problems for Democratic leaders occurred when the state was faced with implementing NRA (National Recovery Administration) and PWA requirements on wages and hours. In 1934, after the NRA proposed a $13 wage in the North and $12 in the South for a 40-hour week for textile workers, the United Textile Workers went on strike. The union demanded uniform wages throughout the country to keep northern textile firms from heading South. When the Saylesville Finishing and the Woonsocket Rayon companies continued to operate, violence broke out at Saylesville, rioters looted stores and set buildings on fire in Woonsocket, and Governor Green summoned the National Guard. In an exchange of gunfire, two strikers were killed and scores were wounded.

Although a truce was proclaimed, more than 19 separate strikes erupted in Rhode Island in 1935 over NRA codes. Not until 1939 did the state pass a 35 cent minimum wage for women and minors in the textile industry. Another costly program resulted from the establishment of an Unemployment Compensation Board in 1936, which paid out $9 million to over 121,000 unemployed workers in two years' time. Nevertheless, Rhode Island still had the highest per capita unemployment rate in the nation, a condition that even the adoption of food stamps in 1939 in Providence hardly relieved.

National Guard soldiers drive strikers away with tear gas at Saylesville. Eight thousand strikers, 51 state troopers, and 32 mill guards battled at Saylesville. In the fighting three strikers were shot and the state arrested a number of people accused of being "communist agitators." When the strike destroyed the Amalgamated Textile Union, in its stead rose the Independent Textile Union (later Industrial Trade Union, ITU) in the Woonsocket-Saylesville area. The ITU's slogan was "uniform wages within all mills." Courtesy, Providence Journal Company

FACING PAGE, TOP: Theodore Francis Green (1867-1966) rose to high office by supporting political and labor reform and through cooperation with the Rhode Island labor movement. He masterminded the "Bloodless Revolution" of 1935 that saw the Democrats take control of the state senate, the last obstacle to the Democratic party conquest of Rhode Island. He served first as Governor (1933-1937) and then as United States Senator (1937-1960). RIHS (RHi x3 4329)

Despite federal help throughout the 1930s, the various recovery and relief measures enacted and funded by the state and municipalities saddled them with heavy financial burdens. In 1939 the state debt stood at $33.5 million, but Providence's was $72.2 million, nearly four times that of 1920 when its debt was among the highest in the nation. An emergency bank loan of $2.5 million allowed Providence to fend off bankruptcy. The state debt was not as pressing but the Tax Study Board recommended to Governor Robert Quinn the enactment of a per-

causes favorable to labor, ethnics, and urban dwellers. The perception that the Democratic party was the "party of the people" was based on the reality that in 1910 over 50 percent of Democratic and only 7 percent of the Republican committee members were manual laborers.

To understand the struggle, one has to return to the 19th century. The Bourn Amendment (1888) had lifted the real-estate property requirement for voting for governor and mayor, but retained it in the city council elections and on financial questions. The office of mayor became largely ceremonial and was held by Democrats, while city councils, dominated by Republicans, had effective control, including appointments and patronage. When Republicans perceived that their grip on the governorship was becoming tenuous, they passed the so-called "Brayton Act" in 1901. It removed most of the powers of the office and vested them in the Republican-controlled Senate, made safe by the malapportionment of seats under the 1842 constitution. It was just in time, too, because a reform Democrat, Dr. Lucius F.C. Garvin, won the governorship in 1902 and 1903. Powerless to effect changes, he supplied muckraker Lincoln Steffens with information used in 1904 for the *McClure's Magazine* exposé of corruption in Rhode Island called "A State for Sale." The alliance of politicians and business interests under the leadership of "Boss" Charles Brayton, Nelson Aldrich, and Marsden J. Perry controlled state politics, patronage, and favors.

The Republican-dominated General Assembly was so conservative and contrary that Rhode Island was the only state to reject as many as three of the progressive era amendments to the United States Constitution. Only the Woman Suffrage Amendment gained Rhode Island's approval, and on it Republicans were too divided to resist. Besides, most suffrage leaders came from the Yankee upper classes upon whom the Republicans depended for support. Leading suffragists included Mrs. Marsden J. Perry, Mrs. John Carter Brown, and United States Senator LeBaron Colt's daughter-in-law; while the leading antisuffragists included Mrs. Rowland Gibson Hazard and Mrs. Charles

Providence's Exchange Place was the location of this "Votes for Women" rally in May 1914. Suffragists toured the state in automobiles and made open-air speeches in their campaign to win the vote, but the conservative, Republican-dominated General Assembly refused to grant the franchise. Eventually Rhode Island ratified the federal suffrage amendment, but the legislature rejected the other progressive amendments: direct election of U.S. Senators, income tax, and Prohibition. Courtesy, Providence Journal Company

sonal property tax, a cigarette tax, and increased levies on corporations, public utilities, and pari-mutuel betting. Quinn, in political trouble, sidestepped the issues. By 1938 state voters were so demoralized that they rejected a slate of relief and capital-improvement bond issues totaling $28 million while approving a state holiday—Columbus Day.

The turbulence accompanying relief measure implementation reflected a half century of struggle which climaxed in the "Bloodless Revolution" of 1935. Democrats ended decades of Republican domination and initiated decades of Democratic domination. The Republican party had dug its own grave by refusing to reform and to broaden its rural, middle-class, Yankee base. The Democrats, on the other hand, tap-danced to power by seeking to lift the franchise restrictions and by backing

ABOVE: Robert E. Quinn (1894-1975), Lieutenant Governor (1933-1935), Governor (1937-1939), and member of the U.S. Court of Military Appeals (1951-1975), takes the oath of office as Governor of Rhode Island in his home in West Warwick on January 5, 1937. He passionately wanted to unite the various factions of the Democratic party, but his efforts to do so created more enemies than friends. His use of martial law in Pawtucket to destroy his chief competitors earned him the nickname of "Huey Long of Rhode Island" and cost him the 1938 gubernatorial election. Courtesy, Providence Journal Company

Warren Lippitt, wife of the former governor.

By the 1920s Democratic legislators in the General Assembly were numerous enough to keep the Republican majority from passing legislation or adopting a budget. In 1928 they used their power to force the Republicans to approve two constitutional amendments which helped end Republican rule. The first modestly reapportioned the state senate to increase urban representation, but every town, regardless of size, still retained one delegate. The second ended the property tax requirement for voters in city elections. The Democrats immediately captured the city councils in the 1930 election, although Republicans retained power in many of the unincorporated, rural areas—the "rotten boroughs."

Democratic victories in 1932 brought Theodore Francis Green to the governorship and Democratic control to the House. But Republicans still retained a 28-14 margin in the Senate; and "Boss" Brayton's successor as head of the Republican party, Frederick S. Peck, controlled the office of State Commissioner of Finance, which supervised the budget and all expenditures. This Republican lock on the fiscal management of the state precluded the Democrats from quickly taking advantage of New Deal programs. When the Republicans appeared to have narrowly retained a majority in the Senate in the 1934 election, Green and his party comrades, Robert E. Quinn, Thomas P. McCoy, and J. Howard McGrath engineered the "Bloodless Revolution" of 1935.

The election of two Republicans was challenged, leaving the Senate with a tie, which gave the deciding vote to Lieutenant Governor Quinn. A Democratic-appointed committee investigated the charges of fraudulent returns and awarded the seats to the Democrats. At last they controlled the General Assembly and the governorship, and they proceeded to break the Republicans. They replaced all five justices of the state supreme court, abolished the office of State Commissioner of Finance, flushed Republicans from the state administration, removed them from the Providence Safety Board, and returned local patronage to the city government. They also reorganized the state government, eliminating devices Republicans had used to thwart and frustrate Democratic growth; and they created the various departments which have operated since then. This political revolution completed the takeover of Rhode Island by the Democratic party. While Republicans occasionally slipped into high office, Rhode Island became the most Democratic state in the Union by the 1970s.

The long denial of power to the Irish-led Democratic party by the Republicans through all manner of constitutional and administrative mechanisms had dammed a normal transition from one party to another. The dam broke, first in the city governments in 1930 and then in the state government in 1935, and led to such a scramble for power, position, and rewards within the Democratic party that it failed to deal with the fundamental problems of the state. After sweeping away Republican obstacles, Democrats turned to the politics of gratification. Instead of addressing the deteriorating industrial base, general shabbiness of the cities, inadequate transportation system, and the low skills and educational levels of the industrial workers, factions set upon each other, demanding rewards and scrambling for dominance within the party.

Thomas P. McCoy, "Prince of Pawtucket," challenged Governor Green for control of the state Democratic party and lost. As absolute boss of Pawtucket, McCoy controlled 10 seats in the General Assembly and had been appointed state budget director. Green ousted McCoy from the directorship. When Green was elected United States Senator in 1936 and Robert Quinn became governor, Quinn inherited the Green machine and its enemies. What followed has been variously called the "Narragansett Race Track War" and the "War of the Wild Irish Roses."

Walter J. O'Hara, a wealthy textile manufacturer, owner of the *Pawtucket Star-Tribune*, and founder and president of the Narragansett Race Track, was a McCoy ally, who first backed McCoy for governor and then sought it for himself. As the racetrack had become a focal point of extensive bookmaking, Governor Quinn

The 1938 hurricane and tidal wave drove water into the heart of Providence, flooding Exchange Place (now Kennedy Plaza). The winds had dropped to "only" 95 miles per hour by the time this picture, looking from the Industrial Trust building toward the northwest and Exchange Street, was taken. By 10 p.m. the water was gone. Courtesy, Providence Journal Company

tried to discredit the McCoy-O'Hara faction by charging that the track was the haunt of thugs and gangsters. After failing in two attempts to use the courts against O'Hara, Quinn sued him for libel, decreed the racetrack area to be under criminal control, proclaimed martial law in October 1937, and occupied the track with National Guard troops. O'Hara was indicted by a grand jury for illegal contributions to political parties. While these charges were later quashed, O'Hara was forced to resign as president of the racetrack, his newspaper went into receivership, and he was finished in politics. McCoy continued to rule Pawtucket until his death in 1945; but Quinn's abuse of the courts and his use of military power in a Democratic party squabble resulted in his defeat in the next election by Republican William Vanderbilt by the largest margin since 1920. Democratic disarray and corruption led to the 1938 Republican sweep of the general offices and the General Assembly. However, this was an aberration; and the Democrats, led by J. Howard McGrath, won the following election, beginning nearly 20 years of Democratic rule.

The 1938 political winds also brought the first Republican mayor to Providence in 25 years and permitted the antiquated city charter to be revised to meet the needs of the 20th century. While the 1928 state constitutional amendment had allowed the Democrats to capture the city council at long last, the city's government was cumbersome and complicated by too many boards, commissions, and independent centers of power. All through the Depression the city's relief and recovery projects were severely hampered by the fact that the head of the Department of Public Works, the Harbor Master, and the City Treasurer were all elected separately and not accountable to the mayor or the city council. Too many individuals had a veto. Democratic Mayor James Dunne, a poorly educated political hack, had neither the imagination nor the power to change the situation during his tenure from 1927 to 1938. Mismanagement and growing corruption led to the victory of John F. Collins, a Republican running for the Independent Citizens for Good Government, promising to clean up fraud and revise the city charter.

Republican State Attorney General Louis Jackvony began the prosecution of voting fraud that involved Democratic leaders and election officials. Unfortunately, the principal cases were lost when the key prosecution witness, Carmine Ruggiero, who had earlier identified the corrupt officials, suddenly "lost his memory" when he was put on the stand to testify. However, the charter revision was far more successful. A bipartisan City Charter Commission was appointed in May 1939. Democrats named former mayor Joseph Gainer, Dennis J. Roberts, and John O. Pastore; and the Republicans selected Jackvony, Walter Farrell, and J. Morton Ferrier. In September the commission filed its report, and Providence voters approved the charter revisions in a special election in November. While these won handily, Republican wards voted heavily against them because they would abolish the Board of Aldermen, the one remaining place where Republicans retained any power in city government.

The revisions provided for a strong mayor with increased administrative and appointive powers, a single-chamber city council of 26 members (two from each ward), the creation of new, streamlined departments and the abolition or consolidation of 26 old ones, a central purchasing department, specified fiscal and budgetary powers, and a civil service system. Collins, the reformer, was not the beneficiary of the new system; instead, Charter Commissioner Dennis J. Roberts swamped Collins in the next mayoralty election, ending the Republican interlude and ushering in another 34 years of Democratic mayors for Providence. Ironically, the Republican refusal for so many years to revise the old charter had saved Providence from Pawtucket-style political bossism. Once the charter revisions were implemented, little could be done by voters to prevent the formation of a Democratic city machine. In the hands of a visionary mayor, the machine could be an effective instrument in reviving a declining city, but it could be an engine of advancement for self-serving politicians, too.

Republican election upsets in 1938 have long since faded from the general memory; but the Hurricane of 1938 is not likely to be forgotten any time soon. It was the worst disaster in the state's history. The great storm, packing winds of 175 m.p.h., slammed into the southern New England coast around three-thirty in the afternoon of September 21, 1938, and within a half hour had done its greatest damage and killed most of its victims. Such was its power that brick factory walls collapsed in New London, Connecticut, and automobiles were sent cartwheeling in Stonington. A tidal wave 30 feet high washed ashore along the southern coast of Rhode Island and swept the beaches clean of human habitations at Napatree Point, Misquamicut, Quonochontaug, and Charlestown. It rolled on to deposit a moraine of shattered cottages and houses nearly a mile inland. More than 50 people died at Charlestown alone. Newport was pounded by raging winds and surf, and Ocean Drive crumbled into the sea along with the fancy beach pavilions of the rich at Bailey's Beach and the boardwalk at Easton's Beach. Towns all around the Bay found yachts and boats in the streets and yards, ferries crushed, and marinas stacked with wrecked vessels. The Rhode Island Yacht Club and the Bristol Yacht Club fell to the storm, as did church steeples all over the affected area. In Providence a tidal surge suddenly pushed water into the streets just about the time that people were heading home from work, drowning a number of them. At 4:16 all electric power and telephone service was lost in the city as the water rose to 13 feet above the mean high-water mark. In Woonsocket, the winds blew down the walls of textile mills and injured a policeman by lifting him from his feet and hurling him against a passing automobile. Even after the hurricane had passed, it caused more misery as the rivers in the region subsequently burst their banks from the torrents of water dumped on New England.

The WPA dispatched thousands of emergency workers to aid in the cleanup and help restore vital services. Rhode Island counted 317 dead and over $100 million in damages out of New England's 680 deaths and $400 million in losses. Nearly 2,000 houses of various sorts were destroyed in the state along with 2,000 barns and other buildings. Almost 900 boats were completely wrecked, including the entire fishing fleet on Block Island. Most of western Rhode Island was a scrapyard of fallen trees, and lumber companies rushed in to salvage millions of board-feet before the wood rotted.

In spite of all the terrible things the storm did, one is forced to recall the old saying, "It's an ill wind that blows nobody some good." Indeed, the Hurricane of 1938 was a cleansing force that swept the coast and upper Narragansett Bay almost clean of beachfront shanties, run-down docks, wharfs, and warehouses, decaying and abandoned amusement parks, waterfront whorehouses, slums, and ramshackle buildings of all sorts. While one might expect a severe economic dislocation from such a disaster, in fact, employment in the state increased. The lumber that was cut from the fallen trees created an enormous stockpile which was immediately available for the emergency defense construction needs that arose within a few years. Like the Great Chicago Fire which allowed that city to build anew and better, so, too, did the Hurricane of 1938 clear the way for new uses and development. Rhode Island was still battling the Great Depression when the hurricane walloped it; and while most set to work picking up the pieces, many wondered if prosperity would ever return. But Adolf Hitler soon rescued Rhode Island from the Great Depression.

Chapter Twelve

THE PATRIOTIC STATE

E ACH FOURTH OF JULY the little town of Bristol swells to a city's population of hundreds of thousands, and the quiet streets resound with the sounds of the nation's oldest Independence Day parade. The tree-shaded streets and warm hospitality of the local folks preserve an atmosphere of an old-fashioned, small-town parade; but this is *the* Fourth of July parade. It is a "must" event for local politicians and groups; some have fought and sued for the right to march. The sound and sight of the drum-and-bugle corps, the marching wind-bands, drill teams, horses, clowns, Knights of Columbus and Shriners, floats, and fire engines add verve and color. The real point of the day is brought home by the military units who march in uniforms that range from the American Revolution to the present. Thus does Rhode Island reaffirm an independent and patriotic heritage.

The Independent State's patriotic heritage grew gradually from seeds planted in the Revolutionary era and has been strengthened by economic, social, and strategic needs. While most Rhode Islanders wanted independence from Great Britain, only a minority favored a strong American union. Those early nationalists (who wanted closer relationships with the Union and ratification of the Constitution) came from the group engaged in oceanic commerce and trade. Although some flouted national trade regulations, they supported a strong navy and coastal fortifications like Fort Adams. When the state's economy shifted from ocean to

industry, industralists wanted protective tariffs, a national banking system, a strong defense, and federal support in securing overseas markets and raw materials. This economic nationalism was complemented by immigrants and their descendants who filled the ranks of the army and navy. Youth from lower socioeconomic orders found military service to be an avenue of opportunity; and the more veterans a family had, the more family pride was engaged. Homegrown veterans were joined by many who settled in Rhode Island after being stationed in the military installations that encircled Narragansett Bay. By 1982 Rhode Island had 152,000 veterans, nearly half of the adult male population. Their presence created a climate celebrating patriotism and traditional values.

The most independent and otherwise-minded colony in British North America had moved early toward concerted action to oppose the new Imperial order. The only way Rhode Island could preserve its independent ways was to surrender some of them to a united effort against the British. Local pride causes some to assert that the American Revolution "really began right here." They point to the cannons firing on H.M.S. *St. John* at Newport in 1764, the burning of a boat from H.M.S. *Maidstone* in 1765, the scuttling of H.M.S. *Liberty* in 1769, and the destruction of the *Gaspee* in 1772. Historians note that violence greeted British press-gangs and revenue agents in other colonies at the same times. Similarly, since 1909 Rhode Islanders have officially maintained that their state was the first to

The 1st Rhode Island Volunteers march down Westminster Street in April 1899 as part of the Welcome home parade for veterans of the Spanish-American War. The regiment, however, never left the country, and the greatest services were performed by the women of the Rhode Island Sanitary and Relief Association. Composed of 577 members, the association collected $21,496 and 18,076 garments for relief, and shipped jellies, mineral water, wine, and medicines to service hospitals. In Newport, Mrs. A. Livingston Mason gave one of her "cottages" to the Surgeon General of the Army as a convalescent home. The famous Casino was the organization's headquarters. Courtesy, Providence Public Library

ABOVE: Nathanael Greene (1742-1786), youngest general in the Continental Army, had no prior military experience before the American Revolution. Commissioned as brigadier general in June 1775, he served as quartermaster general (1778-1780) before taking command in the southern colonies in 1781. Engraved portrait by H. Gugeler. RIHS (RHi x3 582)

RIGHT: Oliver Hazard Perry (1785-1819) led his green-wood flotilla against the British on Lake Erie and won a decisive victory after a furious battle. His flagship, the Lawrence, was damaged so badly that Perry, shown here, transferred his command to another vessel. After the British surrendered, Perry reported, "We have met the enemy and they are ours." He died of yellow fever in 1819. RIHS (RHi x3 4298)

FACING PAGE: Ambrose E. Burnside (1824-1881) was Rhode Island's hero in the Civil War. His military disasters, however, led Ulysses S. Grant to say, "General Burnside was an officer who was generally liked and respected. He was not, however, fitted to command an army." Not only was Burnside a soldier, he was also an inventor, industrialist, and politician. RIHS (RHi x3 4344)

declare independence from Great Britain. This resulted from a misreading of the facts by a determined antiquarian in the 1880s who convinced school committees, the Colonial Dames, the Sons of the American Revolution, and finally the General Assembly of his view.

Still, there is no denying that Rhode Islanders threw themselves into the Revolution and suffered considerably in it. The state's greatest Revolutionary War hero, Nathanael Greene, was arguably the war's best general; and he and George Washington were the only generals in continuous service throughout the war. In his brilliant southern campaign of 1780-1781, Greene, the master of strategic retreats, lost every battle and yet won every objective. In the end the British withdrew from the interior of Georgia, North and South Carolina, and marched off to defeat at Yorktown, Virginia. Heaped with gratitude and land grants, Greene remained on his gift plantation in Georgia, died, and was buried there.

Bristol celebrated its first Independence Day parade in 1785; but coming as it did in the middle of Rhode Island's recession from the Union, the parade may well have reflected the state's attitude toward the Union. The Independent State would eventually submit to the Constitution, but its relationship to the United States was ambiguous until after the War of 1812. During that war, the official actions of Rhode Island were self-serving and obstructive to the national effort, but individual Rhode Islanders made significant contributions. Just as John Brown had given *Providence* to the Continental Navy in the Revolution, James DeWolf gave the United States Navy his *Chippewa* in the War of 1812. At the Battle of Lake Erie in September 1813, Oliver Hazard Perry commanded the American flotilla of 10 small vessels, and decisively defeated the British. One fourth of the Americans in this engagement were Rhode Islanders, five of the vessels had Rhode Island commanders, and 51 of 54 cannons were captained by its sons.

Between 1815 and the War of the Great Rebellion, the ambiguity of patriotism vanished. The state's principal interests were linked to the nation as oceanic commerce gave way to manufacturing for the United States market. Several months prior to the attack on Fort Sumter, Governor William Sprague offered troops to defend the nation's capital; and Rhode Island immediately answered President Lincoln's April 15 call for volunteers. On April 20, 1861, the Rhode Island First Regiment, commanded by Ambrose E. Burnside and accompanied by Governor Sprague, colorfully embarked with the American Brass Band from Providence. The state quivered with patriotic fervor. Within a month the banks and general public subscribed an extra half-million dollars to outfit Rhode Island troops. Little boys joined the Union Guard and Providence High School students formed the Ellsworth Phalanx to drill while men flocked to enlist in the real army. Women and girls sewed uniforms and trimmed hats, and inmates at the Reform School knitted socks for the troops.

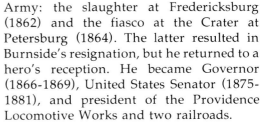

Flags appeared everywhere, but the highest flew from the top of the 185-foot steeple of the First Baptist Meeting House in Providence.

The Rhode Island Second Regiment followed in June, and both units were heavily engaged in the battle of Bull Run on July 21. Governor Sprague served Burnside as a volunteer aide, and in the fighting his horse was shot from under him. While the Second Regiment fought bravely, the First performed badly and fled in panic. Rhode Island lost 167 men that day, and the American Brass Band lost its bass drum. Governor Sprague was so disgusted with the First Regiment's performance that it was disbanded. Nevertheless, honors followed for Burnside: Brown University gave him an honorary degree, and he rose to become the commander of the Army of the Potomac in 1862. However, he was blamed for two of the worst disasters suffered by the Union

Army: the slaughter at Fredericksburg (1862) and the fiasco at the Crater at Petersburg (1864). The latter resulted in Burnside's resignation, but he returned to a hero's reception. He became Governor (1866-1869), United States Senator (1875-1881), and president of the Providence Locomotive Works and two railroads.

As one of the industrial centers in America, Rhode Island secured a flood of war contracts. Builders Iron Foundry cast heavy 11- and 13-inch Dahlgren cannons and massive siege mortars. Mansfield & Lamb made bayonets, Corliss & Nightingale produced cannons, and another company manufactured the Burnside breech-loading rifle. Of course, the textile industry was a leading supplier of cloth for uniforms, blankets, and tents.

As the war ground on, inducements to volunteers were increased. The government offered bounties and improved the system of relief payments to dependents of soldiers and sailors. Total expenditures for bounties and relief in Providence alone amounted to $383,504. Immigrants enlisted in great numbers because service brought more acceptance from native Americans, and the bonuses and bounties provided immediate economic rewards. After the Emancipation Proclamation, blacks were recruited, and in June 1863 the Rhode Island Fourteenth Regiment began forming. One of its earliest duties was to patrol the streets of Providence, protecting military stores and guarding against draft resistance. Later, the Fourteenth spent most of its service in Louisiana, garrisoning captured territory. Before the end, the state contributed over 24,000 men, exceeding its quota by 5,000. The magnitude of that effort grows when one realizes that over 28,000 served in each of the two world wars when the state's population was four times as large.

For the next half century, the defense of the Union was recalled in the public ceremonies and remembrances. Rhode Island first celebrated Decoration Day on May 30, 1869, and in 1874 was the first state in the nation to make it an official holiday. This solemn day memorialized the 1,321 who died in the Civil War and those who joined them with the passing years.

Exchange Place in Providence sprouted several Civil War monuments and statues, and at least a dozen other towns also erected memorials. The General Assembly established the Rhode Island Soldiers' Home in Bristol in 1889; and beginning in 1902 schools celebrated Grand Army Flag Day each February 12, commemorating both the veterans and Abraham Lincoln. Since Rhode Island volunteers moved no nearer to the Spanish-American War than Columbia, South Carolina, only the First World War could begin to match the impact of the Civil War.

Rhode Island never got an accurate view of the conflict in Europe because the state's principal newspaper, the *Providence Journal*, was headed by a flamboyant liar who was determined to bring the United States into the war on the Allied side. Australian-born John Rathom (an assumed name) brought national attention to the *Journal* by filling its columns with exaggerated and often fabricated tales of German espionage, sabotage, and war atrocities. He annoyed the Germans to the point that their Ambassador protested to the United States Secretary of State. The reportage helped to generate a climate of patriotic fervor that spilled over into hysteria. One result was a mammoth Preparedness Day parade in 1916 which saw 54,542 men and women march in a six-hour procession that was cut short by a downpour. A similar parade in Boston the previous week marshaled only 38,000 marchers.

When America entered the conflict, Rhode Islanders enlisted in record numbers, bought war bonds far in excess of quotas, and joined the Red Cross, YMCA, and the Home Guard beyond all expectations. Over 12 percent of Brown & Sharpe employees entered the service, and those who remained behind subscribed $1.4 million in bonds and grew $40,000 worth of produce in the company war garden. War opponents were being arrested in the spring of 1917, and the *Providence Magazine* screamed when it heard of alleged food sabotage by German sympathizers: "The next man or woman caught in the act, or found guilty of destroying food supplies, should be summarily shot. Shoot first! Hold the inquiry afterwards."

The *Providence Journal* urged that Germans and Austrians be watched and suspicious activities reported. A campaign against German influences swept the state. The *Journal* charged that "disloyalty is being taught in American schools. Germanized teachers are everywhere. ... We must now purge our college faculties and public school staffs of every German propagandist." The State Board of Education imposed a loyalty oath on all teachers, and the teaching of the German language and literature disappeared from the schools. Rathom attacked Dr. Karl Muck, Bavarian-born conductor of the Boston Symphony Orchestra as "a man of notoriously pro-German affiliations" and demanded that the BSO play "The Star-Spangled Banner" at its five concerts in Providence. The Board of Police Commissioners refused to grant a license to the orchestra; and when other theaters threatened to cancel the season's concerts, the BSO caved in to the pressure. Dr. Muck resigned. This was patriotism running amok.

Although the war ended, the fear of subversion did not. On Grand Army Flag Day in 1919, the principal of English High School declared, "The Hun is defeated, but other dangers threaten us. The anarchist, the I.W.W., the Bolshevik menace us with loss of public order and security." The Providence City Council outlawed the carrying of the Red flag in any procession, and the Americanization effort was intensified among Rhode Island's foreign-born. As part of the nationwide sweep against foreign-born radicals in January 1920, local police arrested more than a dozen people. Nativist feelings persisted, and some Rhode Islanders enrolled in the Invisible Empire of the Ku Klux Klan in the 1920s. Especially shocking was the discovery in 1928 that the Klan was attempting to use enlistment forms for the Rhode Island First Light Infantry to recruit members for its own ranks. This ploy evaporated in the glare of an expose and legislative investigation.

The antiforeign, anti-Catholic aspects of this warped patriotism faded in Rhode Island in the 20th century. While the immigrant restriction movement had considerable power in Massachusetts and

Australian-born journalist John R. Rathom (1868?-1923) joined the Providence Journal in 1906 and served as its editor and general manager from 1912 to 1922. He brought the newspaper to national influence during World War I with his daring and imaginative reporting of real and imaginary German threats, plots, sabotage, and atrocities. He promoted a climate of hysteria that led to political excesses in the postwar Red Scare. Courtesy, Providence Journal Company

Connecticut, it had little support in Rhode Island; and Senator LeBaron Colt, chairman of the United States Senate Committee on Immigration, was able to block national immigration restriction legislation until his death in 1924. Besides, the coming to power of ethnic voters in the 1920s and 1930s in most urban areas of the state scattered the old nativists. What remained was antiradicalism, which appealed equally to Yankee and ethnic. The Yankee Governor Theodore Francis Green used the heavily ethnic National Guard to break the 1934 strike of ethnic textile workers by blaming the troubles on "outside Communist agitators," and by arresting 15 Communists. He lost little support from Rhode Island's ethnic working class because they shared his sense of patriotism. This patriotism carried Rhode Island headlong into World War II.

World War II converted Rhode Island into an armed camp. The deepwater harbor facilities in the Bay had attracted the Navy in the post-Civil War era; now those modest establishments expanded and were joined by a multitude of other bases and stations. The Naval Training Station at Newport had opened in 1883, but during the summer prior to Pearl Harbor a large portion of the Atlantic Fleet was at Newport and training of seamen accelerated. During the Second World War over 204,000 recruits trained there and additional thousands received instruction at the Anti-Aircraft Training Center and at

the Motor Torpedo Boat Squadrons Training Center. Two naval air bases opened at Westerly and Charlestown, and the Naval Air Station at Quonset Point became the largest in the East. Authorized in May 1939, nearly four months before Germany's attack on Poland, the base eventually covered 1,200 acres and housed

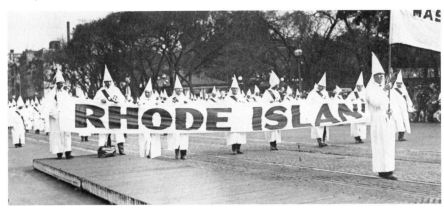

15,000 servicemen. Soon after Pearl Harbor, a training center for naval construction battalions opened at Davisville; and by war's end a total of 100,000 "Seabees" had been trained there. Across the Bay, Melville Fuel Depot had storage capacity for 13 million gallons of fuel in 1937, and this was expanded during the war. The Naval Net Depot at Melville, established in February 1941, trained men in harbor net defenses and constructed antisubmarine nets. The Naval Torpedo Station on Goat Island, established in 1869, expanded to become the nation's principal manufacturer of tor-

ABOVE: Members of Rhode Island's KKK march down Pennsylvania Avenue in Washington, D.C., on September 13, 1926, as part of the National Klonvocation. Klan activities in the state included a rally in Foster Center in June 1924 with an estimated 8,000 participants and a Klan wedding in Georgiaville in 1927 that attracted thousands. The Grand Dragon in the state, John W. Perry, was arrested and indicted for perjury but acquitted in 1929 as the Klan's visibility had disappeared. Courtesy, Providence Journal Company

LEFT: A "human flag" of 1500 schoolchildren and an honor guard of 200 Civil War veterans reviewed the massive parade on "Preparedness Day," June 3, 1916. The parade lasted so long that the children in the flag formation had to be replaced by fresh standbys at regular intervals. RIHS (RHi x3 2103)

pedoes. High-explosive storage facilities and a naval magazine were built on Gould and Prudence islands in 1942.

Other shipbuilding activities deepened Rhode Island's involvement in the war effort. The popular swimming beach at Field's Point became part of the Rheem shipyard in May 1942; and the first vessel, the *William Coddington,* was launched just after Thanksgiving. (It did not matter that Coddington had been an early convert to the Quakers in the 1660s; his Aquidneck Island was now thoroughly militarized and the Newport Naval Base surrounded Coddington Cove.) In February 1943 the Walsh-Kaiser Company took over the shipyard and continued production until July 1945 when the last of 64 vessels, the *Zenobia,* was launched.

Direct employment of citizens in military facilities was only one aspect of the boost to the state's economy. The artificial increase in population by a steady stream of thousands of service personnel afforded bountiful opportunities to all sorts of enterprises, not the least of which were the numerous "white cap" sailor bars and brothels along Thames Street in Newport. In addition, Rhode Island industries received millions of dollars in defense contracts and subcontracts. In the 18 months *before* Pearl Harbor, Rhode Island manufacturers were awarded more than $115 million in defense work, with nearly $75 million going to textiles and most of the rest to the metal trades. The textile industry, which had been in a steep decline since the 1920s, revived momentarily to produce all manner of cloth and uniforms. Belt and webbing manufacturers worked overtime to meet defense needs, and everything from machine guns to gas masks poured out of Rhode Island factories. Payroll disbursements in the state for 1942 reached $379 million, more than double that of 1939.

The war effort had a tremendous economic impact on the state. The Navy Department calculated that nearly $130 million was spent in erecting the Narragansett Bay defenses. Construction of the Quonset Point Naval Air Station commenced in mid-1940 and before completion cost $75 million to build. When the

United States entered the war, Quonset Point Station was still incomplete, so work was accelerated. Nearly 11,000 workers labored nonstop to finish the job, pumping a half-million-dollar weekly payroll into the state's economy and creating an acute housing shortage near the base. Nearly a million dollars were spent on the Wickford housing project, but the statewide housing shortage remained severe. In August 1940 the Newport Housing Authority received $1.1 million from the United States government for a "national defense" low-cost housing project. The old Perry Mill was converted into a dormitory for women workers. Employing more than 12,000 civilians, the Naval Torpedo Station became the "largest single industrial-type employer in the State of Rhode Island" by 1944. Two factories at Davisville, employing 3,000 workers, produced over 32,000 Quonset huts by the end of the war and shipped them around the world.

With such a concentration of military installations, Rhode Island's coast was proclaimed a military district in April 1942, the United States Army superseded civilian authority, and all lights visible from the sea were ordered blacked out. Fear of possible attack caused the Navy to mine the approaches to Narragansett Bay, and antisubmarine nets blocked the passages in the Bay. The antisubmarine devices were deemed necessary because prowling German U-boats sank nine merchant ships off New England's coasts in the first seven months of 1942. In the autumn Rhode Island was declared a "vital war zone" which brought tightened security against espionage and sabotage at military installations. On Chopmist Hill a top-secret, radio-monitoring station eavesdropped on enemy radio transmissions from as far away as Europe, Africa, and South America. The largest of a national network of 13 listening stations, the Chopmist Hill post was the most effective because of its location and atmospheric conditions. By mid-1943 the U-boats had been driven away and threat of attack had declined. Consequently, coastal defenses and artillery units were thinned or reassigned, and the antisubmarine nets in Narragansett Bay were removed in September 1944. Yet, the final battle of the Atlantic occurred in Rhode Island waters.

In early 1945 the Germans sent snorkel-equipped U-boats to the East Coast, but only three reached American waters. Two were destroyed in April, and on May 4 the German High Command recalled the other. The one remaining U-boat operating along the East Coast either failed to receive the message or disregarded it. The next day, the *Black Point,* a coal ship from New York, was torpedoed and sunk three miles off Point Judith, killing 12 crewmen, just 28 hours before Germany's unconditional surrender. The submarine-killer forces swung into action, hunted the U-boat, and destroyed her the following morning near Block Island. The *Black Point* was the last merchant ship sunk in the Atlantic war.

As *U-853* lurked outside the Bay, a few dozen German prisoners-of-war were in Rhode Island participating in a secret anti-Nazi indoctrination program and publishing a newspaper called *Der Ruf,* which circulated in the nearly 400 German POW camps in the country. During the war 370,000 German POWs were interned in the United States, and about 15 percent were clearly anti-Nazi. The government wanted to reeducate these to democratic forms and beliefs so they could assume leadership and police roles in postwar Germany. It started a program in the summer of 1944 at an old CCC camp in New York, but in March 1945 the operation moved to Rhode Island. In May a 60-day indoctrination course commenced at Fort Wetherill with the first class graduating on July 6. For the rest of the year Rhode Island was the "center of the most long-range and idealistic POW re-education efforts ever undertaken by the United States." When the press was allowed to know of the schools in September 1945, they dubbed it the "Barbed Wire College." Before they closed in December, the schools at Fort Getty and Fort Wetherill on Conanicut Island had graduated 1,166 POWs.

Rhode Islanders hailed the victory and the end of sacrifice. Nearly a thousand of her sons had been killed or wounded in combat. Unfortunately, the war-inflated economy began to shrink almost immediately with Japan's defeat in August

1945, causing employment problems for returning veterans and the swollen civilian work force. However, the Navy remained. This seemed only natural because Rhode Island had played a significant role in creating the Navy in the American Revolution, manning it over the years, and serving as a station for decades. Many came to assume that the Navy would always remain since it had invested so much in facilities and because of the state's proximity to the North Atlantic shipping lanes. Rhode Islanders believed that they had a natural affinity for the Navy. They recalled with pride that the first ship in the Continental Navy had been the sloop *Providence* and the first admiral had been Ezek Hopkins. They remembered the exploits of the Perry brothers in winning the Battle of Lake Erie in 1813 and in opening Japan in 1853. But most people forgot that the Navy had no base in Rhode Island until the Civil War.

During the undeclared naval war with France in 1799, the United States government sought a naval base in New England. Some advanced Newport as the site, but George Champlin, a leading merchant, argued that a base would produce too many "disagreeable circumstances." He recommended Fall River as a more suitable place, but the government abandoned the effort. The Navy came to stay during the Civil War when the United States Naval Academy was transferred from Annapolis, Maryland. "Old Ironsides," the U.S.S. *Constitution,* arrived on May 8, 1861, carrying the Academy's officers and professors. Although the Naval Academy returned to Annapolis in the summer of 1865, the Navy had become a part of Newport. Narragansett Bay was increasingly attractive after the war because of its natural facilities and because the social atmosphere of Newport suited the officers and gentlemen of the Navy. The captains of ships and the captains of industry shared many of the same backgrounds, attitudes, and pretensions. Consequently, the Navy established its experimental Torpedo Station (1869), Naval Training Station (1883), and Naval War College (1884) all in Newport. The War College was a postgraduate school "to prepare officers for high command." By

RIGHT: Seamen stand in formation during parade drills at the Newport Naval Training Station in August 1942. Shown in the background, the USS Constellation was used as a training vessel. The presence of thousands of seamen turned the town into a playground for sailors. Courtesy, Naval War College Historical Museum

BELOW: In the spring of 1942 the gun tube of a 16-inch seacoast cannon was hauled past the Stone Bridge Inn in Tiverton enroute to Fort Church at Little Compton. The tube was 68 feet long and weighed 150 tons. Two of these cannons composed "Battery Gray" and required gun crews of 42 men per cannon in addition to control officers, spotters, and security personnel. Courtesy, C.E. Hall & Sons Trucking Company

LEFT: The SS William Coddington is shown here being launched in late November 1942 at the Rheem Shipyard, Field's Point, Providence. Among the 63 ships launched there was the SS Nelson W. Aldrich. Photo by U.S. Maritime Commission. Courtesy, Newport Historical Society

BELOW: The Naval Training Station in Newport provided the setting for this recruit parade around 1915. In the background, Navy ships lie at anchor in Narragansett Bay while the Naval War College looms in the center. On the top right is the Alfred T. Mahan Hall, once the Newport poorhouse. Courtesy, Naval War College Historical Museum

1919 more than half of all flag officers and their staffs were graduates of the War College. Rear Admiral Alfred T. Mahan, twice president of the school, contributed to the college's curriculum; and his international reputation as an advocate of strong navies brought prestige to the institution.

By the time of the First World War, Newport viewed the Navy's presence as an economic necessity. During the war, the Torpedo Station employed some 3,800 civilians producing depth charges, mines, and torpedoes. Increased production of primers occurred in 1918 when women outproduced their male counterparts by six to one. Most of these jobs vanished with the return of peace, but the Newport Chamber of Commerce in the 1920s succeeded in having the Navy concentrate its torpedo manufacture and training operations there. Narragansett Bay was designated as one of two main bases on the Atlantic Coast, and the capacity of the Naval Fuel Depot at Melville was tripled in the 1920s. Of course, World War II greatly increased the Navy's presence at Newport as well as adding the Quonset Point-Davisville complex to the state's naval facilities.

For the state as a whole the Navy continued to be the leading employer through the 1950s, and the extent of Newport's dependency by 1960 was reflected in the fact that 73 percent of its employed residents were working directly for the federal government. As other economic elements in the state declined or stagnated, many regarded the Navy as a comfortable surety; but this proved to be a sand castle. The Navy began a massive withdrawal in 1972-1973, reducing its operations to a hospital, the Naval War College, and a handful of minesweepers and destroyers. However, many naval officers who had been stationed in Rhode Island retired here, adding to the substantial veterans' community and providing a climate favorable to patriotic sentiment.

Rhode Island welcomed the servicemen of World War II and discovered that its percentage gain in veterans was the highest in the nation. Providence gave Davis Park to the federal government for a Veterans Hospital, and the General Assembly adopted a $20-million Soldiers Bonus Act to pay each Rhode Island veteran a $200 bonus. Victory Day (V-J Day) became an official state holiday in 1948, and in the 1980s Rhode Island was the only state that still celebrated the end of World War II. The presence of so many veterans reinforced that uncomplex, general sense of patriotism so deeply felt in Rhode Island's ethnic, working-class population. The continuing presence of the Navy and the dependence of so many upon defense

industries has made Rhode Islanders supportive of patriotic appeals and military needs.

Many people identify various threats to the nation, cherished values, traditions, and institutions; and in the name of patriotism they have supported efforts to suppress alleged menaces. Sometimes this placed them on a collision course with organizations such as the American Civil Liberties Union, American Association of University Professors, and Americans United for Separation of Church and State, which have a different understanding of patriotism. Since the 1950s the state has had a steady diet of controversy over issues of academic freedom, censorship, free speech, public financing of parochial schools, municipally sponsored Nativity displays, antiwar protests, homosexuality, and abortion.

The most intense concern about Communist influences surfaced in the 1950s and early 1960s when being identified as a Communist would get one fired. A student class president at Bryant College was ousted when it was discovered that he was a Communist. When 87 Brown University professors signed a petition urging the abolition of the House Committee on Un-American Activities in 1961, the Rhode Island House of Representatives voted a resolution of support for HUAC, with only four dissenters, who included John Chafee of Warwick. The following year Thomas R. DiLuglio of Johnston introduced a bill to require all editorial writers to sign annual affidavits that they were not Communists. Following an appearance by a Communist speaker at the University of Rhode Island in 1963, a Cranston assemblyman demanded a legislative probe of the university; however, then-Governor Chafee opposed the move and the ACLU denounced it as a threat to free speech and academic freedom. The Vietnam War era brought new demands for intervention in campus disorders and efforts to command respect for the flag. The ACLU and similar organizations found themselves defending unpopular causes such as draft resistance, student rights, and the right of public protest.

A classic example of the clash of concep-

tions of patriotism occurred in 1964 over the issue of the Teacher Loyalty Oath. Since World War I, taking the oath had been a condition of teacher certification in the state, and at Rhode Island College it was administered to all student teachers in their final semester. Unexpectedly in February 1964, 20 seniors refused to sign the oath. The college's chapter of the American Association of University Professors, which had been privately considering the oath for some months, immediately supported the students. Dr. Kenneth Lewalski, chapter president, argued that the oath was vague and ambiguous, abridged academic freedom, and invaded personal privacy. Lieutenant Governor Edward Gallogly, soon to be the Democratic gubernatorial nominee, joined the issue in an address to a labor union gathering at the Naval Construction Battalion Center at Davisville. He declared that the nation faced a crisis when college professors teach that "the words loyalty and honor are vague and indefinite," when they assign pornographic literature such as *Fanny Hill* to students, and when students refuse to sign loyalty oaths. Governor Chafee, Gallogly's Republican opponent, observed at a press conference that the Teacher Loyalty Oath went far beyond the oaths that the governor or the legislators had to take and was unworkable. Subsequently, the State Board of Education, upon the recommendation of a special advisory committee headed by Associate Justice Florence Murray, revoked the oath on December 10.

In the early 1980s a similar clash occurred each Christmas season over municipally sponsored Nativity scenes. On the one hand were those who felt they were defending freedom of religious expression and the idea that America is a Christian nation. On the other hand were the ACLU and various religious leaders who maintained that the patriotic thing is separation of church and state and the preservation of Christian symbols from being reduced to secular objects equal to Rudolph the Red-Nosed Reindeer. Each side believed that the other was trampling on something that is holy. Roger Williams would have found it ironic that both sides invoked his name.

Chapter Thirteen

REVIVAL AND VISIONS

THE SECOND WORLD War was just a respite from a number of persistent problems that plagued Rhode Island. Inasmuch as the national economy escaped the Great Depression, Rhode Island did not tumble back into the Depression, but its recovery was neither complete nor robust. What had been troublesome before the terrible Thirties reappeared to afflict the state. The economy and the physical appearance of cities continued on a path of decay that reached back to the beginning of the century. But from the centers of decay came individuals with visions and programs to arrest the decline, to plan for a better future, and to make it happen. Most of these visions used the federal-urban partnership for money, implementation, and legislation. They revitalized the capital city, recovered Newport's magnetism, and planned for stability in other urban areas and for growth elsewhere. Despite persistent obstacles, Rhode Island held its own, eradicated substantial urban blight, and improved planning and resource management, which promised to guide and guard the future.

The return of peace also brought a return of many of the problems which had vexed the state in the preceding decades. Quite disturbing was the erosion of the industrial base. Some companies fell because of their total dependence upon the war economy. The Franklin Machine and Foundry Company, operating 100 percent on war contracts, went out of business when these were abruptly canceled, and the Walsh-Kaiser shipyard at Field's

Point also closed.

The textile industry resumed its swoon. Cotton consumption for 1945 fell below that of 1935 as military orders ended and civilian demand was slow to materialize. Furthermore, unions struck nearly all of Rhode Island's textile mills during October and November, demanding a closed shop and retention of war-level wages. Within a year the mills began shutting and the jobs began disappearing; and when the Harris Mill closed in 1953, it marked the 15th concern to fold since 1946. In November 1953 the huge Guerin Mills in Woonsocket shut down permanently after the company's 1,000 employees rejected a wage-cut request. A few months later the Lorraine Manufacturing Company of Pawtucket, employing 1,300, closed. Between 1945 and 1982 the work force in textiles declined by 75 percent; and largely because of the loss of nearly 43,000 textile jobs, the number of industrial workers in Rhode Island was 19 percent less than a quarter of a century earlier. Furthermore, the proportion of the total work force engaged in manufacturing declined from 52 percent to 32 percent during that same period.

Two of the old "Industrial Wonders of the World" moved from the state in the decade following the war. In early 1946 the American Screw Company decided to relocate in Willimantic, Connecticut. In 1954 the Nicholson File Company went through a five-month strike from which it never fully recovered, and it moved its operations to plants in Indiana and Pennsylvania. With their departure only two of the five

The Providence skyline will be altered with the construction of a $50 million, 18-story office building next to the Industrial National Bank Building. The structure on Kennedy Plaza resulted from the united effort of the Fleet Financial Group (formerly Industrial National Corporation), Nortek, Incorporated, Gilbane Building Company, and the law firm of Hinckley & Allen. Architects drawing: Helmuth, Obata & Kassabaum, Inc. Courtesy, Fleet National Bank

"Industrial Wonders of the World" remained in Rhode Island: Gorham and Brown & Sharpe. In 1967 the former became a component of Textron, America's first conglomerate corporation, pioneered by Royal Little. Gorham remained a major element in making Providence the jewelry capital of America. When Brown & Sharpe moved its headquarters to a new plant at Precision Park in North Kingstown in 1964, Providence lost its second largest tax-payer. Employing over 1,600 skilled workers, the firm is a mostly Rhode Island-owned corporation, even though it has plants in other states and abroad. Henry D. Sharpe, Jr., spoke publicly of the need for Rhode Islanders to pull together to create an economic climate which will benefit capital and labor, and he urged the people to stop "canceling each other out." Nevertheless, Brown & Sharpe suffered a long strike in 1981-1982 as labor rejected work-rule concessions and management feared the loss of competitiveness in the market.

The state's jewelry industry absorbed some of the lost textile jobs and by 1982 had the largest single industrial force. However, a 1981 exposé revealed that it was afflicted by many of the evils associated with turn-of-the-century sweatshops: health and safety problems, few employee benefits, a largely unskilled work force, exploitation of immigrants, illegal home-work paying wages below minimum requirements and using child labor, and little job security. The industry had 1,200 firms, many of whom were small, marginal, and subject to failure if forced to meet health and safety standards. The state's enforcement of occupational health and safety standards had been slow, and larger, well-managed plants were reluctant to "blow the whistle" on their smaller sub-contractors. Still, when the State Department of Employment Security reported a decline of over 2,000 manufacturing jobs in Rhode Island in 1981, the spokesman noted that most of those lost were in jewelry; and he considered it to be a healthy trend.

The most stunning blow to the state's economy in the past 20 years was the sudden withdrawal of the Navy in 1973. As a result of President Richard M. Nixon's decision to consolidate naval operations and personnel, most of the Newport-based Atlantic Fleet and all of the Quonset-Davisville support operations were reassigned to southern stations. The number of active-duty personnel in Rhode Island fell from 25,881 to about 3,300, and more than 16,000 civilian jobs were eliminated. Eventually more than 30,000 people left in the Navy's wake, a $200-million payroll disappeared, real-estate values around the bases fell sharply, and local schools had to be closed.

While a declining proportion of its workers relied upon Navy employment, Rhode Island still remained significantly dependent upon defense and government contracts. In 1982, defense contracts for Rhode Island amounted to $336 million. In the early 1980s the state's largest defense contractor was Electric Boat, a division of General Dynamics, which employed over 9,000 in its submarine-hull fabrication plants on former Navy land at Quonset. In Middletown, Raytheon Signal Division manufactured sonar and other electronic components. The Robert E. Derecktor Shipyard, located at the former Navy piers at Coddington Cove, won a contract in 1981 to build cutters for the United States Coast Guard. PF Industries, Inc., in Bristol was rescued from bankruptcy in the same year to make military footwear, while the Imperial Knife Company, the largest manufacturer of cutlery in America, frequently supplied bayonets and survival knives. A host of other companies making everything from service pins and insignias to screwdriver bits contributed to the state's economy.

Despite the decline in the number of workers engaged in industry, Rhode Island still has one of the highest industrial ratios in the nation, and overall employment has remained firm. Significant portions of the industrial losses have been replaced in nonmanufacturing fields, principally in the growth of service industries and in state and local government. While the service sector was healthy for the state, the growth in government contributed to Rhode Island's difficulties. The multifarious factions of the Democratic party, reflecting different town organizations, personalities, and ethnic groups which moved into office after the "Bloodless Revolution" of 1935, all demanded their share of rewards for loyal service. In the years since World War II, the growth of government employment in Rhode Island has far outdistanced every sector of the economy. A portion of these jobs undoubtedly resulted from the escalating role of government in providing social services through New Deal, New Frontier, and Great Society programs; however, many government jobs were patronage positions awarded through the "politics of gratification." Repeatedly, the loyal were given jobs somewhere in the maze of bureaus, commissions, and boards. The building and maintenance of the Democratic party has meant places for the various elements within the party, favorable legislation for labor unions, and attractive pension arrangements for the patronage-appointed public employees. These practices have generated problems in the operations of the state's two largest institutions: the prisons and mental health facilities.

As the difficulties of the nation's prisons reached intolerable levels in the 1970s, a study described the Adult Correctional Institution in Rhode Island as "one of the worst prisons" in America. Murders, suicides, beatings, drugs, riots, and disorders occurred almost daily by the late 1970s. And, instead of officials running the prison, it was actually controlled by the prison guards' union and a prisoners' organization. Governor Philip Noel appointed a friend, a trained agronomist without correctional experience, director of the ACI. Conditions became so bad that the federal court intervened, appointed a special prison master, and set timetables for improvement. Governor J. Joseph Garrahy hired a tough, new director, John Moran, who assembled a competent staff, abolished the National Prisoners' Rights Association, and regained control from the guards' union. Instances of violence dropped after certain disruptive prisoners were transferred out of the state and a new maximum-security facility, the Supermax, was opened. Nevertheless, in the early 1980s the ACI remained under the supervision of the courts and many of the underlying conditions persisted.

While treatment at Rhode Island's private mental health facilities such as Butler or Emma Pendleton Bradley Hospital was of high quality, the public system of care deteriorated to scandalous levels. Other states took advantage of Great Society programs to establish comprehensive mental health centers but Rhode Islanders felt that the antiquated Institute of Mental Health met their needs. The IMH tended to be a warehouse for the mentally ill, and it nearly lost national accreditation in 1974. The quality of care was poor and unprofessional, but attempts of new administrators

The principal buildings of the American Screw Company at Randall Square stood empty for the most part from the time the company left the state in 1946 until arsonists destroyed them in a massive fire on July 9, 1971. A similar fate has befallen a number of abandoned industrial properties. Courtesy, Providence Journal Company

such as Joseph Bevilaqua and Robert Becker after 1975 to change the IMH from a custodial facility to a therapeutic hospital collided with an entrenched employees' union. The union's attitude was typified by its president, who responded to the suggestion that all should be concerned about the patients by saying, "I'm not. I'm here to represent my members, that's it. If you want somebody to represent the patients, get somebody else." Deteriorating conditions and the inability to reform the IMH resulted in its being temporarily denied accreditation in 1981. The situation improved as the IMH accelerated its program of deinstitutionalizing patients by placing them in state-operated group homes in communities throughout the state.

The shift from industrial to non-manufacturing employment was one way that the state's economy adjusted to some of its persistent problems. Rhode Island's industries were handicapped by a complete lack of local raw materials, by energy costs that were among the highest in the nation, high shipping rates, aging plants, a modestly skilled labor force, and laws which discouraged new businesses and hurt old firms—namely, unemployment benefits for strikers and soaring workmen's compensation rates. Among the drawbacks cited as long ago as 1950 by the Democratic-appointed Rhode Island Port and Industrial Commission were workmen's compensation and too generous unemployment benefits. These were part of organized labor's reward for its support of the Democratic party. The workmen's compensation tax on employers was already the highest in the nation; and despite such early warnings, actions by Democratic lawmakers in 1969 and 1974 made the benefits even more generous. The 1982 General Assembly reversed the direction and in May passed a business-supported reform of workmen's compensation. Ironically, it was a Democrat, Governor Garrahy, that told the legislature that this measure would be the most important item facing it; and he and the Democratic leadership pushed the bill through despite labor's objections and reservations. This action reflected a new reality and awareness. The new reality was that both labor union and memberhip in Rhode Island and the number of state legislators tied to unions had declined to the lowest levels in years, making the Democratic party less dependent upon organized labor. The new awareness was the general realization that the old compensation laws hindered economic development by making Rhode Island unattractive to prospective industries.

In 1950 the Rhode Island Port and Industrial Commission also urged the state to join 22 other states in establishing a professionally run department of economic development. In 1951 Governor Dennis J. Roberts had the vision to create the Rhode Island Economic Development Council, which centralized the process of planning,

A worker in an unidentified jewelry plant casts molten precious metal on June 24, 1981. The Providence Journal *expose articles on the industry uncovered numerous safety violations, toxic fumes, and unsanitary working conditions in this and many other plants. The Manufacturing Jewelers & Silversmiths of America, a trade association, has denied these findings, rejected health surveys, and dismissed occupational illnesses as the result of "ignorance" on the part of the workers. Photo by Bob Thayer. Courtesy, Providence Journal Company*

promotion, research, and development. Under its first two directors, Harry Whitney, a retired executive of the Nicholson File Company, and Thomas Monahan, president of the Providence Body Company, the council actively campaigned to stem the tide of economic decline and population exodus from central cities. Among the reports and studies it produced was a 1953 survey of industrial conditions. It told the same old story: antiquated buildings, outdated equipment, conservative management, failure to exploit synthetics, growing militancy of the textile unions, southern competition, and high transportation and energy costs. The major drawbacks cited in making Rhode Island attractive for new industries was the scarcity of zoned industrial land and the multitude of old plants. "The Rhode Island scene is dotted with 50- and 100-year-old multi-storied plants which are more symbols of antiquity than of progress," the survey warned. As more factories closed and insufficient new industry moved to the state, the press and business community called for drastic action. Not until Governor Roberts appointed Adolph

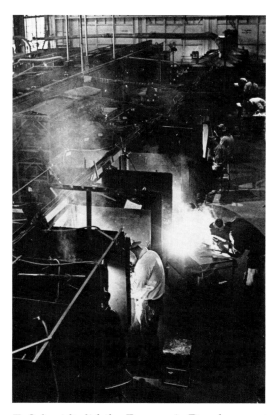

T. Schmidt did the Economic Development Council have professional leadership.

Schmidt was an excellent choice. As chairman of the council, Schmidt set out to improve Rhode Island's economic climate. Working closely with the business community and the legislature, his agency launched a movement for better highways, zoning ordinances designed for industrial purposes in land-rich towns, and development of industrial parks outside of congested cities. It also pressed for the creation of the Rhode Island Industrial Development Authority. The latter had the power to extend low-interest loans of up to $3 million to each firm for building new plants; later the power to finance new equipment was added. Despite the recession of the late 1950s, the council had a banner harvest in the next few years: over $300 million were invested in new plants; Raytheon, Leviton, Kenney Manufacturing, and Amperex Electronic Corporation located plants here, new industrial parks sprang up all over rural Rhode Island, and thousands of new jobs were secured. Although the Navy's departure temporarily crippled the state, the Economic

Development Council under the direction of its new head, James Robertson, acquired much of the surplus land, and by 1982 had sold or leased portions of it to industrial concerns. While the state still received its share of bad press about the economic climate, the situation greatly improved; and for the first time in the state's history orderly, planned industrial development restored a sense of optimism about the future.

The council also worked to improve the vocational training system. In the 1950s Rhode Island experienced great difficulties in enticing prospective companies to locate here, and one reason was the relatively unskilled work force. National enrollment in vocational education classes was more than 5 percent of the industrial work force, but in Rhode Island it was only one percent. Not until Governor John Chafee signed a bill to create a vocational school in 1964 did Rhode Island begin to correct this deficiency. The William Davies Vocational School opened in September 1971, but the state still had a large unskilled labor pool which was continually refreshed by new waves of immigrants in the 1970s and 1980s. In 1982 Rhode Island's workers were among the most highly unionized in the nation, but the average weekly manufacturing wage was almost the country's lowest, higher only than Mississippi and North Carolina. Textiles and jewelry still accounted for nearly 40,000 of Rhode Island's 125,000 manufacturing jobs, and these industries hired large numbers of women and unskilled men and paid them low wages. Because of a large pool of unskilled labor, firms that require highly skilled workers have been reluctant to move to the state; and local businesses, such as Brown & Sharpe, have often recruited people in other states and even abroad.

The problems and weaknesses that plagued Rhode Island's economy in general have affected the older urban areas more severely and deeply than other parts of the state. The aging industrial areas have been the centers of most of the dislocations and decay. Cities which had formerly boasted of their economic power and population growth had to cope with the

These welders are fabricating pieces for nuclear-powered submarine hulls being produced at Electric Boat, a division of General Dynamics, in 1974 at Quonset Point. When the Navy withdrew from the state, Electric Boat was the first industrial tenant to occupy former aircraft hangers and other facilities. In 1981 the company completed a new gigantic hull assembly plant. Offshore oil drilling companies now use the former base as their supply and repair depot. Courtesy, Providence Journal Company

John O. Pastore, the son of Italian immigrants, became Governor in October 1945 when J. Howard McGrath resigned to become U.S. Attorney General. Next he became United States Senator in December 1950, making him the first Italian-American to serve in the Senate. He remained there until he resigned in 1976. Courtesy, Providence Journal Company

reality of decline every decade. On the other hand, suburban areas and the southern portions of the state, where industrial parks and undeveloped land beckoned, grew substantially. People moved to the suburbs, South County, and Aquidneck Island. The state's population increased each decade (except for the 1970s when the Navy left); but Providence, Woonsocket, Pawtucket, and Central Falls all lost inhabitants. Providence had over 250,000 people in 1940, but it has since declined by more than 40 percent. The exodus in the 1950s was so great that the decline was the second highest among cities in the nation. Except for areas on the borders of Johnston and North Providence, all parts of the capital city experienced population loss; and it was most pronounced in the central city areas. In 1900 Providence had been proud to be the 20th largest city in America, but by 1980 it was 98th on the list.

The heart of each city was filled with old factories, dilapidated tenements, and abandoned houses. Companies that stayed in Rhode Island followed the interstate highways and, with state-supported industrial mortgages, headed for the newly created industrial parks. Likewise, upwardly mobile ethnics and the new middle class headed for Johnston, Cranston, Barrington, Warwick, and other towns, leaving behind deteriorated housing around the closed factories and mills. Urban blight spread as the poor became increasingly concentrated

in the central cities, and decaying neighborhoods fell to neglect, vandalism, and arson. Between 1966 and 1980, for example, more than 40 percent of the housing units in South Providence were destroyed, and substantial demolition occurred in the neighborhoods of Smith Hill, Federal Hill, and Fox Point. At a time when thousands of new dwellings were being built in the state, the older cities suffered a net loss.

The older cities have been ground down by the lower millstone of rising welfare and social costs and the upper millstone of a falling revenue base. Empty factories and boarded-up tenements bring no revenue. The rootedness of the poor, the influx of immigrants, and the exodus of the middle class compounded the problem. Swaths were cut through both Pawtucket and Providence in the 1950s and 1960s for the interstate highway system; and while decidedly necessary, taxable property disappeared in its path. Rhode Island ranks sixth in the nation in its percentage of elderly, and veterans constitute an unusually large proportion of the population. Their political power and a sense of generosity and appreciation for both the elderly and veterans produced tax exemptions for them which increased city revenue problems.

Providence in 1982 held about 17 percent of Rhode Island's total population; yet it had 35 percent of the welfare recipients of the entire state. Moreover, Providence

FACING PAGE, TOP: J. Joseph Garrahy, Governor of Rhode Island since 1977, is the son of Irish immigrants. He began his political career as a state senator in 1962 from the Smith Hill area of Providence. He became deputy majority leader in the senate in 1967 and then won four terms as Lieutenant Governor between 1968 and 1974. Courtesy, J. Joseph Garrahy

BOTTOM: Dennis J. Roberts, Mayor of Providence from 1941 to 1951 and Governor from 1951 to 1959, had a distinguished career of public service. Both as Mayor and as Governor, he championed revitalization of industry, reforms in government at both levels (which brought him to the chairmanship of the 1964 Rhode Island Constitutional Convention), and urban renewal for Providence. After leaving politics, he worked to improve public education as a member of the State Board of Regents (1969-1973). Courtesy, Dennis J. Roberts

THIS PAGE: In 1869 the State of Rhode Island purchased land in Cranston and subsequently located most of its institutions there. The old prison on Cove Street in Providence was abandoned and prisoners moved to this new facility—the Adult Correctional Institution—in 1878. Courtesy, Providence Public Library

had more than three quarters of the state's minority welfare cases while cities like Warwick and Cranston had less than one percent. A 1976 study of Central Falls, the tiniest, poorest, most densely populated city, concluded that the city's situation was almost hopeless. It recommended that Central Falls be merged with Pawtucket or Lincoln, but neither of these neighbors cared to shoulder such a burden.

Since World War II the suburbanization of the Providence metropolitan area has produced a boom for the outlying towns. The Garden City development in Cranston began in 1947 as the state's first planned suburban shopping center, and the nearby Dean Estates attracted professional and business people. Subsequently, the huge shopping malls in the towns of Warwick and Lincoln and numerous smaller ones drained the cities of their retail business. One after another of Providence's downtown department stores have either moved to the malls or gone out of business. Providence, which in 1953 commanded 46 percent of the state's retail business, had less than 20 percent in 1982. The suburban, southern, and western parts of the state grew appreciably; but Newport County increased almost four times as fast as the state from 1940 to 1960, and Middletown experienced a 275 percent growth in the 1970s despite the departure of the Navy.

The post-World War II urban decay and exodus from the cities did not go unnoticed, and over the next quarter century various plans to stem the tide and improve the quality of life were advanced. In Providence, Mayor Dennis J. Roberts, the beneficiary of the 1939 "Charter Revolution," employed his newly acquired powers and federal money to initiate plans for a revitalized capital city. In 1943 he accepted the resignation of the entire Planning Commission and appointed a new one with expanded powers, more money, and professional planners. Three years later the commission issued the city's first master plan, something that had been sought since 1914 when the commission was first created. The master plan was devoid of boosterism and its accompanying report was a masterpiece of reality. "This report should not be *alarming*," it pro-

nounced, because "bigger is not synonymous with better." It predicted that Providence's population would continue to decline, that the number of elderly would increase substantially, that the number of immigrants would be smaller, and that blacks and other minority groups would most likely increase. The planners advanced several modest improvement projects: demolition of blighted areas, more units of federally subsidized housing, improvements in vehicular traffic and public transportation facilities, increased parking for shoppers, and a general face-lift for downtown.

Unfortunately, little from this plan became reality because the city faced staggering financial troubles amid a declining tax base. In 1960 a second master plan called for the expenditure of $102 million in urban improvements, including the relocation of the railroad tracks and terminal, a civic center for sports and entertainment, and a pedestrian mall in the shopping district. The Westminster Mall and the Civic Center were constructed, but the plan to relocate the railroad, despite approval by the New Haven Railroad, was shelved because of its prohibitive cost. In the meantime, the city established the Providence Redevelopment Agency to channel federal funds for civic improvement, private interests launched the Industrial Development Foundation of Rhode Island, and students and faculty of the Rhode Island School of Design drew up an imaginative but impractical design for downtown called "Interface." Interface failed to attract the support of the business community because the design advocated the closing of the city's center to vehicular traffic, something merchants did not need in the face of falling retail sales and reduced parking.

By the 1970s Providence's financial situation had improved somewhat and the Great Society programs pumped huge sums of money into inner cities. By the end of the decade, the city had cleared and redeveloped the burned-out Randall Square area and almost all of the blighted sections of North Main Street. A new hotel, state office buildings, a medical facility, and housing for the elderly and middle

class now mark the area. In 1981 the federal government completed the first phase in the development of the Roger Williams National Park on North Main Street on land that had been donated to the city in 1928 by Judge Jerome J. Hahn in memory of his father, Isaac Hahn, who had been the state's first Jew elected to public office. Along South Main Street, old warehouses were converted to attractive shops, offices, and apartments; neighborhoods such as Federal Hill were revitalized with bricked streets, new lights, and individualized street signs. Just as they did in the 1920s, the banking and business community proclaimed their faith in their city and erected the Hospital Trust and 40 Westminster Tower skyscrapers in the financial district and reopened the Biltmore Hotel as a luxury hostelry. In addition, the state government infused new life near a refurbished Westminster Mall when it dedicated the new J. Joseph Garrahy Judicial Complex in 1981, the first building financed by the Public Building Authority.

The hopes for revitalization of downtown Providence received a substantial boost in 1982. In January the city announced that federal officials had approved a $68-million Capital Center Development program, and the Fleet National Bank revealed plans to build a $50-million office complex next to its headquarters facing Kennedy Plaza. The Capital Center project called for the relocation of the railroad tracks and train station to the foot of the State House lawn, a proposal that had been advanced shortly after the "Chinese Wall" had been constructed before the turn of the century. This project would make over 30 acres of land available to private investors for offices, shops, and apartment complexes and shape a second downtown. The Fleet National Bank's office complex would be the largest, most expensive office building ever built in the state and was designed to meet the growing demand for first-class office space in the city.

To make room for urban revitalization, some thought it necessary to demolish some of the state's rich, albeit decaying, architectural heritage; yet much of it has been preserved, restored, and placed on the National Register for Historic Places. Major credit for this accomplishment must be given to two remarkable and visionary women: Antoinette Downing of Providence and Katherine Urquhart Warren of Newport. After her extensive architectural study, *Early Homes of Rhode Island*, Antoinette Downing participated in a citywide historic survey of Newport, and in 1952 she was asked to prepare a survey of Providence so that historic houses could be saved from highway construction. When she learned that the oldest part of Providence was scheduled for demolition, she secured funds from federal housing authorities and the backing of John Nicholas Brown, and launched the Providence Preservation Society in 1956. Her efforts and those of hundreds of volunteers saved the historic College Hill area and turned its houses into the showplace of Providence. But she saved more than College Hill.

In 1963 Governor John Chafee selected her to organize the Rhode Island Historic Preservation Commission. Since then this agency has acted as a watchdog over the entire state, saved many buildings, encouraged private developers to renovate rather than raze, and conducted valuable surveys of historic buildings in almost every town in the state. Other communities have benefited from the work of Antoinette Downing. For example, the towns of Wickford, Kingston, Newport, and Woonsocket also established preservation commissions and historic districts. These efforts immeasurably improved the aesthetic quality of Rhode Island and lured thousands of tourists to the Ocean State. In fact, Downing became a nationally recognized authority on historic preservation, and she was frequently consulted by agencies all over the country.

In Newport, preservation and planning merged after World War II to create an attractive city and tourist magnet. While the rest of the state encouraged industrial development, planning in Newport heeded the advice of a 1926 report by a well-known New England planner, Arthur A. Shurtleff. "Industrial developments are incompatible with the enhancement of the

This view of Garden City in Cranston dates from 1953. Begun in 1947, Garden City was a 233-acre development that included single-family homes, clusters of apartment buildings, a school, and the state's first suburban shopping center. While Garden City's shopping center has been eclipsed by newer and larger malls, such as the Midland, Warwick, and Lincoln malls, it remains Rhode Island's only planned suburban shopping community. From the Rhode Island Development Council. Courtesy, Providence Public Library

city," he wrote, "and should be regarded as a liability." Eight additional planning reports up to 1962 expressed much the same view. Although industrial development did take a backseat in Newport, plans for a better city never fully materialized. The powerful and rich secluded themselves on Ocean Drive and Bellevue Avenue, the Navy occupied the upper harbor and surrounding land, and those who worked for and serviced both of them clustered in the town's run-down colonial castoffs. However, after drastic reductions in war contracts and installations by 1947, some Newporters suggested that the city was at the "crossroads of destiny." Some of the well-to-do summer residents had departed, others had put their cottages up for sale, and still others were simply troubled. After witnessing the construction of the "terrifyingly modern" high school across from her cottage, Idle Hour, Mrs. John Payson Adams (Muriel Vanderbilt) said she feared that Bellevue Avenue "will inevitably succumb to subdividers who will finish the place."

Although a roofing contractor by the name of Louis J. Chartier did buy some cottages on Ocean Drive and converted them into apartments that rented for $5,000 a year, most of the others were spared because of the work of Katherine Urquhart Warren. In 1945 she saved the Hunter House from destruction, launched the Preservation Society of Newport County shortly thereafter, and in 1948 persuaded Countess Szechenyi (Gladys Vanderbilt) to open the family mansion, the Breakers, to the public. Soon several cottages, including the Marble House and the Elms, came under the Society's care and were opened to the public. By 1956 the *Wall Street Journal* carried an article on Newport titled "Hometown U.S.A.," and quoted Mrs. Warren as saying, "All we need is leadership. Money is no object at all. I could raise $100,000 or $200,000 over the lunch table any day in the week. If we only had someone who could take charge." She was too modest. She herself took charge of the preservation movement. While the Preservation Society of Newport County concentrated much of its energy on mansions, tobacco heiress Doris Duke established the

Newport Restoration Foundation in 1968. It purchased houses, restored them to their colonial state, and rented them with strict regulations.

Newport's summer cottages and some colonial homes were saved, but its lifeline was its harbor and wharfs; and these were in deplorable condition when the Navy departed. That area, full of boisterous bars and honky-tonks, was called "Blood Alley" by the locals. But city planners recognized that the city was "adrift from the Navy pullout and tourism would be the life raft." Under the Newport Development Agency the entire wharf area was redeveloped with modern shops and restaurants in both the Brick Market and Bowen's Wharf, America's Cup Avenue was tastefully laid out, and nearby two new hotels and a marina were built. Tourism had already received a boost when, in 1969, the state opened the Newport Bridge, a stunning suspension bridge, the longest in New England, across the East Passage of Narragansett Bay between Jamestown and Newport. Then, as part of the proposed Bay Islands Park, the state spruced up Fort Adams and opened it to promoters of summer concerts. The yachting industry and crowds have never been larger.

The boom was good for the city's work force, which had one of the lowest unemployment rates in the state in 1980, and for retail establishments, which collected over $70 million from the tourist trade a year. Unquestionably, Newport successfully replaced her "solid summer economy" with a "motoring tourist economy." While some locals were glad to ride the crest of prosperity, others dreaded the tourist. One Newporter described her hometown as a "zoo, and every year it gets worse." Indeed, in Newport as in Providence, urban renewal and restoration destroyed ethnic and minority communities dependent upon low-cost housing. What was once a close-knit black community of Newport was in 1982 described by its members as totally disrupted and dispersed all over Newport County. In Providence, blacks, Hispanics, and Laotians were squeezed by higher rents as the Victorian homes on Broad and Elmwood streets were restored. The College Hill area

Antoinette Downing, chairman of the Rhode Island Historical Preservation Commission, and Alfred Van Liew, president of the Heritage Foundation of Rhode Island, stand in the General Assembly room of the Old State House (built ·1762) in Providence. This is where Rhode Island debated the issues of independence in 1776. The restored interior symbolized the work of preservationists all over the state. Courtesy, Antoinette Downing

opened the first portion of the sprawling Bay Islands Park system in Narragansett Bay. Boaters, picnickers, naturalists, and the adventurous gained a public treasure.

In spite of all the problems and difficulties encountered by Rhode Island in the last few decades, the state has held its own. In part, this may be attributed to the reputation of its quality of life which includes excellent recreational, educational, and health facilities. It has seaport potential and is close to the large markets of the Northeast. Life in Rhode Island is less hectic and more pleasant than in Boston or New York; and one is only minutes away from ocean beaches and forests. A substantial amount of credit should go to the men and women of vision and their will to make their dreams come true, to the federal-urban partnership, to those who long for the past but plan for a better future, and to the people of the state whose resilience has been admirable.

The New Federalism and Reaganomics promise to end the Depression-forged federal-urban dependency and return Rhode Island to its former independent ways. The reduction in entitlements and social welfare programs, the elimination of entire agencies and projects, and the cutback in assistance to local governments for water projects, transportation, and civic improvement all throw the state and towns upon their own resources. The New Federalism has struck the state almost as hard as the 1973 Navy withdrawal; but Rhode Island has more than recovered from that earlier dependency. Already it has joined with other New England states to advance regional concerns, and its congressional delegation is part of the Snowbelt caucus in Washington. But it remains to be seen whether the response of Rhode Islanders will be cooperative or individualistic, whether they will "cancel each other out" in a scramble to protect individual, special interests or if they will pull together to create a favorable climate for opportunity and growth while protecting the quality of life in the Ocean State. The history of Rhode Island would suggest that Rhode Islanders will capitalize on the opportunities and forge an advantage out of adversity.

expanded its restoration effort to the once predominantly Portuguese neighborhood of Fox Point, and tension between middle-class restorers and working-class Portuguese was not uncommon.

In rural communities, however, the pressure to preserve and to follow orderly and planned growth created problems of a different sort. Between 1970 and 1980, Foster and Glocester in the northwestern section of the state struggled to protect their agricultural heritage as city people sought homes in the quiet countryside. Zoning ordinances calling for building lots with a minimum size of five acres were enacted, but opposition from smaller landowners and from development-minded residents reduced that to three acres. Nevertheless, real-estate prices skyrocketed to such an extent that even a three-acre parcel was beyond most middle-class families. Glocester and many other rural communities all over Rhode Island have lost their Yankee majority, but they have succeeded in protecting their environment.

A major force in saving wetlands, beaches, water resources, and recreation facilities has been the state's Department of Environmental Management. It has doggedly watched over the state's natural resources, managed the park systems, protected fishing grounds, worked to clean up chemical dumps, and established solid-waste management programs. In 1981 it

RHODE ISLAND

STATE FAIR

CATTLE SHOW!

THE SIXTY-NINTH ANNIVERSARY OF THE

RHODE ISLAND SOCIETY for the
ENCOURAGEMENT OF DOMESTIC INDUSTRY!

WILL BE HELD AT

NARRAGANSETT PARK

SEPT. 23, 24, 25, 26 & 27, 1889

$17,000 IN PREMIUMS

All Departments Open to the World for Competition!

The Amusements and Attractions
Will be Multiplied, and the Display of Live Stock and Poultry will be Doubled. There will be a revelation in Art, Mechanical Science, Merchants' Miscellaneous Display, Agricultural Productions, and Articles of Household Manufacture.

It is the intention of the Executive Committee to make this Fair the Largest and Grandest ever held in New England.

Write to the Secretary for Premium List, and the Annual State Fair Bulletin.

CHAS. H. PECKHAM, - President
DAVID S. COLLINS, - - Secretary

Press of What Cheer Print, Providence, R. I.

ABOVE: Reproduced here is lithographer Moses Swett's 1829 rendition of the Providence Arcade (1828), the first indoor shopping mall in America. W & J Pendleton, Boston, 1829. RIHS (RHi x5 35)/ William C. Gucfa photo

RIGHT: Touro Synagogue (1763), the interior of which is shown here, is the oldest synagogue in the United States. Courtesy, Rhode Island Department of Economic Development

FAR RIGHT: Historic Benefit Street, Providence, has many restored 18th-century houses. It is a part of the College Hill restoration project begun in the 1950s. Courtesy, Rhode Island Department of Economic Development/Chet Browning photo

PREVIOUS PAGE: Although an industrial state, Rhode Island takes pride in its annual town, county, and state fairs. This colorful poster was for the 1889 Rhode Island State Fair. RIHS (RHi x5 46)

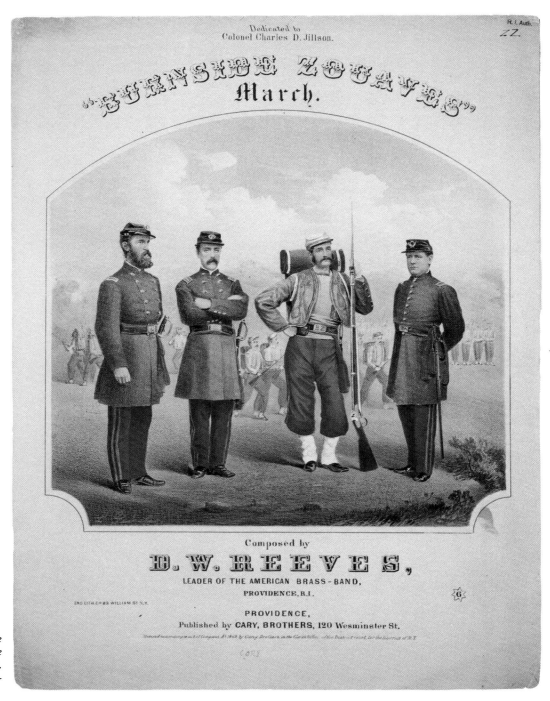

Davis W. Reeves, leader of the American Brass Band, composed the "Burnside Zouaves March" in 1868. RIHS (RHi x5 34)/William C. Gucfa photo

1174.▪ Providence, R. I. Exchange Place, showing the departure of the First R. I. Regiment in 1861.

FACING PAGE, TOP: The Household Sewing Machine Company distributed advertising cards such as this one. The machines were manufactured by the Providence Tool Company in the 1870s as part of its diversification efforts. RIHS (RHi x5 39)

THIS PAGE, TOP: The departure of the First R.I. Regiment from Exchange Place in April 1861 is shown on this color postcard. RIHS (RHi x5 38)

LEFT: Pawtucket, R.I., the birthplace of the Industrial Revolution in America, is seen from the south in this 1870s handcolored engraving by J.S. Lincoln, published by Terry, Pelton & Co. RIHS (RHi x5 37)

FACING PAGE: A shipping label decorated with the trademark for Hope Muslin, produced by the Lonsdale Company of the Blackstone Manufacturing Company, dates from the late 19th century. RIHS (RHi x5 33)/William C. Gucfa photo

LEFT: One of America's architectural treasures is the Meeting House of the First Baptist Church in America. It was built in Providence between 1774 and 1775. Roger Williams had gathered the congregation in 1638. L.C. Lemons photo

BELOW LEFT: "The Breakers," (1893-1895), the summer cottage of Cornelius Vanderbilt, was designed by Richard Morris Hunt. Today it is the star attraction of the Preservation Society of Newport County. L.C. Lemons photo

BELOW: At the turn of the century the Mount Hope, a Block Island-Newport ferryboat, steamed into Newport Harbor, which was filled with ships of the Atlantic Fleet—part of America's "Great White Fleet." Chromolithograph by Forbes, Boston. RIHS (RHi x5 42)

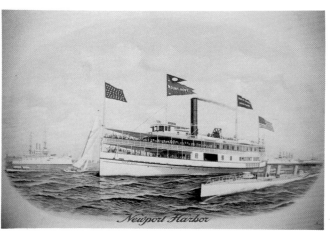

RIGHT: Narragansett Bay resorts did a thriving business in the 19th century as illustrated by this handcolored, photomechanical reproduction of the opening of the bathing season at Narragansett Pier in the 1890s. Drawing by Charles H. Provost from Harper's Weekly. RIHS (RHi x5 41)

FACING PAGE: An art festival takes place at Narragansett. In the background is "The Towers," (1883-1886), the last section of the Narragansett Pier Casino, designed by Stanford White. Courtesy, Rhode Island Department of Economic Development/Chet Browning photo

LEFT: Holy Rosary Church in the Portuguese neighborhood of Fox Point, Providence, sponsors an annual festival during the second and third weekends in September in honor of Our Lady of the Rosary and Santo Cristo. Courtesy, Rhode Island Department of Economic Development

BELOW LEFT: Part of the renewal of downtown Woonsocket is the refurbished Providence & Worcester Railroad station, built in 1882. Courtesy, Rhode Island Department of Economic Development/Chet Browning photo

ABOVE: The battlements of the Cranston Street Armory (built 1907) lend a touch of the mythical Camelot to Providence. Krisjohn Horvat photo

LEFT: This view of South Main Street, Providence, features Providence County Court House (1929-1931), the Joseph Brown House (1774), and the Old Stone Bank (constructed 1854, gold dome added 1898). Courtesy, Rhode Island Department of economic Development

ABOVE: A worker at Gorham polishes a large silver bowl. Courtesy, Rhode Island Department of Economic Development

ABOVE RIGHT: Joseph Mendonza is one of Newport's commercial fishermen. Courtesy, Rhode Island Department of Economic Development/Chet Browning photo

RIGHT: Sunset at one of the many marinas along Narragansett Bay and the south shore. Courtesy, Rhode Island Department of Economic Development/Chet Browning photo

RIGHT: The Heritage Day celebration in Newport, Rhode Island, features the Artillery Company of the Newport, R.I., Militia. This organization was chartered in 1741 and it is the nation's oldest active military organization. Courtesy, Rhode Island Department of Economic Development/Chet Browning photo

BELOW RIGHT: Picturesque Colt State Park in Bristol, R.I., on the eastern shore of Narragansett Bay has nearly three miles of shoreline road, picnicking, bathing, fishing, and boating facilities. Courtesy, Rhode Island Department of Economic Development/Chet Browning photo

ABOVE: A family enjoys the refurbished Providence Arcade. Courtesy, Rhode Island Department of Economic Development

LEFT: The Providence skyline as seen from Fox Point on the historic East Side, 1982. Courtesy, Rhode Island Department of Economic Development/Chet Browning photo

Chapter Fourteen

PARTNERS IN PROGRESS

THE ECONOMY OF Rhode Island, while prosperous almost from the time the first white settlers arrived, can easily be divided into four chronological stages: agriculture, sea trade, the Industrial Revolution, and diversification.

Colonists settled the two major towns, Providence at the head of Narragansett Bay, and Newport at the mouth of the bay. While Providence remained for almost a century a sleepy agrarian community, it was clear by the beginning of the 18th century that the political and economic leadership in Rhode Island resided in Newport— with its wealthy merchants in almost total control. The town's location made it an ideal port, and the golden age of trade resulted in the erection of distinguished residences, churches, and public buildings. Other towns along the bay also reaped the rewards of this prosperous sea trade.

However, the War for Independence tipped the economic scales in favor of Providence. Newport had become an occupied city: British troops controlled the harbor and effectively cut off most trade. Providence first served as the wartime capital, then, as Newport slowly became impotent, it became the business and commercial center as well. After the war ended, Providence maintained its stellar place in the state's economic life.

The following decades saw the city's rise to mercantile prominence in the China Trade. This commerce, as well as trade with the East Indies and India, provided an interim of economic stability, and it was this lucrative business that helped merchants accumulate the capital for later industrialization of Rhode Island.

The Industrial Revolution was actually rooted in the state, beginning when Moses Brown, a Quaker philanthropist from a wealthy Providence family, induced Samuel Slater, an English expert in textile machinery, to emigrate to Rhode Island. Founding the American cotton-spinning industry, they built their first mill in Pawtucket.

By mid-19th century Providence had become the center of the state's economy with its proliferation of banks, railroads, and industries—as well as its harbor. The Civil War proved to be a catalyst for the textile industry, despite a shortage of cotton, providing enormous profits for the mill owners.

With the growth of industry in Rhode Island, there emerged the ancillary institutions to serve the business community: banks to finance the industries; colleges and universities to educate the people; hospitals to care for the sick; and insurance companies, newspapers, architects, and social and cultural institutions.

Rhode Island led the nation in the production of worsted by 1900, and World War I created a tremendous demand for the mills' services. Unfortunately, this was the last hurrah for the great factories. First, labor strikes in the '20s and '30s forced many of them to close. Then, cheaper labor and production costs in the South lured away many of the remaining mills. Today only a few survive.

Although a large part of the state's financial health had been dependent on the mills, the jewelry industry, a number of companies manufacturing machine parts, and high-technology industries began to fill much of the void. Rhode Island now boasts a widely diversified economy.

Allendale Mutual Insurance Company

Allendale Mutual Insurance Company, the oldest and largest company in the Factory Mutual System, was founded in 1835. Although at one time there were as many as 40 individual companies in the system, today there are four: Allendale of Johnston, Rhode Island; Arkwright-Boston Manufacturers Mutual Insurance Company of Waltham, Massachusetts; Philadelphia

Manufacturers Mutual Insurance Company of Philadelphia; and Protection Mutual Insurance Company of Park Ridge, Illinois.

The story of Allendale is also the story of the Factory Mutual System. The concept for the company was the idea of Zachariah Allen, an engineer and enterprising Rhode Island textile mill owner. The year was 1835—a time of financial crisis. Prices were falling, mills were closing, and workers were being laid off. Fire losses were soaring and insurance rates were climbing.

Allen was concerned although his textile mill in Allendale, Rhode Island, a town he had founded in 1822, was constructed more carefully than most.

It had extra-thick plank floors and a large number of fire-extinguishing pumps and pipes, hydrants, and hoses, precautions he had taken to protect his mill from fire damage. He was confident that his insurance company would recognize his efforts and reduce the rate on his property.

Allen could not convince his insurance company, however, which prompted him to turn his attention to the subject of insurance and to study it in detail. He was impressed with the idea of mutual insurance, but none of the companies handling this coverage were insuring factories. Still, Allen was certain that the mutual method could be adapted to serve the textile field.

The new headquarters of Allendale Insurance, overlooking a serene pond in Johnston, Rhode Island, was opened in 1973.

Preventive care and protective equipment also occupied his thoughts, perhaps more than insurance. Only a few mill owners were making an effort along these lines, and the stock insurance companies offered little incentive for them to improve their fire-prevention methods. The insurance companies were acknowledging no distinction between the greater risks and the lesser ones, and none were making efforts to analyze industrial fires to determine their causes.

Allen presented a plan to a group of his friends and associates in Providence. He proposed the formation of an insurance company consisting exclusively of manufacturers operating well-constructed properties carefully protected from fire. He insisted that the

In 1835 enterprising industrialist Zachariah Allen formulated ideas that led to the founding of Allendale Mutual Insurance Company.

principal function of the officers of the new venture be the study of fire loss prevention methods. From Allen's plan came the first of the Factory Mutuals—Allendale Mutual Insurance Company.

The firm has always specialized in the insuring of large accounts, comprising industrial and institutional properties with superior risk qualifications. Today more than 400 of these accounts are purchasing over $100 million of insurance, and 50 other accounts are purchasing in excess of one billion dollars.

The dedication of Allendale and the Factory Mutual System to minimizing loss to industrial and institutional property is most clearly expressed by the Factory Mutual Engineering Corporation/Engineering Association Research Corporation, often described as "the greatest reservoir of knowledge of industrial loss prevention in the world."

Allendale's headquarters is located in a sleek, modern building, constructed in the early 1970s at the edge of a pond in Johnston, Rhode Island, north of Providence.

Amtrol Inc.

The story of Amtrol dates back to 1946 when Chester H. Kirk, a 29-year-old married man with two children and $400, founded American Tube Products, Inc., in a small workshop in a converted mill building in the Natick section of West Warwick. Today Kirk is chairman and chief executive officer), along with his brother, Kenneth Kirk (operations), and Albert N. D'Amico (financial), runs a firm that employs more than 1,000 persons worldwide and has annual sales of more than $60 million.

Four years after Kirk founded his venture, he formed a second company, Kinned Tube Corporation, to manufacture heat exchangers and baseboard-heating elements. Meanwhile, Extrol, a product based on the concept of permanently separating air from water with a diaphragm for the control of water-heating systems, was conceived by Kirk. The Extrol was so successful that within a year sales reached $398,000, primarily due to the sale of the Extrol line to major boiler manufacturers who then added the Extrol products to their boilers for increased efficiency.

Within a few years 90 percent of packaged boilers sold included Extrols. The result was that wholesalers began specifying the Extrol to replace plain steel expansion tanks for use with boilers. In the late 1950s Extrol prod-ucts were introduced into Europe, followed a few years later by the Well-X-Trol pressure tank for water well systems.

A new application was devised for the deep-drawn steel cylinder in 1967, resulting in major production for chemical companies packaging refrigerant gases. In 1968 C.R. Bernstrom Company, a local manufacturer of heat exchangers and air separators, was purchased as a subsidiary, and in Germany the firm introduced the large AX Extrol to the commercial and industrial market. Within four years, with new automation and full production lines for all applications of the company's cylinders, sales approached $20 million and a new plant was built outside Dallas in Plano, Texas.

In 1972 the corporation purchased 35 acres of land in West Warwick and constructed larger, more modern facilities. The following year American Tube and Controls was reorganized and became Amtrol Inc. Two years later a new plant was acquired in Nashville, Tennessee.

When the company reached the $50-million mark in sales a year later, the officers began planning future growth. These plans included the acquisition of a steel-processing company in Massachusetts to augment Amtrol's requirements for its basic commodity, steel.

Its position in the world market was strengthened by the creation of Amtrol International Inc., a wholly owned subsidiary established to administer marketing, sales, and distribution organizations in Southeast Asia and in Central Europe. Another wholly owned subsidiary, Automatic Metal Blanking, Inc., was formed in 1978. Two years later an Indiana pump manufacturing concern, Thrush Products, Inc., was acquired. Amtrol today is moving into the production of equipment for solar systems as well as expanding and improving its other energy-efficient heating products.

Chester H. Kirk, founder and chairman of the board.

Amtrol Inc. corporate headquarters in West Warwick, Rhode Island.

Amperex Electronic Corporation

Amperex Electronic Corporation, with headquarters in Slatersville, Rhode Island, has two plants in the state with 850 employees. The company, an independently managed sub-

in Brooklyn, and eventually changed the name to Amperex.

The main product line remained electron tubes, but it was broadened to include large transmitting and power tubes, as well as diathermy tubes used in medical equipment. Throughout the '30s and '40s, Amperex manufactured the largest line of diathermy tubes in the country. The company also developed a variety of new kinds of tubes, including one that was used in atomic research during World War II.

obsolete Brooklyn operation an moved to a new plant in Hicksvill Long Island, in 1951. Its products no included sophisticated components fc aircraft guidance systems, military an commercial microwave tubes, vacuu tubes for radio and television transmi ters and receivers, and mobile con munications products.

In 1960 Amperex built a facility i Slatersville, Rhode Island, a move tha coincided with the mushroomin growth of solid state semiconducto

Amperex's newest facility is in Smithfield, Rhode Island. A major high-technology manufacturing complex is located in Slatersville, Rhode Island.

sidiary of North American Philips Corporation, makes substantial annual investments in Rhode Island for plant expansion, new equipment, and energy conservation.

Amperex began in 1932 as a small Brooklyn, New York, company named Duovac, making electron tubes for the emerging radio business. Working in small quarters in the shadow of the Brooklyn Bridge, the founders (including a professor of engineering at New York University) had the foresight to realize the importance of this new form of communication; as business grew, they refined their products, moved the company to larger facilities

One of the first radar tubes made by Amperex was exported to England for use in that country's radar equipment during the war.

The year 1944 was a major landmark for the small Brooklyn-based firm; Amperex was among the first companies purchased by North American Philips Corporation, which today ranks among the 150 largest industrial organizations in the United States. Amperex continued to expand its development and production of industrial and vacuum tubes for the communications industry, and by the end of the 1940s was deeply involved in nurturing the infant television industry.

Following the exodus of urban population to the suburbs after the war, the company discontinued its

An enlarged view of a high reliability hybrid electronic circuit. The actual size is approximately 3/4" square.

Amperex's Plumbicon® T.V. camera tube was awarded an Emmy for its contribution to high-quality television reception.

electronic devices; the Slatersville plant was built to manufacture semiconductor devices. Amperex found an excellent work force in Rhode Island, since many of the state's textile mills had recently moved to the South. The excellent local labor supply and the high quality of life combined to make Rhode Island a positive environment for Amperex.

In 1977 Amperex had moved its cor-

Large-scale hydrogen ovens enable precise time and temperature control in the manufacturing process.

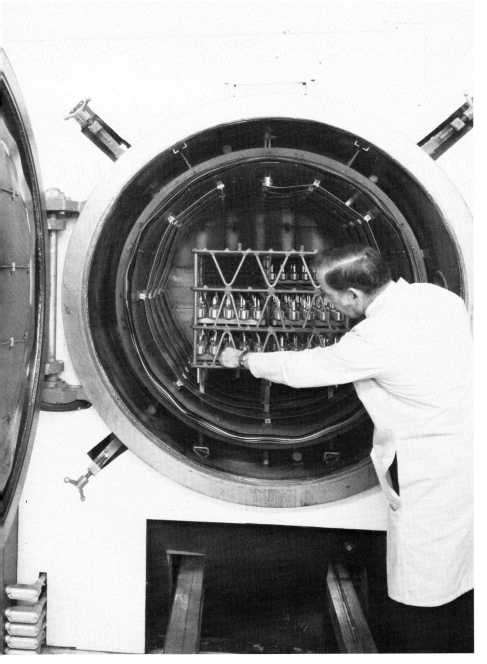

porate headquarters from Hicksville, New York, to Slatersville, Rhode Island. While Amperex is owned by North American Philips Corporation, each of the Philips companies (which include such familiar names as Norelco, Magnavox, Sylvania, Philco, and Baker Furniture) has its own president, corporate staff, and executive management team. In addition, each of the Amperex plants in Rhode Island and New York has a division manager.

The Slatersville division, which employs 600 people, makes electro optical devices and semiconductor devices. The most well-known television camera tube, the Plumbicon® is made in the Slatersville facility. Developed in the early '60s, these tubes demand the utmost precision in manufacture and require the use of ultra-clean facilities and sophisticated processing techniques. The Plumbicon® tube earned an Emmy award from the National Academy of Television Arts and Sciences for "its ability to make television reception comparable to the quality of movie film." The slender golden Emmy award resides in the Slatersville plant, where employees take pride in showing it to visitors.

In 1977 Amperex opened a new facility in Smithfield, Rhode Island. At present the facility is used to house various corporate administrative offices including corporate accounting and a centralized electronic data processing activity.

The Slatersville facility consists of two buildings totaling 135,000 square feet, while the Smithfield facility has one building of 90,000 square feet. In all, Amperex employment now totals over 1,700 people, including those at its Hicksville, Long Island, plant, its Saugerties, New York, plant, and its nationwide sales force.

One of the major reasons for Amperex's growth over the past two and a half decades has been its ability to develop new products and to expand its manufacturing and technology base to serve an ever expanding high-technology component marketplace. Rhode Island, with its stable labor force and high ranking with regard to quality of life, has since 1960 continued to be a significant recipient of Amperex's capital expenditures.

Belcourt Castle

Belcourt Castle on Newport's famous Bellevue Avenue was completed in 1894 as a "summer cottage" for 35-year-old bachelor Oliver H.P. Belmont. The 60-room castle built under the guidance of America's foremost architect, Richard Morris Hunt, took three years to finish with 300 European craftsmen working on it. Hunt, who built many of the great mansions in Newport, used as his inspiration for Belcourt the Renaissance chateaus in France.

The magnificent structure is of granite from Westerly, Rhode Island, brick, and rough cast, with vast mansard roofs, huge oval dormers of stonework and copper, and handwrought iron and bronze grills, balconies, and gates, reminiscent of the Louis XIII hunting lodge at Versailles. The authentically designed wrought iron and bronze entrance gates decorated with 23-carat gold were designed by Donald Tinney and erected in 1981. The total cost of Belcourt Castle was about four million dollars.

The mansion remained in the Belmont family until 1940. Eventually Louis and Elaine Lorillard, tobacco magnates, purchased it for their Newport Jazz Festival workshops, lectures, and seminars. In the fall of 1956 the Tinney family bought Belcourt Castle for a private residence and as a home for their extensive collection of art treasures and furniture from Europe and the Orient. Today the restored mansion is open to the public for tours and private functions.

Oliver Hazard Perry Belmont was the son of August Belmont, a German banker, who with Rothschild backing established his own bank in New York City in 1837. Oliver's mother, Caroline Slidell Perry, was the daughter of Commodore Matthew Calbraith Perry, the American naval officer whose diplomacy opened trade with Japan. He was born in 1858 and named for his grand uncle, Oliver Hazard Perry, famous for his victory at the Battle of Lake Erie.

Little is known of Oliver H.P. Belmont's youth. His health was never good, and he was unable to take up

Belcourt Castle, with its 60 rooms and vast mansard roofs, is seen here in this recent aerial photo.

The Portuguese Coronation Coach was built in Belcourt Castle by members of the Tinney family and took three years to complete. The four-ton coach can be seen by visitors to the castle.

summer residence in his new castle until a year after completion. He remained a bachelor at Belcourt Castle, however, only a short time. He married another "summer cottage" resident, Mrs. Alva Smith Vanderbilt, who by her first marriage was the mother of Consuelo Vanderbilt, later the ninth Duchess of Marlborough. Belmont died 12 years after he was married. But during that time summers at Belcourt Castle were renowned for their lavish entertainments. During formal affairs, the Belmonts' liveried footmen were stationed on every sixth step of the Grand Staircase holding golden candelabra to light the way for the guests.

Belcourt Castle was indeed a splendid place in which to entertain. The Grand Staircase, a replica of one formerly in the Cluny Museum in Paris, connects the first-, second-, and third-floor grand halls. It is suspended from

the top floor and is constructed entirely of delicately hand-carved oak, a work that took three years to complete. The master bathroom had the first shower in Newport. The Italian Banquet Hall, the largest room in the castle, can seat 300 for dinner and 500 for concerts. The floor, of rose marble, took craftsmen from Italy three years to lay.

Visitors to Belcourt Castle will see, in addition, the magnificent architecture of Richard Morris Hunt and John Russell Pope, a remarkable collection of Oriental rugs, European furniture, stained glass, and paintings. In 1964 the Tinney family formed the Royal Arts Foundation, a nonprofit educational organization, to govern the Belcourt Castle Museum and to help ensure its future as a museum.

BIF A Unit of General Signal Corporation

The Builders Iron Foundry was organized in 1853 by Zechariah Chafee; his cousin Amos C. Barstow, the second mayor of Providence; and Apollos Richmond, who purchased the High Street Furnace Company at Coding and High streets (now Westminster Street) in Providence. This property traced its history back to the early 1800s when a blacksmith shop was located there, a shop that later was expanded into a flourishing foundry business which became Builders Iron Foundry.

Barstow was president of the new corporation; Chafee was company agent. Later stockholders included Henry Knight, Gilman Hunt, and James C. Bucklin, architect of the Providence Arcade. Stock in the company was sold to a very select group, and all prospective stock transfers were closely controlled. For almost 100 years, the firm's management was directed by a small network of prominent Rhode Island families, like the Chafees and the Barstows.

The early products of Builders Iron Foundry included ornamental ironwork, iron door and window frames, and cast-iron columns and stairways for homes and commercial buildings. As the demand for architectural iron declined, the company turned to the manufacture of artillery for the military, among other products. During the Civil War, Builders Iron Foundry manufactured a large quantity of shot, shell, and cannons for the Union Army.

In 1880 the company introduced the Globe fitting. This special water pipe, designed by R. Austin Robertson, an officer of the firm, was used extensively by water departments in cities across the country. And in 1887 Builders Iron Foundry began manufacture of the Herschel Standard Venturi tube, the first practical device without moving parts to measure fluid flow in a closed circuit.

The business grew rapidly between 1880 and 1900, its employees increasing from 90 to more than 400. This rapid growth forced expansion to a building at the corner of Kinsley and Sims avenues in Providence in 1902. This structure had formerly housed the marble-cutting operations for the builders of Rhode Island's State House.

By the early 1950s the company emphasized highly engineered products and systems, primarily in the field of water control and filtration for private and public plants. The name "Builders Iron Foundry" was technically inaccurate and misleading, so in 1953 the name was officially changed to B-I-F Industries, Inc.

Two years later the foundry was closed, and the equipment was sold at auction. In 1961 B-I-F Industries became the BIF Division of New York Air Brake Company. The General Signal Corporation acquired New York Air Brake in 1967, and BIF became a unit of that highly diversified corporation.

Today what began as a foundry in Providence before the Civil War is recognized as a world leader in automatic flow control, in the controlled feeding and weighing of liquids and solids, and in waste treatment systems with a 591,000-square-foot modern plant in West Warwick, Rhode Island.

This is an old Builders Iron Foundry ad run in the June 19, 1913, issue of Engineering News, *which shows the type of meter register used to monitor flow through the Newark tube.*

This Venturi meter tube was cast in 1891 by Builders Iron Foundry for the Belleville Reservoir in Newark, New Jersey, and remained in operation until 1949.

Biltmore Plaza Hotel

The Biltmore Hotel in downtown Providence opened its doors to the public on June 7, 1922, amidst an era of wealth and opulence. The opening was celebrated with a banquet and a ball the night before. Twelve hundred guests, including 137 who arrived on a special train from New York City, attended the gala affair.

of its memorable debutante parties transformed the ballroom into a French country estate, complete with authentic landscaping, animals, and musicians in every corner. The general manager of the hotel, L. Duane Wallick, kept a roof garden and "aerial farm" with hens, ducks, rabbits, and monkeys. Presumably he supplied the hotel's kitchens with some of his fresh produce.

By the early 1930s, problems had developed over the recapitalization of the hotel's property, business had declined, and a bankruptcy petition was

York City in 1968 and renamed th Biltmore Hotel and Motor Inn, busi ness never really picked up, and o January 14, 1975, the hotel closed it doors after the Providence Gas Com pany turned off the gas. By now th hotel owed nearly $200,000 in unpai bills and taxes, and it had bee running at less than 20-percen occupancy.

It looked as if the hotel was finall being left to die. However, two year later, a consortium of Providence busi nesses—Textron, the Providence Jou nal Company, the Outlet Compan

The Biltmore Hotel (center) with its distinctive V-shape was only one of the many buildings in downtown Providence that suffered during the destructive 1938 Hurricane. At left is the Providence city hall and at far right, the railroad station.

The idea for a grand hotel had first been raised by the city's Chamber of Commerce during the early 1900s, but it took the energy of community leaders like Henry D. Sharpe, a son of the founder of Brown & Sharpe Manufacturing Company, to organize a civic fund-raising campaign for the money to construct such a hotel.

The unusual V-shaped design of the Biltmore was made to allow all lodgers to have outside rooms. And the 16-story building was constructed of red granite from Westerly, Rhode Island. At the time of its opening, the hotel was referred to as "a city within a city." An inventory showed the hotel included 30,000 pieces of china, 500 full-time employees, a barbershop, beauty parlor, florist's shop, drugstore, laundry, print shop, carpentry and upholstery shops, three seamstresses, a photo lab, a 600-seat ballroom, and six dining areas.

The Biltmore bloomed during the postwar prosperity of the 1920s. One

filed in 1936. It wasn't until 1947 that the hotel began to prosper again. The Sheraton Corporation had taken over the building and renamed it the Sheraton-Biltmore. And for a few brief years, the post-World War II boom once again brought lodgers, parties, and diners to the grand old hotel.

But all of this was short-lived. Hurricane Carol flooded downtown in 1954 and badly damaged the Biltmore. This coupled with the recession found the hotel failing to attract lodgers, and more and more rooms were rented for commercial use. A dwindling residential and business population in downtown also contributed to the demise of the Biltmore. Although the hotel was bought by Gotham Hotels, Inc., of New

and the Business Development Com pany of Rhode Island—bought th hotel, spent $13 million refurbishing i and renamed it the Biltmore Plaz Hotel. A ball attended by 1,200 peopl was held on February 10, 1979, and th hotel opened to the public the follow ing day. Less than a year later hote employees began a strike that was t last 11 weeks and cost the new opened hotel considerable business.

Hotels of Distinction was hired t operate the hotel and supervise i renovation. Today it is managed b Dunfey Hotels Corporation and has es tablished a reputation for, among othe things, its rooftop restauran L'Apogee, reached by a glass "Frenc lift" elevator in the lobby, the onl elevator of its kind in North Americ that is entirely free-standing and n attached to the building. Other high lights of the refurbished hotel include third-floor greenhouse restaurant, street-level cafe, an art gallery, florist shop, and hair salons.

Blue Cross of Rhode Island

Blue Cross and Blue Shield, which today are household words, had their beginnings nationally in 1929, when a plan for prepayment of hospital expenses for schoolteachers was set up by Justin Ford Kimball at Baylor University Hospital in Dallas, Texas.

The original plan provided 21 days hospital care in a semiprivate room for a monthly fee of 50 cents. The concept flourished during those early days of the Depression, and by 1932 programs began forming all across the country.

Locally, Governor William H. Vanderbilt signed an act creating the Hospital Service Corporation of Rhode Island on February 8, 1939. The new corporation, ''Blue Cross,'' was to be a voluntary, nonprofit enterprise that would sell hospitalization insurance at reasonable cost.

The organization opened an office on the third floor of the Hospital Trust Building in downtown Providence with eight employees; Kenneth D. MacColl served as its first president. Initially, only groups were eligible for coverage, but today non-group memberships are offered in several categories.

When Blue Cross outgrew its rented quarters in the mid-1940s, the board of

Banner Days were common in the early open-enrollment campaigns of Blue Cross in Rhode Island. This banner stretched across Providence's Washington Street from the Biltmore Hotel to City Hall in 1947.

directors voted to buy the Insurance Building (as it was known) at 31 Canal Street just across the river from downtown Providence. Both Blue Cross and eventually Physicians Service were housed in the handsome, slender, graystone building until 1968, when they moved to their present headquar-

When Blue Cross of Rhode Island outgrew its quarters on Canal Street in Providence in 1968, it moved to this modern building at the head of the downtown Westminster Mall.

ters at the head of Westminster Mall.

After the company had been in business in Rhode Island for about a decade, it became clear that hospital insurance was not enough; there was a growing need for prepaid medical insurance to handle doctors' bills. For four years Blue Cross negotiated with the Rhode Island Medical Society in an effort to reach agreement on such a plan. In 1949 the Rhode Island Medical Society Physicians Service, Blue Shield of Rhode Island, was established as a voluntary, nonprofit organization for the prepayment of surgical/medical bills.

Almost everyone knew about Blue Cross and Physicians Service by the mid-1950s, but not everyone was enrolled. The late Stanley Saunders, then executive director, decided something must be done to increase membership, so he launched ''Operation Saturation.'' The purpose was to visit every company, business, and shop in the state that did not have Blue Cross coverage. By 1956 enrollment increased by 100 new groups, representing 3,650 new members.

In 1973 the corporation added yet another kind of coverage when it agreed to the joint operation of Delta Dental of Rhode Island, a nonprofit dental insurance program; by April 1982 nearly 200,000 citizens of the state were policyholders.

Today enrollment in the Blue Cross plan, which began as a radical idea in 1929, provides health care benefits to eight out of 10 Rhode Islanders.

Brown and Ives

The history of the economic development of Providence would be incomplete without recognition of the influence of the Brown family. The first Brown to settle in Rhode Island was Chad Brown, who arrived in Providence with his family shortly after Roger Williams founded the town in 1636. It was, however, Chad's great-great-grandsons who left the imprint of the Brown family name so firmly etched on the business life of Providence, of Rhode Island, and of New England. In the mid-18th century, these great-great-grandsons, Nicholas, Joseph, John, and Moses, inherited from their uncle, Obadiah Brown, a prosperous business that included the manufacture and selling of spermaceti candles and a growing shipping operation.

Each of the brothers in his own way contributed to the social and economic growth of the city and the state. Joseph was more inclined to the study of philosophy, astronomy, and architecture and was instrumental in the early development of Brown University. Moses, while studious, was a lover of mechanical experiments and was responsible for bringing Samuel Slater from England to Rhode Island where together they established the first cotton mill in this country. Slater Mill still stands today in Pawtucket, Rhode Island, as a national historic site. John was the more aggressive of the brothers. Throughout his life he displayed the same confidence that had led him, as a boy, to write in his "Cipher Book" the words "John Brown the cleverest boy in Providence Town." It was no mere accident that he sent the first Rhode Island ship to China or that he built the finest house in Providence. But it was Nicholas, the eldest, who appears to have had the best balanced and most fully rounded mind of them all, and who, with his cautious and methodical business ways, founded the firm of Brown and Benson, which later became known as Brown and Ives.

By the time Nicholas died in 1791, leaving his son Nicholas and his son-in-law Thomas Poynton Ives in charge, the firm already was gaining a worldwide reputation with its shipping trade. The fleet sailed to almost all co[r]ners of the world, bringing back sug[ar] from the West Indies, gin and linse[ed] oil from Amsterdam, brandy, wine[,] fruit, and spices from the Mediterr[a]nean, hemp and new sable iron fro[m] Russia, and tea from China. The firm['s] maritime business came to a gradu[al] close after the War of 1812 as t[he] partners turned their interests to t[he] Industrial Revolution. By 1838 Brow[n] and Ives had sold its last ship, markin[g] the end of an era which had its begi[n]nings in the mid-18th century.

As its maritime fortunes were de[c]lining, however, Brown and Ives wa[s] developing a number of other busine[ss] interests, including banking, in[-] surance, turnpikes, canal buildin[g,] land investments, and cotton manufac[-] ture. Some proved more lucrative tha[n] others, especially the latter two. Th[e] firm was an early speculator in land i[n] New York State, Ohio, Vermont, Penn[-] sylvania, and, later in the 19th centur[y,] the Midwest and Far West. Closer t[o] home, the firm was involved in th[e] enormously profitable manufacture [of] cotton through its interests in severa[l] mills, including the Blackstone Mi[ll] and the Lonsdale Company.

By the early 1960s Brown and Ive[s] ceased ownership of any investmen[ts] and became a partnership devoted t[o] managing the personal affairs of i[ts] members, Robert Hale Ives Goddar[d] and his son William H.D. Goddard.

Nineteenth-century sketch of the Joseph Brown House on South Main Street, Providence, which has been the headquarters of Brown and Ives since 1926. (Courtesy of the Rhode Island Historical Society.)

Nicholas Brown, son of Nicholas Brown, the founder of Brown and Ives, successfully ran the firm with his brother-in-law, Thomas Poynton Ives. (Courtesy of the Rhode Island Historical Society.)

The Ann & Hope, a trading vessel of the firm of Brown and Ives during the China Trade. (Courtesy [of] Robert Hale Ives Goddard.)

Brown & Sharpe Manufacturing Company

Although no members of the Brown family are active today in the firm of Brown & Sharpe, Henry D. Sharpe, Jr., grandson of one of its founders, is still active as its chairman and guiding spirit of an enterprise that grew from a tiny shop on South Main Street in Providence to become a worldwide manufacturer. Today the company makes precision metrology equipment, machine tools, and industrial hydraulics in five countries and employs approximately 4,000 people.

The story of Brown & Sharpe began in the late 1820s when Joseph R. Brown, son of an itinerant razor sharpener, set up a small shop to repair and build watches and clocks. In 1833 his father joined him, forming the partnership of D. Brown & Son at 60 South Main Street. This makes Brown & Sharpe one of the oldest manufacturing concerns still in business in its own right in the United States.

The firm was struck by a disastrous fire in the late 1830s which resulted in the dissolution of the father-and-son partnership. The senior Brown moved west to settle in Illinois, but his son Joseph continued alone.

On September 12, 1848, Lucian Sharpe came to work for Joseph Brown. While still in his apprenticeship, Sharpe moved ahead to become a full partner in the enterprise and the firm became known as J.R. Brown & Sharpe.

The 1850s found the fledgling enterprise introducing the world's first vernier caliper, graduated on Brown's precision dividing engines. Later the American Standard Wire gauge, sometimes called the B&S Gauge, was perfected and Brown took out his patent on the world's first universal milling machine.

By 1868 the firm was also growing. It moved from South Main Street to much more spacious quarters on Promenade Street in Providence and constructed what is generally considered to be the first steel-framed fac-

Joseph R. Brown took in Lucian Sharpe as his apprentice, and soon the two became partners.

Lucian Sharpe, one of the founders of Brown & Sharpe, is shown here in a photograph taken in 1860.

Workers spill out windows and stand in front of the Brown & Sharpe shop on South Main Street in 1872.

tory building ever erected in the United States.

In 1876 Brown died, but only after having first invented and patented the formed tooth cutter, the universal grinding machine, and the hair clipper. He also had sponsored many other important mechanical "firsts," notably the mass production of the micrometer caliper.

In 1899 Brown's partner, Lucian Sharpe, also died, but shortly thereafter, Henry D. Sharpe, Lucian's son, quickly emerged as the new leader of the company to replace him. Throughout Henry Sharpe, Sr.'s, career, the firm prospered during both peacetime and two world wars (reaching a Rhode Island employment record of 11,119 at the height of World War II). The company also weathered the crashing Depression years of the 1930s when machinery production in

America came to a virtual standstill.

In 1951, at the age of 28, a third-generation Sharpe, Henry D. Jr., succeeded his father as president on the latter's retirement. During his 29 years as chief executive officer, the most recent of the three Sharpes saw Brown & Sharpe grow from a multistoried plant in the center of Providence, Rhode Island, into a modern, worldwide manufacturing concern with diverse operations located not only in Rhode Island, but also in Michigan, North Carolina, Great Britain, Switzerland, West Germany, and France.

In 1980 Donald A. Roach succeeded Henry D. Sharpe, Jr., as president and chief executive officer. The firm's long tradition in the application of precision to increasingly sophisticated manufacturing technologies continues today.

179

Brown University

The history of Brown University reaches back more than two centuries and tells of a university constantly undergoing change. Brown was established under a charter from Rhode Island's General Assembly in 1764 as the seventh college in America and the third in New England. In September 1765 the first student enrolled at the college, then known as Rhode Island College and located in Warren. Five years later the school was moved to a hill on the east side of Providence, and in 1804 its name was changed to Brown University in recognition of the generous contributions of Nicholas Brown, a member of the socially and economically prominent Brown family of Providence.

Shortly after the college moved to Providence, the Revolution broke out and the college was closed so that faculty and students could serve their country. University Hall, the main campus building, was used as a barracks and hospital for American troops and for the French soldiers of General Rochambeau. After peace was restored, President Washington visited Providence with Thomas Jefferson and was awarded the honorary doctor of laws degree. The illumination of University Hall for President Washington is now recalled on Class Night, Christmas Eve, and Rhode Island Independence Day, when candles are placed in every window of the building.

A number of eminent scholars and administrators have guided Brown since its founding. Francis Wayland, who in 1827 became the fourth president, attracted widespread attention in academic circles by introducing his "new system" at Brown, a curriculum radical for its era, which emphasized applied science and engineering and gave students some choice in the election of courses. Elisha Benjamin Andrews, who became the eighth president in 1889, was responsible for creating nine new departments of instruction and tripling the size of the faculty. The 11th president, Henry Merritt Wriston, who served from 1937 to 1955, brought the university from an important regional school to a posi-

Francis Wayland was the innovative fourth president of Brown University.

This is the way the Brown University campus at the corner of Prospect and Waterman streets appeared in 1840.

These students are celebrating the rites of spring behind Hope College, the second oldest building on the Brown University campus. Constructed in the early 19th century, the structure is currently used as a dormitory.

tion among the leading universities of the country. He introduced important curriculum changes, hired many outstanding faculty members, and instituted an ambitious building program.

Dr. Wriston was succeeded by Barnaby Conrad Keeney, a member of the history faculty, who embarked on several major fund-raising programs to spur educational and physical plant growth. In 1969 a highly flexible curriculum was introduced. Under president Donald F. Hornig, a medical school became a reality in 1972 when the university's corporation approved a medical education program leading to a doctor of medicine degree. Under the leadership of Howard Swearer, political scientist and former president of Carleton College who took office in 1977, the university has undertaken the largest fund-raising campaign in its history and has established itself as one of the most selective institutions in the country in undergraduate admissions.

The school has been coeducational since 1971 when Pembroke College, the women's college founded in 1871, merged with the undergraduate program. Brown has been commended by the New England Association of Schools and Colleges for "its ability to attract first-rate students, the flexibility of its undergraduate curriculum, and its success in maintaining the balance between attention to undergraduate education and a collegiate atmosphere on the one hand and emphasis on graduate work and research on the other."

Carey, Richmond & Viking

Newport, Rhode Island, at the southern tip of Aquidneck Island, is famous for its fairy-tale mansions by the sea and its handsome restored colonial homes. Carey, Richmond & Viking, an amalgamation of four older, separately owned insurance and real estate companies on the island, has been in the forefront of the restoration and revitalization of the historic seaport.

The firm traces its history to 1948, when William L. Carey and John W. Richmond formed a real estate company to service the town's estates and

"Bird's Nest Cottage," built in 1872, has been restored by Carey, Richmond & Viking and serves as its Newport office.

summer colony. In 1972 Victor M. Andrade of Bristol purchased Carey and Richmond, adding it to Viking Associates, a real estate and insurance agency he had acquired the previous year—hence the name Carey, Richmond & Viking. Viking Associates had been founded in 1963.

In March 1973 Andrade acquired the Herbert W. Smith Agency, founded in

1926 by Smith, who was known as the "Father of the Mount Hope Bridge." Smith had been a leading promoter of the bridge which today connects the mainland of Rhode Island with the island of Aquidneck.

The following year Andrade acquired the George Spiratos agency on the island, and two years later the firm expanded its real estate division with a branch office on the northern end of the island joining the Pierce Insurance Agency he had opened in 1961. Another branch office followed in 1979 in Bristol.

Today Andrade is the sole owner and president of Carey, Richmond & Viking, one of the largest real estate and insurance agencies on the island. The company employs more than 30 full-time real estate sales associates and

four managers in its offices, an insurance division with one general manager and three sales representatives, and an administrative staff of five. The agency continues to handle estate sales and rentals, and since 1974 has been well known for sales of period homes, many of them dating to the 18th century.

Carey, Richmond & Viking brought restoration to its own front door in 1972 when it discovered it needed larger quarters for an expanding staff. The firm purchased the historic "Bird's

Nest Cottage" next door and began to restore it to its original Victorian splendor. When it was built in 1872 across from the Redwood Library on Bellevue Avenue by Samuel F. Pratt of Boston, it was typical of Newport architecture of that period. The exterior was distinctive with its mansard roof, colorful slate siding, and intricate trim.

In 1874 *Harper's* magazine thought it was so typical of the Newport cottages

Victor M. Andrade, president of Carey, Richmond & Viking, in the "Bird's Nest Cottage," which has been remodeled to accommodate the real estate firm.

of that era that the house was sketched for a magazine illustration. Pratt used the house for a summer residence from 1872 until about 1917. Then the years began to take their toll; small additions were built, some of the intricate trim was destroyed, and the layers of paint accumulated.

Andrade recognized the architectural importance of the cottage and restored it. Although the interior has been remodeled to accommodate a modern business, the handsome marble fireplaces have been retained and the interior woodwork is in keeping with that of the period. Today, with its exterior repainted the original Victorian colors of burgundy and gray, the house looks much the way it did to 19th-century Newport passersby.

CE Maguire, Inc.

The architectural, engineering, and planning firm of CE Maguire, Inc., has left its professional mark on many areas of Rhode Island life in the years since it was founded (as Charles A. Maguire and Associates) in 1938 by Charles A. Maguire, a civil engineer. The firm's name is synonymous with architectural and engineering design of military, transporation, environmental, and building projects throughout the state and the region.

When Maguire organized his 12-employee company after leaving his post of director of public works, he in all likelihood never realized that this firm would one day grow to 700 employees throughout the United States with far-flung offices in Hawaii and Africa. After his death in 1953 the company continued to be privately owned under the direction of Grant Potter, Howard Holmes, Harold Bateson, and Gordon Bronson. In 1970 the business was purchased by Combustion Engineering Corporation of Stamford, Connecticut, and the name was changed to CE Maguire, Inc. Nine years later Maguire, now one of the leading architectural/engineering

firms in the world, returned to private ownership as an employee stock ownership company under the direction of John Slocum, Vincent Cangiano, and Frank Pierce, all of whom worked under Maguire as young engineers in the early 1950s.

The firm is now located in its own building at recently renovated Davol Square. The firm's earliest assignments were with the U.S. Navy in designing new and expanded military facilities at Newport, Quonset, and Davisville at the outset of World War II. This initial involvement with the Navy has continued for over 40 years. At the present time Maguire is designing a major naval port facility in the Mariana Islands in the South Pacific.

As the war years slipped into history and the automobile became the dominant element of a suddenly mobile society, Maguire began designing interstate highway systems in Rhode Island, Massachusetts, and Connecticut. Since the mid-1950s the company has designed many of the interstate highways in Rhode Island as well as several of the state's major bridges, including the Henderson Bridge, the Sakonnet River Bridge, the Washington Bridge, and the Pawtucket River Bridge.

During the late 1960s Maguire worked with the University of Rhode Island in the design of several of its new buildings, including the Chemical Engineering Building, the Industrial Engineering Building, and the Inde-

pendence Hall classroom building. Perhaps the best-known Maguire project is the nation's first automated post office in Providence. The building, which from the air resembles an open parachute, was dedicated by the postmaster general in 1960.

Maguire has continually responded to the environmental needs of Rhode Island society. For four decades the firm has been the foremost designer of sewage systems, treatment plants, dams, water supply, and treatment and distribution facilities throughout the state. These projects, large and small, all attest to the firm's professional contribution to the betterment of life for the citizens of Providence and Rhode Island.

Charles A. Maguire, the director of public works in Providence, organized the firm of Charles A. Maguire and Associates in 1938.

CE Maguire, Inc., was the consulting architectural/ engineering firm for the country's first automated post office, completed in 1956.

Cranston Print Works

The story of the Cranston Print Works is bound inextricably with the once powerful and tragic Sprague family of Rhode Island. While it has been almost a century since the name "Sprague" was deleted from the mangement rolls of the company, the history of the print works cannot be told adequately without first telling the story of the Spragues.

The first William Sprague came to Rhode Island from England in 1620. Little is known about him or his early descendants. However, one of the later descendants, also named William Sprague, converted a grist mill to a spinning mill in 1808, and a few years later he purchased half the water power at Natick Falls, Rhode Island, and built a 42-loom cotton mill for carding and spinning. In 1824 he began converting a spinning mill in Cranston into a print plant, and a decade later he and his brother Amasa renamed it A. & W. Sprague. This was the forerunner of the Cranston Print Works.

The brothers developed the first power-printing machine with rollers. By 1840 their plants were turning out thousands of prints of about 40 yards each per week. And when William was elected governor of the state and then a United States senator, it looked as if fate were smiling on the Sprague family. Unfortunately, a few years later, in 1843, Amasa Sprague was murdered. A man named John Gordon was hanged for the crime, but later, fearful that the wrong man had been executed, Rhode Island abolished the death penalty.

Two years after his father's murder, Amasa's son William, the second William to become a governor and a United States senator, joined the firm. When his uncle William died in 1856, the 26-year-old man assumed full responsibility for what by then were vast holdings. He was elected governor of Rhode Island in 1860, and a year later he led Rhode Island troops into battle at Bull Run. In 1863 he was elected a United States senator, and while serv-

William Sprague, who first converted the old spinning mill to a print plant under the name A. & W. Sprague, went on to become governor of Rhode Island and a United States senator.

ing in Washington, he met and married Kate Chase, daughter of President Lincoln's secretary of the treasury.

Sprague holdings were at their peak at the beginning of the Civil War. The plant in Cranston was the most extensive in New England, including homes for families and single workers, a private fire company, a private gas line to supply fuel, stores, an ice house, and a vegetable farm. In fact, Sprague holdings were said to be the largest in the world, with assets of about $25 million.

But the depression following the

This 1915 photograph was taken a few years before the William G. Rockefeller interests bought the plant and reorganized it as the Cranston Print Works.

Civil War marked the beginning of the end of an empire already overextended. The Sprague fortunes began to wane and dissension within the family diminished its assets. William and Kate Sprague were divorced. He remarried, and eventually moved to Paris where he died a broken man.

When the Sprague empire collapsed, Zechariah Chafee was installed by the creditors of the Sprague family as trustee of all Sprague mill interests. Eventually they passed to B.B. and R. Knight, and in 1920 the William G. Rockefeller interests bought the plant in Cranston and reorganized it as the Cranston Print Works. William Rockefeller at the time was associated with his brother, John D. Rockefeller, in the Standard Oil Company.

Cranston Print Works became one of the most important textile printing plants in the country. Today it also has print plants in Webster, Massachusetts, and Fletcher, North Carolina, in addition to cloth-supplying companies, a trucking firm, and a chemical company to supply dyes and other chemicals necessary to the textile printing industry. The printed textiles made by the Cranston Print Works are sold around the world. The president of the corporation is Frederic L. Rockefeller, a descendant of William Rockefeller.

Cumberland Farms

Vasilios and Aphrodite Haseotes bought a farm in Cumberland, Rhode Island, in the spring of 1939, hoping to make a better life for their growing family. They then bought a cow and a calf, rebuilt the barn, and a family dairy business was born. Today known as Cumberland Farms, it operates the largest privately owned convenience-store chain in the country.

Vasilios Haseotes was born in 1892 in Epirus, a rural region in northern Greece. The youngest of 13 children, he came to America after he received a letter from an older brother telling him of the opportunities here for a better life.

He arrived at Ellis Island, New York, at the age of 12, and went on to settle in Maine with his brother where he quickly learned English working in a textile mill. Soon he was serving as an interpreter for his fellow Greeks there. He later moved to Lonsdale, Rhode Island, to continue working in the textile industry. During World War I he joined the U.S. Army Infantry under the command of General John "Black Jack" Pershing. Once again he served as an interpreter, relaying orders to his fellow Greeks who were fighting beside him. He emerged from the war a hero (with shrapnel wounds and suffering the effects of mustard gas), decorated by both the French and American governments.

Haseotes returned to Rhode Island, became involved in the bakery business in Providence, and in 1927 married Aphrodite Bassis. The Depression years were difficult, and he left the bakery business to work for the State Division of Roads and Bridges for 10 years.

Like her husband, Aphrodite also had come to America from Greece as a young child. Her home had been in the region of Macedonia, the birthplace of Alexander the Great. An independent and liberated woman for her times, Aphrodite worked during the 1920s in the jewelry business in Rhode Island. This was the same business that had been her family trade in Greece for many generations. She worked hard and by age 25 owned her own automobile.

In retrospect, it seemed that Vasilios and Aphrodite had only been marking time until they bought their farm in Cumberland. They were living in Providence with their children, but when they saw an opportunity to buy the land in Cumberland, they didn't hesitate, even though they were entering a business new to both of them.

Once on the farm, they bought a cow and a calf for $84 and then spent the next three years paying for them. They bred the animals and eventually had a herd of milking cows. Their young family, consisting of three boys—Demetrios, George, and Byron—and five girls—Hytho, Erato, Anastasia, Lily, and JoAnn—worked together and soon they had established a local milk delivery route. Aphrodite encouraged Vasilios to expand the milk route. They bought a dairy in Connecticut at an auction and moved all the equipment to Cumberland. Within six years the family was peddling more than 1,000

Vasilios S. Haseotes, a Greek immigrant, was the founder of Cumberland Farms, which grew to be the largest privately owned convenience-store chain in the country.

The 1,000th Cumberland Farms store was opened in April 1975 in Pawtucket, Rhode Island, by Mrs. Vasilios S. Haseotes (foreground), Demetrios Haseotes (second from left), Mrs. Lily (Haseotes) Bentas (second from right), and company and state officials.

quarts of milk a day.

One of the main reasons for the success of the Haseotes operation was the hard-driving vitality of the three sons. They were known throughout the area for their unfailing strength and hard work. The girls, as well as the boys, contributed a great deal to the business. Hytho was a licensed pasteurizer at the age of 14. She and her sisters also drove the farm equipment, tended to the cows, and helped with the other farm chores. All of the children were encouraged to go to college by their parents, but felt that their first obligation was to the family and the business. Three of the girls attended college and

eventually chose their own careers while two remained actively involved in the business along with the three sons.

The turning point for the family business came in 1954 when Byron, the youngest son, returned from a vacation in Wisconsin. In his suitcase he had an empty gallon jug for his family's inspection. He hoped the family would onsider selling gallon jugs of milk in a tore. At first the family was apprehensive, but after a year of debate, they decided to open the first Cumberland arms store in Bellingham, Massachusetts, selling milk in gallon jugs along vith other dairy products.

Going to the store to buy milk was a new concept in New England. The

ing public controversies.

The company continued to receive more opposition from conventional milk companies that still specialized in home deliveries. When it entered the Boston market in 1958, these disputes were carried to the Massachusetts courts. But Cumberland Farms continued to expand. While the 1960s

Today Cumberland Farms owns more than 1,200 stores and 400 gasoline units, and employs approximately 8,000 people in 10 states. The stores are supplied by five milk plants and an ice cream plant. In addition, the company owns and operates a large automated farm in Bridgewater, Massachusetts, and a 600,000-square-foot

The Haseotes men are shown here in 1951 with the newest addition to their dairy herd. From left are Byron, Vasilios (the father), Demetrios, and George.

Haseotes family was, in effect, revolutionizing the region's milk industry by shifting the emphasis from home delivery to store pickup. Eventually, the family opened more stores in the Massachusetts, Rhode Island, and Connecticut areas. They had bought new pasteurizing and homogenizing equipment, as well as huge tank trailer-trucks to haul milk from northern New England. Cumberland Farms was growing, but its revolutionary ideas and aggressiveness were arous-

were a time of bitter court battles for the firm, it successfully eliminated retail milk price-fixing in several states. This opposition to price-fixing continued through 1981 when the battle finally was won, and minimum milk pricing was eliminated in all states chainwide.

By 1962 Cumberland Farms had diversified its product line to add groceries, beverages, and nonfood items, and its stores opened earlier and closed later then most of its competitors. A decade later Cumberland Farms was the second largest convenience-store chain in the country and the largest privately owned chain.

complex in Westboro, Massachusetts, housing a distribution warehouse, a bakery, and a beverage plant. It also operates a cranberry processing plant located in Hanson, Massachusetts, and thousands of acres of cranberry bogs and land in southern Massachusetts.

Vasilios Haseotes died in 1980. Aphrodite still contributes to the business, which is operated by the Haseotes sons and daughters. Today when the children talk about their parents, they make it clear that it was the combination of their father's hard work, humility, and compassion and their mother's will to win and achieve that made their family business a success.

Danecraft

On a foggy morning in New York Harbor in 1910, hundreds of European immigrants huddled together to catch their first glimpse of America. One of these new arrivals was Victor Primavera, whose family traced its history to the 17th century in Italy as noted designers of jewelry for royalty and the wealthy families of the region near Pescara on the Adriatic Sea.

Often one of the Primavera artisans would go directly into the home of a patron to design and reproduce as jewelry some cherished object of art.

Danecraft remains a family-oriented business. Victor Primavera III (left), his sister Gail, and their father and president of Danecraft, Victor Primavera Jr., discuss a new product line.

Before it moved to new facilities on Baker Street in Providence, Danecraft was housed in this building on Bucklin Street.

world, purchased one of the top costume-jewelry manufacturers in Providence. And, in May of that year, "The House of Primavera" began operation as the maker of high-fashion costume jewelry in addition to designing and producing high-quality sterling silver and gold jewelry.

Usually the young son would go along, and it was there by candlelight that the craftsmanship was passed along, father to son, generation to generation.

Although Victor Primavera was a young boy when his family came to America, he began at a young age to design jewelry—and on March 1, 1934, founded an enterprise in rented quarters at 144 Pine Street in Providence. Since the company was making jewelry with primarily a Danish influence, the name Danecraft was selected. Soon major retailers were looking to Danecraft as one of the innovative leaders in the precious-metals industry.

In 1942, continuing the family tradition, Victor Primavera, Jr., joined his father in the business and began implementing changes—combining the Old World artistry of his father with modern manufacturing techniques. He was instrumental in building the new facility at 24 Baker Street, in broaden-

ing retail distribution of the firm's products from specialty shops to major department stores, and in introducing the computer to Danecraft. Initiating the first national fine-jewelry television campaign, he also instituted the first national ear-piercing program in major department stores.

In early 1982 Danecraft, which now sells directly to retail stores around the

Danecraft has headquarters at 24 Baker Street, Providence.

As did his father, Victor Primavera Jr., personally supervises all Danecraft designs. The company remains a family enterprise; Victor Primavera III and his sister Gail are the third generation of Primaveras to continue its tradition of jewelry artistry in this country.

Dixon Industries Corporation

Ezra Dixon, Sr., founder and first president of Dixon Lubricating Saddle Company, forerunner to Dixon Industries, came from Massachusetts to Bristol, Rhode Island, after the Civil War to install spinning frames in a textile mill there.

While he was working in the Bristol textile mill, Dixon became aware of the need for a more modern and productive saddle, the wooden bearing that weighted the top rolls on the spinning frames.

Dixon eventually developed a metal bearing that proved to be an important labor-saving device in the mills, and soon these saddles became the standard used around the world. The original saddle made by Dixon now rests in the Smithsonian Institution in Washington, D.C. By the end of the century these saddles were used worldwide, and as synthetic fabrics were developed more than 250 variations of the lubricating saddle were on the market.

By 1876 Dixon had borrowed enough money to set up his own office in a foundry in Providence where the foundry could manufacture the saddles and Dixon could supervise. Four years later he moved his operation to Bristol. By the time of his death in 1936, his invention had made him a millionaire.

Dixon Industries Corporation opened its new plant on Metacom Avenue in Bristol in 1963.

Dixon's sons, Ezra Jr. and William, ran the company until 1946 when Robert Rulon Miller, a Brown University graduate who had married the senior Dixon's granddaughter, Ann Leahy, took over as manager.

Few spinning frames were built during World War II, but once the war ended the textile industry geared up again and the demand for frames, and lubricating saddles, surged. It soon became obvious to Miller that the original saddle was sadly outmoded. His goal then was to develop a more efficient saddle. Investigating newer materials, Miller experimented with Teflon, a plastic material that Du Pont had recently developed, and arrived at a formula for a new, long-wearing saddle bearing. That formula, under the trade name "RULON," still remains a secret today.

The new saddle marked a resurgence of the Dixon company. As the firm moved into the 1950s competition was forcing it to diversify. It was found that "RULON," because of its unique properties as a low-friction, high-wear resistance material, had many potential industrial applications. Dixon moved from its shop on High Street in Bristol to a new location on Burnside Street and began to develop these applications under the technical leadership of Saul Ricklin and the market leadership of John Feeley.

In 1963 Dixon moved to a new plant on Metacom Avenue, sold its textile machinery division, and decided to devote itself to the high-performance plastics business, making use of many new "RULON" formulations as well as other specialized polymers.

The company became Dixon Indus-

Dixon Industries was still called Dixon Lubricating Saddle Company and its headquarters was in this building on High Street in Bristol when this photograph was taken of the employees in the early 1950s.

tries Corporation with the acquisition of Penntube Plastics (Clifton Heights, Pennsylvania) and Danco (Putnam, Connecticut) as divisions, as well as joint ventures in Japan and licensees in the United Kingdom, Italy, Holland, and Australia.

Dixon is now a recognized world leader in the production of high-performance plastic parts used as essential components in every type of machinery. Since 1973 the company has been operating as a wholly owned subsidiary of Bundy Corporation in Detroit, Michigan. Dixon employs 625 employees at its three locations under the leadership of Bert Katzanek, president.

EG&G Sealol, Inc.

When the Lunar Excursion Module touched down on the moon's surface in July 1969, the "Moon Dust" seal made by EG&G Sealol of Warwick, Rhode Island, kept abrasive dust out of the radar system that guided the astronauts to a soft and safe landing. That seal was one of many critical Sealol components that helped make this and many other space flights a success.

EG&G Sealol was founded in East Providence in 1939 under the name Stevenson Engineering Company. With the backing of civic leader John Nicholas Brown, an inventor named Robert L. Stevenson began making mechanical seals for Pratt & Whitney and Wright aircraft engines. Stevenson had devised an improved means of preventing leakage where a rotating shaft passes through a housing con-taining a fluid, as in an engine crankcase or gearbox.

In 1941 the company, which had changed its name to Sealol, took a giant step forward with the invention of the first pressure-balanced seal, an ingenious design that overcame a basic problem. Previously, as fluid pressures rose, the rotating seal faces were forced together and soon destroyed them-selves. Robert Stevenson and Justus Stevens, still active as an engineering consultant to Sealol, devised a means whereby the pressure of the fluid being sealed could be made to work against itself, cancelling out all but a small amount of force necessary to maintain face contact.

Rapid expansion began during the presidency of Clement Williamson, who served from 1951 to 1975. In 1955 the firm built a modern 70,000-square-foot plant in Warwick, Rhode Island.

In 1957 Sealol proposed to the U.S. Navy that seals for submarine pro-pellor shafts be fabricated in two 180-degree sections to facilitate installation and repair. Today every U.S. nuclear submarine is equipped with Sealol split seals, as are many submarines and sur-face vessels of other free-worl[d] nations.

Chempro, Inc., in Cranford, New Jersey, was acquired in 1962 to serv[e] the sealing needs of the petrochemic[al] industry. Seven years later Seal[ol] acquired Rotary Seal Corporation i[n] Chicago, considered to be the fir[st] company in this country, if not th[e] world, to manufacture face-typ[e] mechanical seals.

In 1969 Sealol was acquired b[y] EG&G, a Fortune 500 company. Today under the direction of J.R. Erkelbou[t] EG&G Sealol has 33 corporate office[s] manufacturing plants, or service cen[ter]ters in 14 countries on 5 continent[s] Products from the firm that began i[n] East Providence are found throughou[t] the world—in refineries, chemica[l] plants, jet engines, and aboard ships—providing dependable solutions to th[e] complex problems of 20th-centur[y] technology.

The first pressure balanced seals (inset), developed by EG&G Sealol, permitted marked improvements in the efficiency of aircraft engines such as this Pratt & Whitney Twin Wasp.

When existing seals were unable to withstand the hostile conditions found in the early U.S. rocket engines, EG&G Sealol developed the first welded-bellows seals. Sealol seals and bellows devices have been aboard every major U.S. space flight.

Federal Products

Federal Products became a corporate entity on January 10, 1918, in Providence, as an outgrowth of the Federal Screw Corporation which had manufactured ordinary wood screws. Leonard Tingley, one of the founders of the new enterprise and its first president, was faced with the prospect of running a faltering company during the bleak days of World War I.

But the end of the war and the prosperity of the '20s meant a demand for bigger and better products. By 1923 Federal had 14 workers in its shop on Harris Avenue and two men and two women working in the office. Federal began gaining recognition for its technical competence in the highly specialized field of precision measurement. With the rapid growth of the automobile industry, Federal took on the regrinding of auto engine cylinders. This resulted in the development of the company's first specialized gage for checking inside diameters, the Federal Cylinder Gage with its accurate and easy-to-read dial indicator.

Federal celebrated its 10th anniversary in 1928 by moving to newer and larger quarters at 1144 Eddy Street on the edge of downtown Providence.

A branch office had been established in Detroit during the '20s to coordinate business with the automobile industry, and now a branch was set up in Chicago. About this same time the Federal Testmaster®, a universal-type test indicator, was introduced; it would eventually become one of the firm's most widely known products.

In 1937 a young engineer named Fred C. Tanner joined Federal to design what was then a new concept in the company, the custom-engineered gage. This was the beginning of a new era for Federal and the beginning of a new career for Tanner, who in 1950 became the second president of the firm.

World War II saw business at Federal grow by leaps and bounds. Dial indicators, mechanical and air gages, and machine control and automatic gages were in such great demand that a special training program was started with the help of the Providence School Department and hundreds of new

Heavy-duty model Formscan^{TM} 3000 Modular Circular Geometry Gage, incorporating a microcomputer to measure roundness, squareness, parallelism, and concentricity.

In 1928 Federal Products Corporation moved to these offices at 1144 Eddy Street.

employees were taught precision work.

Federal has always been an innovator in employee relations. The firm was among the first to adopt a no-time-clock policy and flexible working hours. It established recreation programs for employees, in-house training, educational assistance, and recently instituted plant-wide Quality Circles programs to increase employees' participation in improved quality- and productivity-related decisions. Under Tanner's direction the company also

founded the Federal Products Foundation for charitable work and the awarding of scholarships to employees' children.

In 1962 Federal Products International was established in Switzerland to coordinate sales in Europe; Federal has since expanded its marketing efforts worldwide, with manufacturing, sales, and service facilities in England and Brazil. In 1969 Federal was purchased by Esterline Corporation (NYSE) and is the key company in Esterline's Metrology Group. Under the leadership of its third president, John J. Kane, Federal's product lines have grown rapidly, including electronic gages, geometry and surface finish gages, and many computer-assisted and microprocessor-based gaging products. And, through expanded research, engineering, manufacturing, and marketing efforts, Federal is entering the 1980s as an innovator in the development of precision measuring instruments and the application of state-of-the-art technologies to the science of industrial metrology.

Hasbro Industries

Hasbro Industries' roots were planted when Henry and Helal Hassenfeld, Jewish immigrants from Eastern Europe, started their textile-remnants business in a small room on North Main Street in Providence in 1924. The venture eventually emerged as one of the major toy manufacturers in the world.

The brothers bought used fabrics and sold them as remnants. Deciding it would be more profitable to do something creative with the scraps, they began making pencil boxes and covering them. The company, by now called Hassenfeld Bros., Inc., prospered and moved to larger quarters on Orange Street behind the Outlet building. About this time the brothers determined their product would be even more viable if they filled the boxes with pencils.

In 1930 the firm moved to Broad Street in Providence, where it remained for the next decade. It was here that the business really expanded and moved into the area for which it finally would become famous—toys.

The organization was also manufacturing photo albums, scrapbooks, and picture frames in 1937 when Henry's son, Harold, joined the operation. A year later his other son, Merrill, became associated, and Hassenfeld Bros., Inc., made its first toys: doctor and nurse kits, and paint sets.

In fact, the toy business had evolved from the stationery-supplies business. At that time salesmen would distribute both toys and stationery supplies since the buyers and outlets were often the same for both. Since Hassenfeld Bros., Inc., already was making stationery supplies, it seemed logical to add toys.

The company purchased its pencils from other manufacturers until suppliers raised the prices, and Henry decided it was time to make their own. Shortly before World War II he and his wife traveled to Germany, where they bought pencil-making equipment and hired a man to teach them its operation. This was the beginning of what one day would become a separate and very successful business.

In 1944 the corporation ventured into plastics—then a new concept, especially in the toy business. It was this plastic molding of toys that became the basis for today's Hasbro toys.

The pencil-making division of the company flourished to the point that the organization decided to make it a separate entity in 1946. Later that year it acquired the Empire Pencil Company in Shelbyville, Tennessee, and Harold moved there to manage the operation. Henry and Merrill continued to supervise the Rhode Island plant; Helal had died some years before.

The year 1952, a landmark for the

TOP: *Stephen D. Hassenfeld, chairman of the board and president of Hasbro Industries, Inc.*

ABOVE: *Super Potato Head is a superb combination of the crazy play pieces for Mr. and Mrs. Potato Head and includes the latest 1983 design features.*

RIGHT: *The headquarters of Hasbro Industries, Inc., are located at 1027 Newport Avenue in Pawtucket, Rhode Island.*

firm, marked the arrival of Mr. Potato Head. Four million were sold that first year, and the toy held the distinction of being the first advertised on television.

As the toy division was rapidly expanding during the 1950s, the company was slowly phasing out its pencil operations in Rhode Island. In 1954

Hassenfeld Bros., Inc., purchased the Mallard Pen and Pencil Company in Kentucky. About the same time, became a major licensee of Disney-toy products.

In addition to its plant in Central Falls, the corporation added the Newport Avenue facility in Pawtucket in 1960, and three years later built warehouse and distribution center in that city.

The year 1964 is a notable one in Hasbro history for two reasons. Stephen Hassenfeld, the son of Merrill, joined the family business; and Hasbro introduced its G.I. Joe toy. The pro

uction of the toy, in which Stephen was immediately given key responsibilities, increased sales from $13 million to $35 million. The result was that, for the first time, Hasbro began subcontracting for overseas work. And G.I. Joe went on to become one of the most successful toys ever marketed.

During the 1960s the organization expanded into the Canadian market and today it has a large operation based in Montreal. Hasbro acquired Romper Room Enterprises in 1969 and developed a broad line of preschool products, which now constitute its largest single category of toys.

That decade witnessed a phenomenal growth, with the company advertising its toys nationwide. The name Hassenfeld Bros., Inc., was becoming known as Hasbro, and was officially changed in 1968 when Hasbro became a public corporation and a member of the American Stock Exchange.

In 1974 Merrill Hassenfeld named Stephen president of the company, and another son, Alan, who had become associated with the firm several years earlier, executive vice-president. Five years later, upon their father's death, Stephen succeeded him as chairman of the board. Hasbro Industries and the

Empire Pencil Company split in September 1980 and became two separate corporations, with Stephen in charge of Hasbro and Harold as head of Empire.

In the late 1970s the company made a decision to concentrate on a fewer number of proven toys—such as Mr. Potato Head, Sesame Street characters, preschool products, and Peanuts characters. The corporation by 1981 had annual sales of more than $100 million. Early in 1982 G.I. Joe, which had been placed on the inactive list in 1976, was reintroduced to a whole new generation of children.

New England Butt Company

The Wanskuck Company has three manufacturing plants in Rhode Island, two in Los Angeles, and one in Fort Wayne, Indiana. The corporation manufactures an extensive line of wire and cable machinery, braiding machines, plastic granulators, heavy-duty press room equipment, abrasive belt centerless grinders, steel reels, plastic and wood-metal spools, and metal stampings.

The decade from 1950 to 1960 marked the greatest change for the Wanskuck Company, which had been founded almost a century earlier as a woolen mill to manufacture uniforms and blankets for the Union Army during the Civil War. During the 1950s the business changed from a textile firm to a modern holding company. Wanskuck expanded and diversified by a combination of new-product development, purchase/license of product lines, and acquisition of other companies. It is now a very different corporation than its textile mill ancestor.

Wanskuck, named after a local Indian chief, was founded by three Rhode Island businessmen, Stephen T. Olney, Jesse Metcalf, and Henry J. Steere, in 1863. Soon after it was started, the mill complex consisted of buildings forming a typical New England mill village. By 1870 it had added a machine shop, a waste house, a blacksmith's shop, a bleach house, and an engine house. In 1883 Wanskuck became the first mill in the state to invest a large sum of money in electric lights. The firm continued to prosper throughout the 19th century, making high-quality worsted cloth which remained in great demand well into the 20th century.

In 1955 the Wanskuck Company merged with the New England Butt Company, a manufacturer of braiders and wire machinery. During this merger the Metcalf family, active in the Wanskuck Company since its inception and now 100-percent owners of the venture, sold it to local investors. Two years after the merger of the two

A New England Butt Planetary Cabler (circa 1915).

firms, Wanskuck closed the three textile mills and sold their machinery. This was the end of the Wanskuck Company as a textile operation. However, it was just the beginning for the modern Wanskuck Company.

That same year Wanskuck purchased the Mossberg Pressed Steel Corporation, which became a division of the parent organization. In 1960 Wanskuck bought the Production Machine Company of Greenfield, Massachusetts, and moved it to Providence a year later. In 1966 the company acquired the Edmands Company of Cranston, Rhode Island, and added it to the rapidly growing group under

During the period from 1910 to 1915, Frank B. Gilbreth did pioneer time-and-motion studies as a consultant to the New England Butt Company. He made numerous motion pictures of manufacturing operations there. In this picture, Gilbreth (right) and John G. Aldrich, president of New England Butt, are examining one of these films. Gilbreth was the subject of the best-selling biography Cheaper By The Dozen, *published in 1948.*

the Wanskuck Company's umbrella. During the 1970s Wanskuck bought the Hubbard Spool Division of Gulf and Western, Inc., of Fort Wayne, Indiana, the Wayne Plastics Division of AMF, and Ramco Industries of Worcester, Massachusetts. The company's latest acquisition, in 1980, was Regal Industries of Huntington Park, California, a manufacturer of heavy duty press room equipment.

The New England Financial Group

The name "New England Financial Group" brings to mind a group of high-powered businessmen sitting around a long oak table in a corporate board room making intricate decisions. In fact, the New England Financial Group is controlled by one man. Henry E. Kates has a large and exceptionally well-trained staff working with and for him, but essentially it is his company and his business.

Kates grew up in Colorado. At the age of 13 he became the youngest eagle scout in the state. After graduation from the University of Colorado, he joined an insurance company in Colorado Springs and soon became fascinated with real estate. The offer of a statewide insurance franchise brought him to Rhode Island in 1967, and two years later he formed the Kates Corporation to handle his growing real estate interests in the state.

In the early 1970s Kates began buying buildings in downtown Providence, some of them slated for demolition and many of them historic. As his real estate interests grew, he formed the New England Financial Group, an umbrella organization which has expanded to include businesses ranging from property development and restoration to investment advice, estate planning, and insurance.

In 1976 Kates purchased the historic Lauderdale Building in the heart of the downtown financial district, which today is his firm's headquarters. The building was vacant and headed for demolition when Kates acquired it. In spite of its deteriorated condition, he and his advisors determined the building was structurally sound. They then began a renovation process that eventually brought them an award from *Buildings Magazine*, which selected the Lauderdale as "an exemplar of adaptive reuse of a building almost surely destined for destruction." Kates, a physical fitness advocate, even had a paddle tennis court built on the roof and enlivened the reception area with paintings and sculptures by Rhode Island artists.

Kates, through his restoration work in the city, has become one of the leaders in downtown development. *Town and Country* magazine has called him "foremost" among the city's businessmen interested in restoring and saving the historic city. The magazine noted that Kates "is gaining unanimous respect for his extraordinary artistic renovations that have all the modern conveniences demanded by the 20th century."

Real estate, while one of Kates' major interests, is only one aspect of the New England Financial Group. With his background and expertise in the insurance business, Kates has put together an impressive array of organizations in the last decade.

These diverse businesses include Mutual Benefit Financial Service Company, Plantations Capital Management Corporation, Kates Properties, Inc., Kates Properties Management Company, and the Westminster Group.

The historic Lauderdale Building in downtown Providence was purchased by Henry Kates and renovated for his firm's headquarters.

During the 14 years he has been in Rhode Island, Henry E. Kates has graduated from head of the Providence office of Mutual Benefit Life to become one of the city's most prominent businessmen.

New England Institute of Technology

James Gouse opened one of the first trade schools in New England, the Massachusetts Trades Shop School, in 1936. He trained apprentices in his Boston machine shop at the facility, which grew steadily. When the country became involved in World War II, the federal government recognized the importance of the trade school—and took it over for the duration of the war to train machinists and other skilled workers necessary to the war effort.

After the war Gouse offered an even larger array of courses for the GIs returning to civilian life in need of skills for the work force. At this time his son, Julian, became associated with the operation. In the early 1960s Julian founded the Rhode Island Trades Shop School. A short time later the Massachusetts Trades Shop School merged with International Telephone and Telegraph (to be known as ITT Tech), and the Rhode Island Trades Shop School was sold.

The Julian B. Gouse campus, in Warwick, of the New England Institute of Technology was named after the school's late benefactor.

In 1971 the Gouse family again became involved in trade schools when Julian Gouse assumed the direction of the New England Technical Institute. Its curriculum had grown from initial programs in plastics technology to a successful school with a broad curriculum during and after the world war years. However, by 1971, the enrollment was down to 70 students and Gouse made a personal financial commitment to keep the school operating. When he died a few months later, his son, Richard I. Gouse (then 23), personally assumed all financial commitments and became the president of the school.

Under the direction of president Richard Gouse, the school showed dramatic growth in enrollment and in prestige through intensive and aggressive program development, physical plant renovation, and faculty and administration restructuring. In 1977 the state board of regents granted the institution the authority to offer associate-degree programs in addition to non-degree programs. It was then the name was officially changed to the New England Institute of Technology.

Today the school has an annual enrollment of more than 2,000 students. It is a private, nonprofit, coeducational, technical college accredited by the Accrediting Commission of the National Association of

Richard I. Gouse has been the president of the New England Institute of Technology in Rhode Island since 1971.

Trade and Technical Schools and i affiliated with the New England Association of Schools and Colleges, Inc.

The college has two campus loca tions in Rhode Island. The Providenc campus is housed in a three-story bric structure at 184 Early Street. Most ad ministrative offices are in this buildin The Julian B. Gouse campus on Pos Road in Warwick is named after th late trustee and benefactor of th college.

Old Colony Cooperative Bank

Rhode Island's banking industry of the 1890s was very different from what is today. At that time, there were five savings and loan associations in the state, each chartered by the state legislature. With no laws to govern their operations and no provisions made to supervise their activities, they could do business pretty much as they pleased in any part of the country. To remedy this situation, the State Building and Loan Act was passed at the January session of the legislature in 1895. Soon after the law was enacted, a bill was introduced to charter Old Colony

Cooperative Bank. It was approved on May 22, 1895, and Old Colony opened its doors on June 30, 1895, upstairs in the old Industrial Trust Building on lower Westminster Street in downtown Providence.

Growth came slowly to the fledgling bank. In 1927 the main offices of Old Colony moved to their present home, a 10-story building at 58 Weybosset Street. By 1945 Old Colony was the second largest savings and loan association in the United States.

Old Colony has been an innovator in the banking industry. It pioneered with the direct reduction mortgage, which few associations offered until after 1930. Excluding a ceremonial

The main office of the Old Colony Cooperative Bank was built in 1927 in the financial district of downtown Providence.

closing in Washington, D.C., Old Colony processed and closed the first G.I. mortgage in the country. In fact, more than $44 million in veterans' loans were made to over 6,000 ex-servicemen following World War II. In the field of operations, Old Colony was the first financial institution in Rhode Island to install a complete electronic data-processing system in 1955, and it was the first financial institution in the country to provide its customers with the convenience of complete "on-line" direct communication between tellers and an in-house computer.

In 1962 Old Colony completed its first merger, with the East Greenwich Savings and Loan Association. Later mergers included the Roger Williams Savings and Loan Association in 1970 and the Mayflower Savings and Loan Association in 1980. One of the most significant events in Old Colony's history took place in 1971 when it acquired 95 percent of the stock of The Newport National Bank. As a result, Old Colony became the only savings and loan association in the United States to have a national bank affiliate, allowing it to increase greatly the scope of services to its savings customers.

The history of The Newport National Bank is both proud and long. Founded in 1803, Newport National is the 12th oldest bank in the United States. In the year of its inception, Newport National helped provide funds for the Louisiana Purchase. Its home at 8 Washington Square, Newport, is the nation's oldest banking office in continuous use. This building, which once was the home of John Gardner, deputy governor of Rhode Island, is also known as "the birthplace of Brown University." In 1764 James Manning and others met with Gardner at his home to discuss the founding of Rhode Island College, later to become Brown University with Manning as its first president.

Today, with 21 offices and assets of more than $620 million, Old Colony Cooperative Bank is the largest savings and loan association in Rhode Island and the third largest in New England.

The Newport National Bank was founded in 1803 in this house erected in 1740 as the residence of John Gardner, deputy governor of Rhode Island. This is the oldest bank facility in continuous use in the United States.

Old Stone Corporation

The Providence Institution for Savings opened its doors for the first time on Saturday, November 20, 1819, the eighth mutual savings bank in the country. The *Providence Gazette* described the bank as an institution designed "to promote habits of economy." Despite such a descriptive name, the bank eventually became known during the mid-1800s by a nickname, the "stone bank." More than 100 years would pass before this nickname became the bank's official title.

The bank's first home was a rented room at 41 South Main Street, right on the city's busy waterfront. By 1837 it had moved its operations to rented quarters in the basement of another bank, the Providence Bank, located in a brick building at 50 South Main Street. The institution continued to grow and

by 1854 was housed in a newly built, handsome granite structure at 86 South Main Street. Customers going to the nearby commercial bank (which did not welcome savings accounts) were instructed to take their business to the "stone bank." Thus, it was the good citizens of Rhode Island who actually named the Old Stone Bank.

The institution's incorporators included 126 prominent Providence men. The first election of bank officers took place on November 4, 1819, in the

Washington Insurance Company o[f] Washington Row. Thomas Poynto[n] Ives, a partner in the well-known me[r]cantile house of Brown and Ives, wa[s] elected president. A wealthy mercha[nt] in the China trade, Thomas L. Halse[y] was elected first vice-president, an[d] John Howland, the father of the fr[ee] school system in Rhode Island, wa[s] elected treasurer.

The Old Stone Bank weathered th[e] financial panics of 1837, 1873, an[d] 1907, the stock market crash of 192[9]

Old Stone's famous "Gold Dome" is a familiar Rh[ode] Island landmark.

An aerial view of the Old Stone Corporation complex on South Main Street in downtown Providence. From left to right are the beautiful "Gold Dome" banking office; Guild Loan & Investment Company (a corporate subsidiary situated in the historic Benoni Cooke House); corporate headquarters; and Old Stone administrative offices.

and was still flourishing in 1954 wh[en] it opened its first branch outside Providence, in the town of Warren. [By] 1982 Old Stone had a statewide bran[ch] system totaling 32 offices serving t[he] Rhode Island banking public.

The bank initiated the first steps [of] converting to a stockholder-own[ed] bank holding company in 1973. Th[e] following year the conversion wa[s] complete and 111,000 savings accou[nt] holders became partners in Old Ston[e.] It seems fitting that the people who[se] ancestors had chosen the name of th[e] organization now owned it.

Entering the 1980s, Old Stone Co[r]poration, a one-bank holding com[pany, owns realty, investment, an[d] mortgage companies throughout t[he] United States. The corporation h[as] over 1,200 employees and assets ov[er] two billion dollars.

A.J. Oster Company

The A.J. Oster Company had its beginnings in Chelsea, Massachusetts, originated by Aaron J. Oster in 1922 as a one-man scrap-metal operation. Today, with headquarters in Providence, Rhode Island, the corporation is engaged in the creation of the finest combinations of alloys and other sophisticated metals that are sold worldwide.

He was inspired in his enterprise by his father, Solomon, a former barrister in Russia who had emigrated to the United States; in the early 1930s the founder moved his business to Providence. There he met and married Ruth Beach who served as the company's first secretary and bookkeeper, ultimately holding the positions of vice-president and treasurer until her retirement on January 1, 1979.

Oster gained a national and international reputation in his field. He served under President Franklin D. Roosevelt from 1941 to 1943 to help secure strategic metals for the war effort, and later was often called upon as an arbitrator to settle business disputes among dealers throughout the country. After his death in 1967, the Oster family established a philanthropic foundation in memory of Aaron J. Oster to provide support for a broad spectrum of charitable, educational, and religious organizations and projects in Providence.

Since 1967 Richard and Stephen Oster have been leading the firm their father founded, now housed in a building once owned by one of the company's earliest clients. When his business was still very young, Oster established a price for a large amount of metal with the president of the Builders Iron Foundry in Providence. When he admitted that he did not have enough money in the bank to cover so large a purchase, the president replied, "You look like a fine young man. Take it, sell it, make a profit, and then pay me." Oster sold the metal the following day and personally returned to pay his bill; a long business relationship was thus established. Richard and Stephen Oster eventually purchased the old Builders Iron Foundry Building.

With additional factories in Waterbury, Connecticut, Chicago, Illinois, and Allentown, Pennsylvania, the company's Providence plant deals mainly in brass, steel, pewter, jewelry-casting alloys, and Bismuth alloys—one of which was developed by Richard Oster. Known as "Ostalloy," it is used in many hospitals as a shield in radiation therapy.

In January 1979 the corporation was acquired by L.I.G., Ltd., of the United Kingdom. However, Richard M. Oster still serves as president of A.J. Oster, and Stephen A. Oster is the executive vice-president. Both have been instrumental in the acquisition of numerous firms for L.I.G., Ltd., and Richard Oster was appointed to the board of L.I.G., Ltd., as an executive director in 1980.

Aaron J. Oster, inspired by his father, Solomon, founded the A.J. Oster Company in 1922.

The Outlet Company

The Outlet Company was founded in Providence in 1894 as a retail business, and as recently as 1960 operated one radio station, one television station, and one retail store in that city. By early 1981 the company operated five television stations, seven radio stations, and 72 women's specialty stores located in 15 states and the District of Columbia.

This is a long way from the early days when the Samuel brothers, Joseph and Leon, established a small retail shop on Weybosset Street in Providence where they immediately began to offer dry goods at the lowest prices around, encountering hostility from the city's more conservative businessmen as well as from the *Providence Journal*, which refused to print the advertisements of the progressive Manufacturer's Outlet, as it was called then.

Shortly after the turn of the century the store expanded, buying up nearby buildings on Weybosset Street. In 1903 the new block-long store opened with more than 35 departments, making the Outlet Company one of the largest department stores in New England. By 1924 the store occupied the entire block bounded by Pine, Eddy, Weybosset, and Garnett streets. The Outlet Department Store, although sold in 1980 to United Department Stores of Trenton, New Jersey, still stands on this site.

From the beginning the Outlet's advertising and public relations were unlike any to which Rhode Islanders had been exposed. Much of this was due to Leon Samuels, who was the artistic and creative force behind the company, while his brother, Joseph, was the astute businessman who guided the Outlet's growth and expansion until his death in 1939. It was Leon who was responsible for the firm's venture into wireless broadcasting, an interest that developed in 1919 and 1920 and eventually led to the formation in 1922 of WJAR, the second (by only a few months) radio station in Providence. Continuing its pioneer role in the broadcasting industry, in 1949 Outlet's WJAR-TV went on the air in Providence. It became the seventh TV station in the NBC network and only the second TV station in Ne[w] England.

The Outlet name also was ke[pt] before the public by its various form[s] of philanthropy. The most impressiv[e] was the establishment of the Josep[h] Samuels Dental Clinic for Childre[n] opened in 1931 at Rhode Island Hosp[i]tal to provide free dental services t[o] children whose parents could n[ot] afford proper treatment. The Outl[et] was also known for its paternalis[m] toward its employees. For years th[e] company sponsored outings, and bot[h] brothers, particularly Joseph, made their business to keep informed abo[ut] the health of their employees and the[ir] families.

Joseph and Leon Samuels each ha[d] one daughter. It was the son [of] Joseph's daughter who eventuall[y] assumed management of the fami[ly] business after the brothers died. Josep[h] S. "Doty" Sinclair became a full-tim[e] employee in 1947 after serving in th[e] Navy. In 1968 he became chairman [of] the board.

In October 1980 the Outlet Compan[y] sold its department stores and men[s] wear divisions—91 stores in all—an[d] under the leadership of its presiden[t] and chief executive officer, Bruce [G.] Sundlun, made a decision to concen[trate] its efforts on broadcasting an[d] broadcast-related businesses. All 12 [of] the companies' broadcasting propertie[s] are located in the nation's top 5[0] markets.

The original Manufacturer's Outlet store at the turn of the century.

The ultra-modern Broadcast House in downtown Providence, home of the Outlet Company Broadcasting Division.

The Paramount Line, Inc.

The Paramount Line, Inc., among the largest firms producing greeting cards today, traces its beginnings to the Japanese Wood Novelty Company, which opened its doors in Providence, Rhode Island, in 1906. Its founder was Samuel Markoff, an artist and poet.

Markoff's early products were calendars and post cards made by burning the designs on a thin material known as Japanese Wood. These sold well, not only because of their quality, but also because of America's fascination at

wife, Ruth, was chairman of the board from 1964 to 1978, and today The Paramount Line, Inc., continues to be a family-run enterprise. Samuel and Ruth's three daughters play an active role in the business. Dorothy Markoff Nelson is corporate secretary; Bernice Markoff Gourse is editorial director, and her husband, Samuel Gourse, is director of industrial relations; Gloria Markoff Winston is director of community relations, and her husband, James W. Winston, has served as company president since 1964.

James Winston is involved in many Rhode Island cultural, humanitarian, and business organizations, and occasionally takes his expertise to Washington, D.C., to appear before Congress

Paramount now has a sales force covering the United States, and worldwide licensing brings Paramount greeting cards to 39 countries.

The tradition of employee concern and community philanthropy started by the founder, Samuel Markoff, is carried on today by the current owners and management.

Paramount greeting cards express thoughts in a very special way for people who otherwise might not have the time or ability to say what they feel, giving true meaning to the company's present-day slogan, "Paramount . . . from the Heart."

The four Markoff brothers—Samuel, Allen, Charles, and Ted—at a meeting in the conference room of the old Summer Street Building.

that time with Japanese culture. As business grew, his brothers joined the company: Charles as the sales and credit manager, Allen as the production chief, and Ted as the creative director.

Eventually the firm added greeting cards, which were called the Paramount Line. They became an immediate success, and in 1932 the company adopted The Paramount Line, Inc., as its corporate name and began producing greeting cards exclusively.

By the time he died in 1932, Samuel Markoff had developed his business into a leader in the greeting card industry. After his death his brothers continued to run the organization, with Charles and Allen each serving terms as president. Samuel Markoff's

and the Postal Rate Commission as the spokesman for the greeting card industry. He has served three terms as president of the National Association of Greeting Card Publishers.

Paramount's first home was on North Main Street in Providence, later moving to Summer Street in that city. In the 1950s the company moved to Pawtucket, where it is presently located in the restored historic mill complex formerly occupied by the Coats & Clark Company. Additional property was acquired in the early 1970s to house its international division.

"Jimmy," Paramount's president and chief executive since 1964, James W. Winston.

199

Providence and Worcester Railroad Company

As early as the 1790s, Providence merchants were studying the possibility of a convenient transportation system between their city and Worcester, Massachusetts, some 45 miles to the north. The flow of goods between the cities already was heavy, and Providence merchants felt that a workable transportation system between the two cities would divert a sizable amount of commerce from the Boston merchants.

Finally, about 30 years later, the Blackstone Canal was built, but an insufficient water supply and legal problems led to its eventual failure. It was completely run out of business by the construction of a railroad between the two cities.

The Providence and Worcester Railroad, a much more economical alternative to the Blackstone Canal, was incorporated in 1844. As soon as it began operations, the Providence and Worcester Railroad prospered. The one-way trip between Providence and Worcester was $1.25 first class and 85 cents second class. The trip took about two and one-half hours.

In 1866 the railroad began experimenting with coal locomotives, finding these more economical than the old wood-burning ones. And in 1868, the railroad was constructing a branch line from the docks in East Providence, Rhode Island, and leasing lines in nearby Massachusetts, all aimed at making the company more efficient and profitable.

Finally, in 1888, the Providence and Worcester Railroad Company became inactive. That year the New York, Providence and Boston Railroad Company took a 99-year lease on the line, but four years later that lease was cancelled in favor of the New York, New Haven and Hartford Railroad Company.

It wasn't until December 1966 that a group of businessmen led by Robert H. Eder, a New York lawyer, and Raymond Finizia, an East Providence busi-

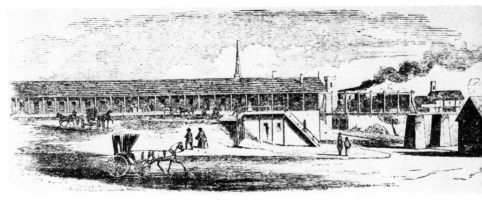

The railroad depot in Woonsocket, Rhode Island, as it looked in 1855. Woonsocket is about half-way between Providence, Rhode Island, and Worcester, Massachusetts, the terminals of the original line of the Providence and Worcester Railroad.

The Providence and Worcester's engine No. 16 stands in the Woonsocket railroad station about 1890. In the background is a warehouse for wool storage, built in 1855.

nessman, assumed control of the railroad, which remained a leased line of the New Haven company. But Eder and his associates realized the importance of the line to the economy of New England. In the late 1960s its owners began working seriously toward the goal of autonomy for the railroad. And on February 3, 1973, after innumerable legal difficulties, the firm gained the right to become an independent line.

Now the officers had to assemble a team to operate a railroad system. Most of the 30-member staff they hired had extensive experience, and as added inducements the employees were given

a guaranteed annual wage and profit sharing.

The next step was to begin a rehabilitation of the railroad's lines, as well as acquiring new lines which would make it more efficient and economical to operate. In 1976 the company acquired a substantial number of lines, doubling its size and extending its area of service into Connecticut. This rehabilitation and acquisition process continues today.

In 1977 the railroad moved back into the depot in Woonsocket, Rhode Island, built in 1882. The facility was fully restored and now serves as the company headquarters.

rovidence Journal

For the past 150 years the *Providence Journal* has played a major role in the city-state of Providence and Rhode Island.

Throughout the years, the newspaper, the state's largest daily, has had a lively relationship with its community. In its earliest period, after it began publication as a daily in 1829, the newspaper was the voice of the Republican party. But late in the 19th century it was formally read out of the party as being too independent. From that point on, the *Providence Journal* has had no formal ties with any political party, and it takes pride in being denounced in turn by both the Democrats and the Republicans or sometimes by both at once.

The *Journal* was first published as a semiweekly, starting on January 3, 1820, under the name of the *Manufacturers' and Farmers' Journal and Providence and Pawtucket Advertiser*. It became the *Providence Journal* when it began publishing as a daily. The hyphenated name, the *Providence Journal-Bulletin*, which often appears in connection with the company, is not the result of any merger, switch, or consolidation with another paper. Rather, the *Journal*, a morning newspaper, began publishing the *Evening Bulletin* on January 26, 1863, to bring

Today's Journal *was first published as a semiweekly, starting in 1820, under the name of the* Manufacturers' and Farmers' Journal and Providence and Pawtucket Advertiser. *It became the* Providence Journal *when it began publishing as a daily in 1829.*

its community the latest news of the Civil War, in which Rhode Island was heavily involved. Today the *Evening Bulletin* publishes five afternoons a week and has a circulation of 137,630. The *Providence Journal* remains the morning newspaper with a weekday circulation of 81,110, and a Sunday circulation of 236,798.

Many men and women have played prominent roles in the publication of the *Journal* throughout the years, but several names stand out above the others.

Henry B. Anthony, 23, and just a few years out of Brown University, moved into the editor's chair nine years after the *Journal* became a daily newspaper. It was Anthony who enunciated so clearly the policy that no matter what the editorial views of the newspaper, those of opposite opinions were to have a hearing in its columns. Anthony relinquished his editor's chair in 1858 when he went to Washington, D.C., as the new U.S. senator from Rhode Island.

John R. Rathom came to the *Journal* in 1906 as managing editor. In 1912 he became editor and general manager. His stories, claimed to be generated by a worldwide spy system, played a dynamic role in overcoming the neutralism of Woodrow Wilson and getting the United States into World War I. Despite the dubious sources of much of his material, he was an accomplished reporter and writer and brought many improvements to the newspaper.

Rathom's successor, Sevellon Brown, left his distinct imprint on the editorial policies of the *Journal.* In 1925 he decided that, since Rhode Island had all the aspects of the city-state, the newspaper should cover it that way, and he set up a state staff with reporters and news bureaus in every part of the state, a method that remains unique in local newspaper coverage. His strong interest in improving the quality of newspapers in general led to the formation of the American Press Institute now located in Reston, Virginia, where newspaper men and women attend concentrated seminars to exchange ideas and gain proficiency by contact with leaders in their profession.

Under its current chairman and chief executive officer, John C.A. Watkins, the company continues to place major emphasis on news and editorial excellence. In addition, it began a program of diversification and today operates two radio stations, WEAN-AM and WPJB-FM in Providence; a television station, WPHL in Philadelphia; Colony Communications, Inc., with cable systems in seven states; and Providence Gravure, Inc., one of the country's largest printers of quality rotogravure and offset products.

The Providence Journal Company is headquartered at Fountain Street.

Providence Marriott

Greater Providence and the Randall Square area in particular received a major economic boost when the Providence Marriott officially opened on November 14, 1975. The hotel, located on a 5.7-acre site in the heart of one of

Shortly after the completion of a new wing, the Marriott began renovations of its Providence Provision Company Restaurant and Lounge. The work was completed early in 1981 and the opening concluded a month of activities held at the hotel to benefit the American Cancer Society. Cancer Society Month was the grand finale of three months of intense involvement by the Marriott with local charities. February had been Heart Fund Month at the

and lodging headquarters, the Marriott. More than 2,500 people were housed at the hotel for more than three days, at a time when the hotel's normal capacity was 600 guests. Procuring food was a top priority, and the Marriott staff and guests went to such lengths as forming a human chain to carry eggs from a truck stranded near the hotel. Another chain was formed to reach a produce truck snowed in on Interstate 95, and more than 10

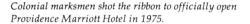
Colonial marksmen shot the ribbon to officially open Providence Marriott Hotel in 1975.

The 1980 addition to the Providence Marriott was highlighted by a giant Christmas tree hoisted to the roof.

the city's redevelopment areas, has proven to be an anchor in the massive effort to transform the once-blighted historic area. The three men responsible for the hotel, which has become an important factor in the city's economic life, were Arthur Robbins, a native Rhode Islander, and Edward A. Perlow and Milton Fine, both of Pittsburgh.

The opening of the new hotel was marked by an official proclamation designating it the city's Bicentennial Hotel, and the Kentish Guards Militia Company fired two volleys of musket fire.

The hotel opened with 250 rooms, 23 parlors, 8 meeting rooms, a grand ballroom, restaurant, and cocktail lounge. Five years after the official opening, an expansion program was undertaken to meet increasing demands.

hotel, with the Marriott sponsoring a variety of activities to raise money for that charity. In March the hotel supported the Muscular Dystrophy campaign, and the Cancer Society activities were held in April.

From the outset the Marriott took its commitment to the community seriously by supporting many worthwhile causes in the greater Providence area. The Marriott began a series of programs to support the local Toys for Tots effort and the Head Start Program with annual Christmas parties for the youngsters.

The event that best describes the Marriott's involvement with the community was an unplanned one—the Great Blizzard of 1978. The February blizzard reached its peak during the afternoon rush hour, forcing many motorists to abandon their vehicles on Interstate 95, its exits, and nearby roads. Many of these people trudged through the snow to the closest food

volunteers trekked to the Star Market, a walk that took nearly an hour instead of the usual five minutes, to bring back badly needed supplies.

First-aid stations were set up in the hotel to assist the stranded people, including a busload of schoolchildren and members of a funeral procession who got caught unexpectedly in the blizzard near the Marriott. None of the guests were charged for the tremendous additional expenses incurred by the hotel during the week of the blizzard, and letters of thanks from guests were received for several months afterwards. Many of the letters included checks for the food and lodging, but all were returned with the suggestion that the money be sent to charities.

Raytheon

A group of scientists and inventors, firmly believing that water was the most reliable medium for transmitting signals to ships, organized themselves to develop this idea in 1901. A year later Professor Reginald A. Fessenden joined the company, and presently created what became known as the Fessenden Oscillator—a device that revolutionized submarine signaling and doubled and tripled the range at which signals could be sent through the water.

The U.S. Navy, recognizing its value, was quick to adopt the innovation for use on warships and submarines. After more experimentation the inventor perfected a unit that allowed warning signals and coded messages to be sent 50 miles and more, ship to shore, shore to ship, and even ship to ship.

While Professor Fessenden and his associates were developing the oscillator, the *Titanic* struck an iceberg in the north Atlantic and sank; an additional feature was then incorporated to allow the device to detect obstructions in the water from the signals it sent. Tests in 1914 off the Grand Banks showed that the oscillator could detect echoes from objects in the water as well as echoes from the ocean bottom. The origin of this oscillator established the principle upon which all echo-ranging and echo-sounding equipment is based.

The Fessenden Oscillator, as well as other sound-sensitive equipment for underwater use developed by the Submarine Signal Company, played an important role in World War I. By the end of the militant years, the firm had developed submarine-detecting and

A modern seaman uses a computerized display terminal to monitor underwater objects.

direction-finding apparatus more accurate and useful than any developed by foreign countries during this period.

After the war the organization returned to work on developing even more advanced echo-sounding equipment and radio echo-ranging devices. One of the high points in its history came between the two world wars, but it was many years before this achievement ever became public.

By 1930, when the Naval Research Laboratory first began to study the problem, the Submarine Signal Company already had developed a primitive system called a "Radameter." The U.S. Navy, fully aware of the military significance of this radar development, requested that all further work be kept secret.

Continuing its scientific research, Submarine Signal Company was the principal supplier to the Navy during World War II for sonar equipment so vital to the success of the campaign against submarines in the Atlantic.

The firm was acquired by Raytheon Company in 1946. Its headquarters has been on West Main Road in Portsmouth, Rhode Island, since 1960. Today the Submarine Signal Division of Raytheon, with plants in Portsmouth, Middletown, Newport, East Providence, and Bristol, supplies sonar for all the Navy's attack submarines and for many of its surface ships.

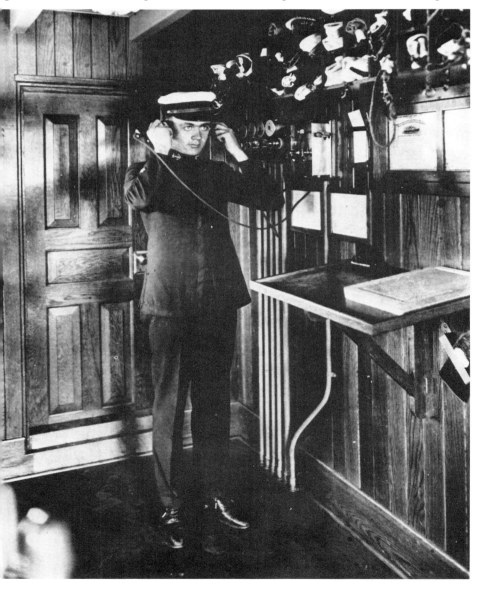

A seaman listens for underwater sounds and underwater objects, circa 1914.

The Rhode Island Historical Society

The Rhode Island Historical Society was founded on April 19, 1822, by a dozen of the state's most prominent citizens who, meeting in the law office of William Aplin at 3 South Main Street in Providence, realized the value of historical artifacts and documents and took steps to collect and preserve them. In June the founders received a charter from the General Assembly, and the following month, with the venerable Moses Brown presiding, the Society elected Governor James Fenner its first president.

From the outset the Society went to work collecting. Among its first major acquisitions was a lengthy file of the *Providence Gazette* owned by Dr. Solomon Drowne. The newspapers became the basis for what is now the longest run of an American colonial newspaper still in existence, lacking only four issues out of a file covering nearly 80 years. Today the Society strives to collect every daily newspaper printed in the state and preserves most of them on microfilm.

But newspapers and books form only a part of the Society's collection. It began to collect museum objects—what early Society reports called relics—soon after it was founded. Today the Society's collections encompass objects dating from the mid-17th century and include the compass of Roger Williams, who founded Providence in 1636, and the jacket worn by Oliver Hazard Perry, a Rhode Island native, in the Battle of Lake Erie in 1813. The collection contains paintings by well-known American artists, a rare set of Chinese export porcelain, silver, glassware, and textiles.

Between 1822, when it was founded, and 1844, when it built a new "cabinet" on Waterman Street across from the Brown University campus, the Rhode Island Historical Society lived in rented quarters. In 1942 the Society acquired the magnificent 1786 John Brown House on nearby Power Street, a gift of John Nicholas Brown. The Society spent the next three decades restoring and refurbishing the

mansion, which now serves as its headquarters and contains one of the finest collections of late 18th- and 19th-century American furniture. It is open to the public as a house-museum.

The Society's collection of books, manuscripts, maps, and photographs soon outgrew the shelves of the John Brown House, and in 1964 they were moved to the former Tockwotton Branch of the Providence Public Library at 121 Hope Street, which the Society had purchased. Today the library houses more than 100,000 books and pamphlets, several million manuscript documents, more than 50,000 graphic images, and three million feet

The 1786 John Brown House was acquired by the Rhode Island Historical Society in 1942, and today it serves both as a house museum and the Society's headquarters. (Photo courtesy of the Rhode Island Historical Society.)

of television film.

In 1974 the Society was given the home of former Ambassador Winthrop W. Aldrich, which it uses for museum galleries, lectures, receptions, and editorial and curatorial offices. The house is located at 110 Benevolent Street, a few blocks east of the library and the John Brown House.

From its beginning, the Society has served all Rhode Islanders. It offers a half-dozen or more lectures annually, many open to the public. It also publishes a quarterly magazine containing articles about Rhode Island history and has published about two dozen books pertaining to the state's history, including the letters and papers of the Revolutionary War hero and Rhode

Moses Brown, shown here in a portrait by Martin Johnson Heade, was one of the founders of the Rhode Island Historical Society in 1822. Brown was a local Quaker merchant and philanthropist. (Photo courtesy of the Rhode Island Historical Society.)

This is the dining room of the John Brown House in Providence as visitors to the handsome 18th-century mansion see it today. (Photo courtesy of the Rhode Island Historical Society and Warren Jagger.)

Island native, General Nathanael Greene.

The Rhode Island Historical Society is a responsibility handed down from one generation to the next, and it takes this responsibility seriously, gathering and preserving historical evidence to document the story of the Rhode Island community for future generations.

The Robinson Green Beretta Corporation

The Robinson Green Beretta Corporation was formed in 1969 but its beginnings go back to 1946, when the architectural and engineering firm of Cull and Robinson was established in Providence. That same year Joseph A. Beretta, who had studied civil engineering at the University of Rhode Island, joined the firm, a move that was the beginning of a long and successful career for him. In 1958 he became a partner of Knight D. Robinson, one of the original founders, and Conrad E. Green, a local architect and a nephew of Rhode Island's Senator Theodore Francis Green. The firm then became known as Robinson, Green & Beretta. In 1969 the company was incorporated, and Beretta became the president. In 1976 he was named chairman of the board.

Today Beretta heads a firm that employs a staff of more than 50, including architects, engineers, landscape architects, and interior designers. Other principals in the firm are George V. Jezierny, Jr., A.I.A., senior vice-president; Raymond A. DeCesare, A.I.A., senior vice-president and secretary; and Dana M. Newbrook, A.I.A., and Gerhard H. Graf, P.E., vice-presidents.

Since its inception, The Robinson Green Beretta Corporation has been instrumental in designing and overseeing a number of well-known Rhode Island building projects. Three of its earliest projects included remodeling the First Federal Savings Bank in downtown Providence, designing the addition to the Adolph Meyer Building at the Institute of Mental Health in Cranston, Rhode Island, and designing the Fox Point Elementary School in Providence.

During the '50s and '60s, the firm concentrated on schools, office buildings, and work for the U.S. Navy in Rhode Island. Some of these projects included the Refectory and Living Center at the Rhode Island School of Design, the Walter Wilson Laboratory at Brown University, the Memorial Library at the University of Rhode Island, the multipurpose building at Portsmouth Priory, the Bachelor Officers' Quarters complex at the naval base in Newport, and the Howard Building and IBM Building in Providence.

The '70s saw The Robinson Green Beretta Corporation focusing on public and multifamily housing, nursing homes, and schools. Some of the firm's major projects during that decade were the Rhode Island Veterans' Home in Bristol and dormitories at Providence

---

Joseph A. Beretta, chairman of the board of The Robinson Green Beretta Corporation.

College, Brown University, and the University of Rhode Island.

The company also has been involved in the design of multifamily housing developments in Florida, Pennsylvania, Texas, New York, Delaware, and New Jersey. And The Robinson Green Beretta Corporation was selected to design the athletes' housing for the 1980 Winter Olympics at Lake Placid, New York. Closer to home, the company was the architectural and engineering firm chosen to design the six-story Judicial Complex in downtown Providence that opened in mid-1981.

Since 1951 The Robinson Green Beretta Corporation's headquarters has been in the handsome Hoppin Villa on the east side of Providence. The villa, one of the largest and most elegant homes built in the city during the mid-19th century, is a fitting headquarters for an architectural and engineering firm.

As The Robinson Green Beretta Corporation looks ahead to the next two decades, it will continue to explore and expand its interests in ecology and energy with an emphasis on using more active renewable energy sources in its designs.

The J. Joseph Garrahy Judicial Complex in Providence, Rhode Island, was designed by The Robinson Green Beretta Corporation.

Rhode Island Hospital Trust National Bank

The name of Rhode Island Hospital Trust National Bank is unique in financial circles. The history behind the name began in the spring of 1863, five years before the bank accepted its first deposits. As the nation was embroiled in the Civil War, the idea of a hospital had provoked considerable discussion and enthusiasm, and a group of public-spirited citizens embarked on a fund-raising campaign for the proposed facility, to be named Rhode Island Hospital. The first benefactor was a 29-year-old medical student, John Poynton Ives, who pledged $10,000. Two years later he died, and his will provided an additional $50,000 for the hospital. Earlier he had persuaded his father, Moses Brown Ives, to leave a bequest of $40,000 for building such a facility. Moses Brown Ives died in 1857. There were other donors, and a war-conscious public responded generously so that construction of the hospital was assured.

Looking ahead, the hospital's trustees foresaw the need for some

The Rhode Island Hospital Trust Company Building is shown under construction in 1919. It was completed in 1920 (construction had begun in 1917) and was placed on the National Register of Historic Places in 1979.

continuing source of income to overcome the deficits incurred in the operation of the hospital. They therefore decided to form a banking institution that could share earnings with the hospital. A charter was obtained from the state legislature, and the Rhode Island Hospital Trust Company, the first trust company in New England, was incorporated in 1867, and accepted its first deposits early in January 1868. The new hospital admitted its first patient on October 1, 1868. The bank continued to share its profits with the hospital until 1880, and today the hospital still owns 6 percent of the bank's stock.

When the third decade of the bank's history came to an end, the trust company had a magnificent new home in downtown Providence, assets were at an all-time high, almost $16 million, and it had survived a severe financial panic that had jolted the country a few years earlier. The 1890s in general were years of growth for the bank as well as the community. The bank had quite suddenly doubled its trust business. Many of these accounts were charitable trusts, the handling of which laid the foundation for Hospital Trust's management of charitable and

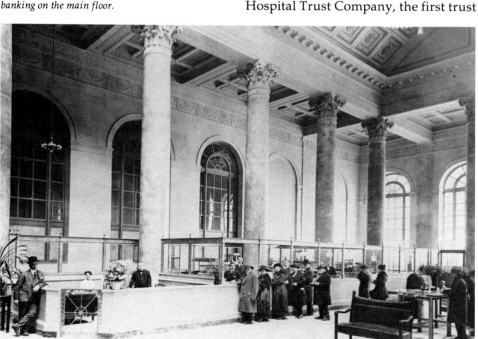

Opening day, 1920. Customers line up to do their banking on the main floor.

stitutional trusts. In 1896 trust accounts represented property inventoried at about $6 million. Four years earlier, the comparative figure had been not quite $3 million. The bank had become the agent for several prominent organizations, among them the Providence Public Library, Brown University, the Shelter for Colored Children, and Rhode Island Hospital. And it had developed facilities for handling a great diversity of business.

Over the years, the bank has had a number of homes. The founders met to elect officers in the Providence Horse

Guards' Armory at 15 Westminster Street in downtown Providence, the same geographical location as the bank's corporate headquarters today. The bank had offices across the river on South Main Street until 1891, when it moved back to 15 Westminster Street to a new building on the site of the old armory. In 1917 this structure was replaced by a 12-story facility designed in the grandeur of the Italian Renaissance. Although this building was carefully constructed, no planning could foresee the tidal waves of the 1938 Hurricane which washed through downtown. The staff worked around the clock that September to save the bank's documents, which were pressed with flatirons and pressing machines operated by kerosene.

Sixty-two reams of blotters were used for drying out safe deposit boxes in the wet area of the vault.

It seemed that no sooner had the state and the bank recovered from the devastating effects of the hurricane than war broke out. During the first years of the war, 2 of the bank's directors, 5 officers, and 41 employees had joined the armed services. The skylights in the main office were removed and replaced by non-shatterable material, and an air-raid shelter was arranged in the basement. By the spring of 1943, the real estate and mortgage departments were forced to move elsewhere, and their offices were occupied by the War Activities Department. Finally, on December 31, 1945, at 12 p.m., President Truman declared the ''hostilities of World War II closed.'' And as if to start fresh after the war, the head office building of the bank was washed in 1946.

In the early 1970s the headquarters was renovated to accommodate the bank's corporate banking division. This coincided with the construction of a 30-story Hospital Trust Tower, adjacent to the 15 Westminster Street building. The tower, which serves as the corporate headquarters, was one of the cornerstones in the redevelopment of downtown Providence.

Over the years, some of Rhode Island's most distinguished citizens have played prominent roles in the history of the bank. The names of Taft, Sharpe, Metcalf, Lippitt, Goddard, Ives, Chafee, Freeman, and Ballou can be found among the board of directors. Senator Nelson W. Aldrich, whose daughter married John D. Rockefeller, Jr., was a member of the board for almost 20 years, during which time he was one of the most powerful members of the United States Senate.

In 1968, with the bank on the threshold of its second century of service, the directors successfully sought a federal charter for the bank, and it became Rhode Island Hospital Trust National Bank. A year later, a one-bank holding company was formed to provide management with greater flexibility and diversity. That company became Hospital Trust Corporation in 1973, taking a name that more readily identifies it with its principal subsidiary, the bank.

The Rhode Island Hospital Trust Company Building, completed in 1920, stands in the shadow of the bank's tower, erected in the mid-1970s.

Roger Williams College

Although Roger Williams College was founded in 1948, it dates back to 1919 when Northeastern University in Boston established a branch in the Providence YMCA offering courses in business and law. One of its most famous students was John O. Pastore, who honed his legal and oratory skills there. He later became governor of Rhode Island and an influential United States senator.

In 1948 the state authorized granting the associate degree. The school was chartered under the name Roger Williams Junior College, the first recognized junior college in Rhode Island. It was named after the founder of the state upon recommendation of faculty member J. Harold G. Way. The president of the college was Harold W. Schaughency, who served from 1950 until 1963.

Within a decade it became obvious that the facility was outgrowing its rented quarters in Providence. A search for land was undertaken. Dr. Ralph Gauvey, who had become president in 1963, envisioned a seaside campus. Land was purchased on Mount Hope Bay in Bristol, about a half-hour's drive from Providence. The new campus was opened in the fall of 1969 to 1,500 students, with another 1,000 remaining at the Providence location. The liberal arts programs were established in Bristol; the professional studies programs were in Providence.

Roger Williams College received accreditation as a four-year institution in 1972 by the New England Association of Schools and Colleges. At about the same time, a decision was made to move all day classes to the new Bristol campus. The college had enlarged its educational programs, increased its student body, and was firmly ensconced in its new 63-acre waterfront campus—to which another 17 acres were later added.

Dr. Gauvey resigned in 1975 and William H. Rizzini was named acting president. He became president in 1978. That same year the Bristol campus was renamed in honor of the late

The Bristol campus of Roger Williams College overlooks Mount Hope Bay.

Roger Williams College offers more than 25 academic programs that combine practical and theoretical studies.

Dr. Marshall Fulton on whose former family farm the campus is situated.

Today Roger Williams College has an enrollment of 2,200 undergraduate day students and 1,500 part-time evening students. It offers career-oriented courses as well as those in the liberal arts and sciences, with more than 25 academic programs that combine prac-

tical and theoretical studies. Amor the newest academic offering introduced in the fall of 1982, are five-year professional bachelor of a chitecture degree and three comput majors: computer informatio systems, computer engineering, an computer science mathematics.

Uncas

When Vincent Sorrentino, a 15-year-old immigrant from Castellamare di Stabia, Italy, arrived in New York City in 1906, he made his way north to Providence and became first a plumber's apprentice at two dollars a week and then a jeweler's apprentice. Five years later he bought some jeweler's tools and went into business for himself, marking the beginning of a firm which later would be incorporated as Uncas Manufacturing Company and become known as "America's Largest Ring House."

The first shop was housed in a single room at 9 Calendar Street where Sorrentino made jewelry findings for other companies. The business prospered and in 1919 moved to larger quarters at 85 Sprague Street. Ten years later the firm moved to its present location at 623 Atwells Avenue. Today the plant is a modern, four-story structure with ample room for machines and equipment as well as the skilled craftsmen and semiskilled workers who turn out the finished jewelry.

The name of the company comes from the legendary Indian sachem in James Fenimore Cooper's book, *The Last of the Mohicans*. During his first

years in this country, Sorrentino attended night school to study English. As a part of his schooling, he read Cooper's novel and was impressed by the sachem, Uncas, who befriended the white man. When the firm moved to its present quarters, the employees presented Sorrentino with a bronze figure of Uncas along with a plaque bearing this inscription: "Presented to Vincent Sorrentino by his employees on the occasion of the 14th anniversary of Uncas Manufacturing Company as a pledge of loyalty to his high ideals and sound business principles upon which the business was established and maintained and as a token of their wishes for a continuation of well-deserved prosperity." This plaque is still prominently displayed in the office which he occupied for many years.

Over the years Uncas has grown and expanded, even during unstable economic times. During the Depression the company made the popular "10-cent sterling silver wedding band," and the firm's expansion included the purchase of 12 smaller ring companies. During World War II Uncas produced military uniform buttons and insignia and other metal military items. In the 1950s and 1960s the business turned from steel die-stamped rings to the lost-wax casting method, and more recently Uncas has pioneered in the development of heavy gold electroplating on quality rings.

Uncas was the first to install an auto-

matic barrel-plating line, providing closer control, more uniform results, and manufacturing economies. During the 1960s the company started a Canadian operation which today employs 50 people. The Providence plant, which continues to grow, now has an average employee force of 400 producing many types of jewelry in addition to the 10 million rings that are manufactured at Uncas each year.

Stanley Sorrentino, the son of the founder, heads the corporation today. He entered the business after his graduation from Colby College in 1951 but did not move into management until he had apprenticed in each of the firm's major departments.

Vincent Sorrentino, an Italian immigrant, was the founder of Uncas Manufacturing Company in Providence, a jewelry firm named after an Indian sachem.

A drawing of the Uncas Building in Providence as it looked in 1929.

Salve Regina-The Newport College

Salve Regina-The Newport College is a coeducational college of arts and sciences in the Catholic tradition that is situated along cliffs that border the spectacular Atlantic seacoast. Offering associate's, bachelor's, and master's degrees, the college has an enrollment of 2,000 men and women from across the country who participate in a broad-based academic curriculum of value-centered education.

Located within a historic district of a city known primarily for its impressive architecture and geographic beauty,

The Wakehurst estate was purchased by Salve Regina-The Newport College in 1972. The structure, now a student residence, is a replica of Wakehurst Place in Sussex, England.

The college's history is traced to 1934, when the General Assembly of Rhode Island granted its charter. The 14 original incorporators included 11 Sisters of Mercy, a Dominican priest, the state superintendent of education, and a priest from the Diocese of Providence. The planning of these men and women became visible 13 years later when the college formally opened following the gift of Mr. and Mrs. Robert W. Goelet of their 50-room, oceanfront Newport estate, Ochre Court. Offered to Salve Regina for its corporate purposes, the opulent turn-of-the-century Richard Morris Hunt structure housed the entire institution during its formative years. The magnificent French-paneled library became the school library, the huge state dining room with double-hearth fireplace became the college dining room, and the elaborate sitting rooms, bedrooms, and suites were transformed into classrooms, student residences, and offices.

Dr. Lucille McKillop, R.S.M., has been president Salve Regina-The Newport College since 1973.

Salve Regina's 60-acre campus joins 22 historic and exceptionally significant structures within a one-half mile radius of the central administration building, Ochre Court. The adaptive reuse of several 19th-century "summer cottages" that serve the college has provided administrative, educational, and student facilities that are both functional and splendid.

Under the leadership of its first dean, Sister Mary James O'Hare, and an administration and faculty of 13 Sisters of Mercy and one priest, Salve Regina's doors opened to a freshman class of 58 women in September 1947. Sister Mary James O'Hare and Sister Mary Hilda Miley, moving forces in the early development of the college, assisted with the establishment of a strong

liberal arts curriculum intended clarify, refine, and deepen the art critical thinking within the context Catholic values.

The groundwork of the early found ers has been carried forward. Enroll ment climbed slowly for the first 1 years. While the college charter did n mandate the incorporation of a singl sex college, the school did not see a flux of males until the 1960s; in 1973 deliberate effort to recruit men was nade. Today a planned enrollment oal of 2,000 students has been met. r. Lucille McKillop, R.S.M., president nce 1973, has guided the institution hrough recent years of planned growth, has assisted with the development of an expanded curriculum, and has promoted the solid commitment to coeducation that was made during her first year as president.

The physical facilities of the college are clearly outstanding. Beauty and of Mercy since its inception, the college strives to help students with their goals and dignity as persons and with their roles as members of society through the continued implementation of a curriculum that cultivates intellects, ripens capacities for sound judgments,

Salve Regina-The Newport College borders Newport's Cliff Walk and overlooks the Atlantic Ocean.

history have been preserved and renewed to produce one of the country's most visually attractive campuses.

Ochre Court, one of the first of the grand Newport mansions, derives its name from the tint of the cliffs bounding the estate. Today it serves as a reminder of our national heritage and functions as a strong symbol for the college. It houses central administrative offices and a chapel (the former grand ballroom for the Goelet family) and serves the college and the public on many special and festive occasions. Fronting Cliff Walk on "Millionaire's Row," Hunt's design is constructed of Indiana limestone and modeled after the chateaux of the Loire Valley. Its late French Gothic architectural detail with high turrets, tall chimney, and elaborate dormers is said to be based on King Edward VII's castle in Paris.

Under the sponsorship of the Sisters

and deepens knowledge and understanding. The Salve Regina curriculum provides opportunities for more than 25 areas of concentration leading to undergraduate and graduate degrees. In addition to the usual liberal arts areas of concentration, special disciplines include computer science, accounting, nursing, criminal justice, special education, and management. Master's concentrations in several areas of human development, management, criminal justice, and health services administration were expanded in 1981 to include a master of arts in liberal studies. Plans to add horticulture and anthropology to the undergraduate curriculum during the 1980s are being developed.

he 14th-century stained glass window, in Ochre ourt, is from the Spitzen collection of Germany.

Textron

In 1923 Special Yarns Corporation was started in Boston by a 27-year-old Harvard graduate and veteran of World War I, Royal Little, to process yarns made of rayon, at that time the principal synthetic textile material. Five years later partnership with a Providence firm expanded facilities and brought in new capital. The new venture, Franklin Rayon Corporation with headquarters in Providence, became a leading dye and spinning company for synthetic yarns. In 1938 Little bought out his co-owners and changed the name to Atlantic Rayon, setting the stage for the eventual name change to Textron, a corporation that soon emerged as a major multinational organization with operations in 19 countries, generating $3.3 billion in sales in 1981 alone and employing more than 2,000 people in Rhode Island.

After World War II began Atlantic Rayon lost its exclusive distributorship for processed yarn from manufacturers, and in a search for new business, the firm began manufacturing nylon parachutes for the military. But as the war ended and parachute orders dried up, Royal Little looked for a solution to keep his company's sewing and cutting plants busy. What he decided on was a novel approach in business, vertical integration. This meant that one firm handled all production and marketing operations from weaving of the cloth to distribution of consumer products, all directed from a single company headquarters.

Textron soon became the name of the corporation. "Tex" was for textiles and "tron" was for synthetics. By the end of 1946 Textron's operations had grown to more than 30 plants employing 16,000, with sales reaching $125 million annually.

But by 1952 Little had become dissatisfied with the highly cyclical nature of the textile business and its low rate of return on investment. Little believed that diversification would protect one against industry cycles, encourage participation in new markets and technologies, permit the greater financial backing to divisions with the highest rates of growth, and potentially increase returns to shareholders.

Today Textron is a diversified, multinational manufacturing organization with operations in seven areas — Aerospace and Electronics, Outdoor Products, Specialty Con-

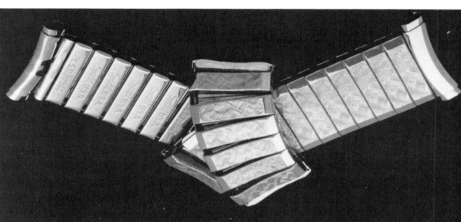

Seen here is the Bostitch plant in East Greenwich, Rhode Island, in the 1920s, a plant that later was replaced by a large, modern facility on the edge of the town.

Introduced in 1959, Speidel's famous Twist-O-Fle[x] watchband quickly became the division's best-kno[wn] product.

sumer, Machine Tool and Precision Bearing, Engineered Fasteners, Industrial Products, and Venture Capital and Financing. The corporate headquarters is at 40 Westminster Street in downtown Providence, where 225 people are employed.

Through the past two decades, the chief executive officers who succeeded Little have first worked with their predecessors for many years, guaranteeing a continuity of management style. Little, who retired in 1962, was succeeded by Rupert C. Thompson, Jr., a Providence banker. In 1968 G. William

Miller, an engineer and lawyer, to[ok] over. When Miller became chairma[n of] the Federal Reserve Board in 1978, [he] was succeeded by Joseph B. Collins[on] who had been with Textron since 19[ ]. When Collinson retired in 19[ ] Robert P. Straetz, the company pre[si]dent, became chairman and chi[ef] executive officer, and B.F. Dola[n,] executive vice-president of operation[s] was named president and chief opera[t]ing officer.

The oldest of these companies [is] Gorham Corporation, founded b[y] Jabez Gorham, who in 1831, began th[e] manufacture of silver spoons in a sma[ll] shop in Providence with 10 employee[s.] The business grew to be the large[st] producer of sterling silverware in th[e] world, receiving gold medal awards [at] expositions in the late 19th and earl[y] 20th centuries. Along the way it estab[-]

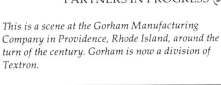

This is a scene at the Gorham Manufacturing Company in Providence, Rhode Island, around the turn of the century. Gorham is now a division of Textron.

electronic research and development firm. In 1967 Textron acquired Gorham and expanded into the table-top field, so that in addition to making silver products, Gorham was manufacturing fine china and designing and marketing full-lead crystal and other giftware products.

Bostitch began in 1896 when Thomas A. Briggs built a wire-stitching machine in his home workshop in Arlington, Massachusetts. His stitcher was an immediate success, and his firm, the Boston Wire Stitcher Company, eventually changed its name to Bostitch and outgrew its quarters. It moved first to Woonsocket, Rhode Island, and in 1904 to East Greenwich where it is today. Bostitch, which was acquired by Textron in 1966, is a leading manufacturer of staples, staplers, and power-nailing equipment. In addition to three plants in the United States, Bostitch manufactures and distributes worldwide with plants in France, England, Spain, Mexico, Canada, and Australia.

Speidel was started in the late 1800s with capital equivalent to $10 by a craftsman named Frederick Speidel, who began making gold and silver chains in his home in Pforzheim, Germany. He then developed a new way to create "couple," a bi-metal with gold plating on a base material, and soon he was the head of the largest jewelry factory in Pforzheim.

In 1904 he opened a branch in Providence and not long after that his brothers joined him in Rhode Island at his business located at 70 Ship Street. The company's foresight in recognizing the possibilities of automating the manufacture of an entirely new kind of watchband led to the development of the Twist-O-Flex in 1959. In 1965 Speidel established a new division and entered the men's fragrance business with British Sterling, the first in a line of Speidel toiletries. A year later Textron acquired the firm. Speidel continues to manufacture and distribute watchbands, identification bracelets, neckchains, fashion jewelry, and men's toiletries.

obert P. Straetz, chairman of the board and chief executive officer of Textron, at left, and Beverly F. Dolan, president and chief operating officer of the company, at right, talk with Royal Little, the founder of Textron, who holds a model of a Bell helicopter made by a Textron-owned company.

ished a bronze division, which cast uch famous heroic statues as that of Theodore Roosevelt outside the Museum of Natural History in New York and the figure of "The Independent Man" which stands atop Rhode Island's capitol in Providence. Gorham later entered the cemetery bronze memorial market.

In 1959 Gorham began a diversification program, acquiring Eaton Paper Company, a producer of fine stationery, and Pickard and Burns, Inc., an

Vennerbeck & Clase Co.

The Vennerbeck & Clase Co. traces its history to the late 19th century and a Providence firm founded by Horace Remington and his partner, Charles Barber. In 1879 the two men, who had worked for a number of years in local cotton mills and refining and smelting plants, decided to set up a gold and silver refining business. Three years later Barber left the business and the partnership was dissolved. Remington continued what had become a successful enterprise, and in 1888 his son, Albert A. Remington, joined him. That same year they purchased land and erected a five-story brick building at 91 Friendship Street on the edge of downtown Providence. Remington's other sons, Horace E. and Clarence G., were admitted to the business in 1901, and the corporation called Horace Remington & Son Co. was formed.

The firm prospered during the years before World War I. Remington was elected an alderman for the city and became one of the largest landowners in the city's Elmwood section. The company expanded and purchased real estate and other business interests.

In 1909 the firm entered into a transaction that was to remain a secret for the next 39 years. Horace Remington & Son purchased the controlling interest in the firm of Vennerbeck & Clase, which had been started in 1881 around the corner from the Remington company to manufacture gold, gold-filled, and sterling silver wire and sheeting stock for the jewelry and optical businesses.

Remington purchased a 51-percent controlling interest in the firm, and Albert S. Vennerbeck, the last surviving Vennerbeck in the company, became the treasurer and general manager. But for reasons best known to the principals, Remington's ownership was kept a secret until 1948 when Vennerbeck died. When his will was read, his widow learned that her husband had owned only one third of the family business.

In 1949 the Remington company bought out the remaining Vennerbeck shares from Mrs. Vennerbeck and became the sole owners. However, the firms continued to operate as separate entities. Horace Remington had died in 1928, and his son, Albert, had died in 1935. Clarence died in 1943, so by 1949 the company was being run by Albert's son, A. Andrew Remington, Jr., and his uncle, Horace, one of the founder's sons.

A. Andrew Remington, Jr., took over management of Vennerbeck & Clase in 1961 and improved and upgraded the company. His son, Albert A. Remington III, had joined the family business in 1954 after graduation from college, and by 1963 he was in charge of the Horace Remington & Son Co.

Both A. Andrew Remington, Jr., and his uncle, Horace, died in 1969, leaving the management of both firms to Albert A. Remington III. The following year he bought out the shares owned by Horace from his heirs, and in 1970 after 91 years in operation, the refinery of Horace Remington & Son Co. was closed and the stock was merged with the Vennerbeck & Clase Co.

In 1976 a new plant was constructed in the town of Lincoln, Rhode Island, north of Providence. The 24,000 square-foot plant of Vennerbeck & Clase employs 38 and continues to manufacture gold, gold-filled, and sterling silver wire and sheeting stock for the jewelry and optical businesses.

Albert A. Remington III has served on the board of directors of the Travelers Aid Society, the Jewelers Board of Trade, and The Jewelry Institute. He is a former chairman of the Greater Providence Advisory Board of the Salvation Army.

Albert A. Remington III, great-grandson of the founder of Horace Remington & Son, presides over Vennerbeck & Clase today, the product of a merger between Remington and Vennerbeck & Clase.

Lindbergh's transatlantic flight provided the inspiration for this advertisement in the early 1930s in which the Horace Remington & Son Co. pointed out the importance of gold in everyday life at that time.

GOLD

THE foremost metal of all—the WORLD'S money standard. Every household has more or less old gold and silver, Jewelry, Watches, Dental Crowns or Bridges, Mutilated Coins, Sterling Silver Spoons, etc.
Let us interest you in our Treasure Chests for Churches, Societies and Clubs.
A card or telephone and our representative will call.

Horace Remington & Son Co.
Gold and Silver Refiners
91 FRIENDSHIP STREET, PROVIDENCE, R. I.
Telephone Gaspee 5481 — Est. 1879

The Washington Trust Company

Six months after George Washington died, the Washington Bank of Wester-y, with a capital stock of $50,000, opened its doors. It was the third bank n Rhode Island. And on Washington's irthday in 1801, the bank paid its first dividend, a tradition carried on for any years. Today the bank's suc-essor, The Washington Trust Com-any, is the nation's ninth oldest bank

ur members of the well-known Westerly banking mily in the new building just after it opened in 25. From left are Arthur L. Perry, Charles Perry, , Arthur Perry, and Thomas Perry.

nd Westerly's only hometown bank-ng institution.

Situated on the Pawcatuck River in e southwestern corner of Rhode sland, Westerly in those early days of e Washington Bank was a remote illage with 400 residents and 50 omes. The principal occupation in the arrow valley of the Pawcatuck was rming. And as the farms prospered, e farmers needed a bank to serve oth as an institution for savings and r loans. Because Providence was too r away, the Washington Bank was es-ablished. A few years after the bank's pening, Timothy Dwight, the presi-ent of Yale College, came through Vesterly and found it worthy of pecial mention that "a bank has lately een established here."

For its first 36 years the bank had headquarters in the Paul Rhodes Hotel, and built into a hill in the rear of the building was the bank's massive stone vault. By 1836 the bank's capital stock had increased to $100,000, and the stockholders voted to give the bank its own home. A committee charged with overseeing the construction of the new building decided that the architecture should be similar to the Parthenon in Athens. The result was "the little Greek temple," as it became known in Dixon House Square. It was said to be the first building constructed of the now-famous Westerly granite.

In 1864, when the national banking system was established, the bank sur-rendered its state charter and the following year became the Washington National Bank. In 1901 the bank purchased the town's second oldest financial institution, the National Phenix Bank, and in 1904 the Wash-ington National Bank and the Westerly Savings Bank formally united to create The Washington Trust Company.

Over the years the bank has suc-cessfully weathered the country's financial crises. It took in stride the Panic of 1907, meeting every demand for payment without delay. Westerly was spared the worst effects of the Great Depression, but for those resi-dents who needed assistance the bank

opened a small loan department and enabled hundreds to work their way out of the financial difficulties created by the hard times.

A history of The Washington Trust Company would not be complete with-out a mention of the Perry family of Westerly, a family whose name has been closely associated with the bank almost since its doors opened in 1800. The first banking Perry was Thomas Perry, who began his career with the bank in 1805 as a cashier. Succeeding generations of Perrys worked in the bank, holding important positions including the presidency. Harvey C. Perry II, an officer of the bank, is a tri-ple great-grandson of that first Perry.

Today the bank's headquarters is in a building constructed in 1925, designed in a modified Italian Renais-sance style with a distinctive red tile roof. During the '50s and '60s the bank acquired more land around the build-ing and constructed drive-in windows. Two branches of the bank, one in Wyoming, Rhode Island, and one on Franklin Street on the outskirts of Westerly, serve the residents in the surrounding area.

Finishing touches are put on the new home of The Washington Trust Company in Westerly. The building, designed in a modified Italian Renaissance style with a distinctive red tile roof, was opened in 1925.

The Westerly Sun

The name "Utter" has been synonymous with publishing in Westerly since 1858, when John Herbert Utter came there to buy the town's first newspaper, *The Literary Echo,* which had begun publication on April 3, 1851.

George H. Utter joined the family newspaper in 1886. Later he served as governor of Rhode Island and as a United States congressman.

Utter had learned his craft in New York City from his brother, the Reverend George B. Utter, who published *The Sabbath Recorder,* a denominational weekly with principal circulation among Seventh Day Baptists in the nation. John Herbert changed the name of *The Literary Echo* in 1858 to *The Narragansett Weekly,* and in 1861 his brother moved his *Sabbath Recorder* aboard a sailing vessel from New York City to Westerly where the brothers joined forces under the name G.B. and J.H. Utter, Steam Printers. The latter half of the name referred to the steam engine which furnished the power to operate their equipment.

In 1886 John Herbert Utter died, leaving the operation of the newspaper to his brother. By then the paper had been renamed *The Westerly Narragansett Weekly.* The Reverend Utter was joined by his only son, George H. Utter, and the two men ran the paper until the Reverend Utter's death in 1892.

It wasn't until the following year that George H. Utter, perhaps the most remarkable and certainly the most famous publisher the paper has had, realized his dream of a daily newspaper in Westerly. On August 7, 1893, *The Westerly Sun* began daily publication, and soon thereafter, *The Westerly Narragansett Weekly* ceased publication.

It had been written of George H. Utter that "he could set type, make up a newspaper, or travel to some corner of the state to make a speech." He had been a state representative from Westerly, speaker of the House of Representatives, a state senator, and secretary of state, all within the space of eight years. He served as governor of Rhode Island from 1905 to 1907, a period during which the governor's office in the state house was closed on Saturdays. He served in Congress from 1910 to 1912, and on November 3, 1912, just three days before the national elections, George H. Utter died.

Upon the death of the congressman, his son, George B. Utter, who had ably stepped into his father's shoes during his years in political office, became both editor and publisher of *The Westerly Sun.* In 1914 he was joined by his youngest brother, Wilfred B. Utter, who became the advertising manager. Upon the death of their mother in 1939, the brothers became co-publishers.

The newest co-publishers of the fourth generation of Utters in Westerly are Charles Wilbar Utter and George H. Utter II, two sons of the late George B. Utter. Today *The Westerly Sun* is published in the same building on Main Street that published *The Narragansett Weekly.* This is probably the oldest continuous use of a building for publishing a newspaper in this country. The *Sun* continues to be published six days a week, Sunday through Friday, still holding the distinction of being the only daily newspaper in the United States that is printed on Sunday afternoon.

Circulation averages above 11,000 daily, except Saturday, and the newspaper is printed by offset. In all it employs about 56 full-time and 9 part-time employees, and 235 news carriers.

Typesetters prepare the day's Westerly Sun *in the newspaper's composing room in 1897.*

Woonsocket Savings and Trust

The Woonsocket Institution for Savings, chartered in June 1845 by the Rhode Island General Assembly, was created not for profit but to provide dividends for the owners of the bank — its working-class depositors.

Originated within another bank, the Woonsocket Falls Bank (later known as the Woonsocket National Bank) at Main and Bernon streets, it moved with that institution to Cook's Block on Main Street in 1867. In 1928 the Woonsocket Institution for Savings constructed its own office on Main Street.

From the beginning the bank provided safety for the holdings of the small investor. During the years between its opening on August 23, 1845, until 1891, it paid a minimum of 5-percent interest, with all profits being returned to the depositors.

John Osborne was the first president of the bank, serving in that position for 12 years. Under his direction, savings deposits rose to more than $250,000 — a sizable amount of money considering the average mill worker only earned from 5 to 10 dollars a week.

One of the most prominent local men to be associated, however, was Aram Pothier who later served as governor of Rhode Island from 1908 to 1915 and from 1925 to 1928. He became president of the bank in 1912 and remained in that position until his death in 1928.

The institution grew slowly yet steadily. It weathered the Depression, when larger, stronger banks were forced to close their doors permanently. By 1945, its centennial birthday, it had assets of $18.5 million.

Rapid growth began during the 1950s, and by the early 1960s the bank had established branch offices at Park Square and Walnut Hill Plaza. Deposits reached $100 million.

Until the mid-1960s the Woonsocket Institution for Savings had been successful in gathering small deposits, which provided a significantly large source of funds. However, as a mutual savings bank it could not offer check-

Before the Woonsocket Institution for Savings moved to its new building at 144 Main Street in 1928, it was briefly located in the Harris Block Building, now the tax division/finance department of the Woonsocket City Hall.

ing accounts — another large source of funds. In order to compete in this area, it created the Woonsocket Institution Trust Company to provide checking accounts and other commercial banking services.

Even though the Woonsocket Savings and Trust, as it now is known, acts as one bank, it is comprised of two organizations that have individual charters as well as distinct limits on the services each can provide.

During the 1970s the bank grew from three offices to nine, three of which are located in growing communities outside the greater Woonsocket area. Staff, equipment, and operations also kept pace with the expansion.

The Woonsocket Savings and Trust, entering the 1980s with completion of a modern headquarters complex on John A. Cummings Way in Woonsocket, is the second largest mutual savings bank in Rhode Island.

Woonsocket Savings and Trust entered the 1980s by moving its headquarters into this modern building on John A. Cummings Way in Woonsocket.

PATRONS

The following individuals, companies, and organizations have made a valuable commitment to the quality of this publication. Windsor Publications and The Rhode Island Historical Society gratefully acknowledge their participation in *Rhode Island: The Independent State.*

Allendale Mutual Insurance Company*
Amica Mutual Insurance Company
Amperex Electronic Corporation*
Amtrol Inc.*
Belcourt Castle*
BIF A Unit of General Signal Corporation*
Biltmore Plaza Hotel*
Blue Cross of Rhode Island*
Mrs. John Nicholas Brown
Brown and Ives*
Brown & Sharpe Manufacturing Company*
Brown University*
Carey, Richmond & Viking*
R.A. Cataldo & Associates Inc.
CE Maguire, Inc.*
Cranston Print Works*
Cumberland Farms*
Danecraft*
Dixon Industries Corporation*
Eugene A. Eddy
Robert F. Eddy
EG&G Sealol, Inc.*
Federal Products*
Mr. & Mrs. Theodore Armington Fisher
General Dynamics Corp., Electric Boat Division, Quonset Point Facility
Hasbro Industries*
Island Interrelated Library System
Manasett Corp
Moody Tools, Inc.
New England Butt Company*
The New England Financial Group*
New England Institute of Technology*
Old Colony Cooperative Bank*
Old Stone Corporation*
A.J. Oster Company*
The Outlet Company*
The Paramount Line, Inc.*
Vincent D. Pellegrini

Providence and Worcester Railroad Company*
The Providence Gas Company
Providence Journal*
Providence Marriott*
Raytheon*
Rhode Island AFL-CIO
Rhode Island Hospital Trust National Bank*
The Robinson Green Beretta Corporation*
Roger Williams College*
Salve Regina-The Newport College*
Starkweather & Shepley Inc.
Telesis, Inc.
Textron*
Uncas*
Vennerbeck & Clase Co.*
WPRI-TV, Knight-Ridder Broadcasting, Inc.
The Washington Trust Company*
The Westerly Sun*
Woonsocket Savings and Trust*

*Partners in Progress of *Rhode Island: The Independent State.* The histories of these companies and organizations appear in Chapter 14, beginning on page 169.

INDEX

Italized numbers indicate illustrations

THIS BOOK WAS SET IN PONTIAC, PRINTED ON 70 POUND WARRENFLO AND BOUND BY WALSWORTH PUBLISHING COMPANY. HALFTONE REPRODUCTION BY ROBERTSON GRAPHICS.